RIVER ROAD RECIPES

PUBLISHED

BY

THE JUNIOR LEAGUE

OF

BATON ROUGE, INC.

BATON ROUGE, LOUISIANA

10,000 COPIES PER PRINTING

FIRST PRINTING	SEPTEMBER, 1959	ELEVENTH PRINTING	DECEMBER, 1965
SECOND PRINTING	JANUARY, 1960	TWELFTH PRINTING	MAY, 1966
THIRD PRINTING	JANUARY, 1961	THIRTEENTH PRINTING	NOVEMBER, 1966
FOURTH PRINTING	FEBRUARY, 1962	FOURTEENTH PRINTING	APRIL, 1967
FIFTH PRINTING	NOVEMBER, 1962	FIFTEENTH PRINTING	JULY, 1967
SIXTH PRINTING	JULY, 1963	SIXTEENTH PRINTING	DECEMBER, 1967
SEVENTH PRINTING	DECEMBER, 1963	SEVENTEENTH PRINTING	MARCH, 1968
EIGHTH PRINTING	AUGUST, 1964	EIGHTEENTH PRINTING	JUNE, 1968
NINTH PRINTING	FEBRUARY, 1965	NINETEENTH PRINTING	DECEMBER, 1968
TENTH PRINTING	AUGUST, 1965	TWENTIETH PRINTING	JANUARY, 1969

20,000 COPIES PER PRINTING

TWENTY-FIRST PRINTING	APRIL, 1969	FORTY-FIFTH PRINTING	FEBRUARY, 1977
TWENTY-SECOND PRINTING	SEPTEMBER, 1969	FORTY-SIXTH PRINTING	MAY, 1977
TWENTY-THIRD PRINTING	FEBRUARY, 1970	FORTY-SEVENTH PRINTING	DECEMBER, 1977
TWENTY-FOURTH PRINTING	AUGUST, 1970	FORTY-EIGHTH PRINTING	JUNE, 1978
TWENTY-FIFTH PRINTING	JANUARY, 1971	FORTY-NINTH PRINTING	NOVEMBER, 1978
TWENTY-SIXTH PRINTING	AUGUST, 1971	FIFTIETH PRINTING	APRIL, 1979
TWENTY-SEVENTH PRINTING	JANUARY, 1972	FIFTY-FIRST PRINTING	OCTOBER, 1979
TWENTY-EIGHTH PRINTING	MAY, 1972	FIFTY-SECOND PRINTING	APRIL, 1980
TWENTY-NINTH PRINTING	OCTOBER, 1972	FIFTY-THIRD PRINTING	NOVEMBER, 1980
THIRTIETH PRINTING	JANUARY, 1973	FIFTY-FOURTH PRINTING	JULY, 1981
THIRTY-FIRST PRINTING	MAY, 1973	FIFTY-FIFTH PRINTING	DECEMBER, 1981
THIRTY-SECOND PRINTING	SEPTEMBER, 1973	FIFTY-SIXTH PRINTING	JULY, 1982
THIRTY-THIRD PRINTING	JANUARY, 1974	FIFTY-SEVENTH PRINTING	FEBRUARY, 1983
THIRTY-FOURTH PRINTING	MAY, 1974	FIFTY-EIGHTH PRINTING	OCTOBER, 1983
THIRTY-FIFTH PRINTING	AUGUST, 1974	FIFTY-NINTH PRINTING	MAY, 1984
THIRTY-SIXTH PRINTING	DECEMBER, 1974	SIXTIETH PRINTING	OCTOBER, 1984
THIRTY-SEVENTH PRINTING	MARCH, 1975	SIXTY-FIRST PRINTING	OCTOBER, 1985
THIRTY-EIGHTH PRINTING	JUNE, 1975	SIXTY-SECOND PRINTING	AUGUST, 1986
THIRTY-NINTH PRINTING	OCTOBER, 1975	SIXTY-THIRD PRINTING	MAY, 1987
FORTIETH PRINTING	JANUARY, 1976	SIXTY-FOURTH PRINTING	JUNE, 1988
FORTY-FIRST PRINTING	MARCH, 1976	SIXTY-FIFTH PRINTING	AUGUST, 1989
FORTY-SECOND PRINTING	JUNE, 1976	SIXTY-SIXTH PRINTING	JULY, 1990
FORTY-THIRD PRINTING	SEPTEMBER, 1976	SIXTY-SEVENTH PRINTING	JUNE, 1991
FORTY-FOURTH PRINTING	NOVEMBER, 1976	SIXTY-EIGHTH PRINTING	JUNE, 1992

30,000 COPIES PER PRINTING

SIXTY-NINTH PRINTING	JULY, 1993

The object of this League shall be to promote voluntarism and to improve the community through the effective action and leadership of trained volunteers. Its purpose is exclusively educational and charitable.

Copies may be obtained by addressing *River Road Recipes*, THE JUNIOR LEAGUE OF BATON ROUGE, INC., 5280 Corporate Blvd., Baton Rouge, La. 70808.

Printed in the USA by

WIMMER
The Wimmer Companies, Inc.
Memphis • Dallas

Cover Design and Illustrations by
YVONNE PULLEN LEWIS

FOREWORD

The River Road, from Baton Rouge along the Mississippi River to New Orleans, is a section famous for good cooking, which is so much a part of our heritage and tradition here in Louisiana. Our culinary history is old. Influenced principally by the French and Spanish, it is Creole Cooking. And it is truly Southern!

The French enhanced their own outstanding cuisine with the great abundance found in Louisiana — the herbs, seafood, games, meat, vegetables, and fruits. The Spanish added zest and the African slaves contributed their knowledge and use of herbs.

South Louisianians today are proud of this heritage — cooking that is truly an art. Delightful creations, such as gumbos and crayfish bisque, courtbouillons and jambalayas, shrimp Creole, hushpuppies, pralines and just a good cup of coffee — these are distinctly ours to share. To a glorious past and a gourmet future we dedicate "River Road Recipes."

ORIGINAL COMMITTEE

Sara Fidler Barrow
Martha Myatt Bowlus
Betty Hummel Cadwallader
Jean Pearce Collier
Sara Menefee Downing
Elizabeth Farnsworth Geheber
Nettie Lemoine Kean
Carolyn Blanchard Landry
Mary Frances Moreland
  MacCurdy

Doris Reid McCall*
Nona Reddy McInnis
Jane Porter Middleton
Katherine LaCour Miller
Camille Cade Raggio
Anne Roberts Reitzell*
Emily Roberts Robinson
June Heroman Scheffy

Eloise Arbour Selig
Betty Smith Siegel
Carolyn Neal Simpson
Amy Blanche Slowey
Mary Jane Laidlaw Smith
Evelyn Wilsford*
Barbara Sevier Womack*

*Deceased

River Road Recipes was named by Ann Wilbert Arbour.

The Junior League of Baton Rouge, Inc., proudly announces that as of August 1, 1991, the combined sales of *River Road Recipes* and *River Road Recipes II, A Second Helping*, have earned $2,000,000 to fund League projects in the Baton Rouge community. Projects supported and sponsored by the Junior League of Baton Rouge, Inc. include, but are not limited to the following:

Baton Rouge Speech and Hearing Foundation
Louisiana Arts and Science Center
Baton Rouge Association for Retarded Children
City Beautification
Baton Rouge Area Council on Alcoholism
Community Volunteer Bureau
East Baton Rouge Parish Family Court
  Volunteer Program
Keyettes Sponsorship
Academic Readiness
Arts and Humanities Council — Community
  Development
Baton Rouge Youth
Oral History of Baton Rouge
Arts for the Elderly
Children's Emergency Shelter
Magnolia Mound Plantation Kitchen
River Road Recipes in Braille
Fine Arts Series
Monterey Reading
Friends of LTI
Library Information Service
Public Radio
Battered Women's Shelter
Crisis Home

Human Devleopment Program
Parenting Center
Respite Care
Discovery Depot Children's Museum
International Summer Special Olympics
Symphony at Twilight
Drug Awareness Task Force
Playmakers Theater for Children
Artists in Action
USS Kidd Docent Program
Adopt-A-School
Greater Baton Rouge Food Bank
Hospice
LSU Museum of Natural Science
Parenting Center Outreach
Media Literacy
Teen Pregnancy Prevention
Volunteer Baton Rouge
Arts in Education
Excellence in Teaching
East Baton Rouge Parish School Quiz Bowls
Peer Helpers
Shared Reading Experiences for Children
  and Parents

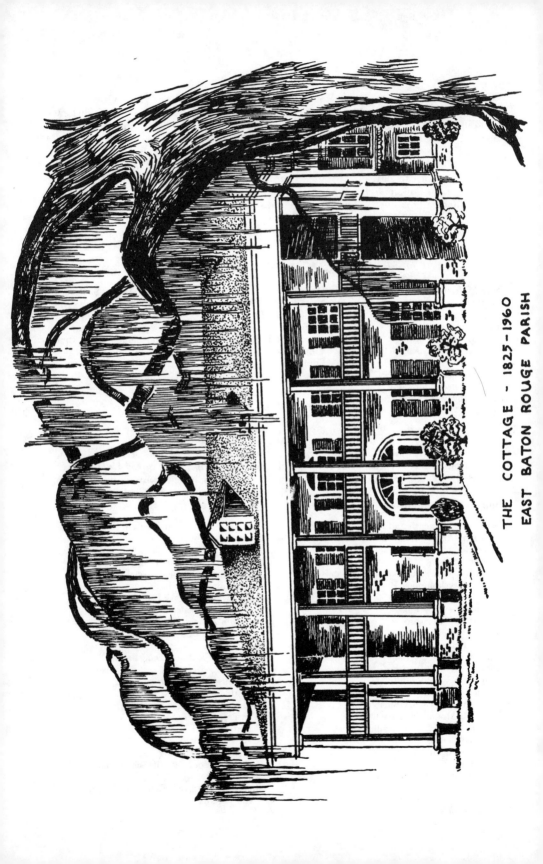

THE COTTAGE - 1825-1960
EAST BATON ROUGE PARISH

CONTENTS

For three years we have dreamed cookbook. We collected furiously, tested prodigiously, edited relentlessly, typed incessantly, proofread continuously and highly hoped . . . that our book would be enjoyed and used by you.

Trade names of products are given only when necessary.

BEVERAGES

CAFÉ NOIR, *the early morning cup or after dinner demitasse, and* CAFÉ AU LAIT *at breakfast time are highlights in the day of a South Louisianian! Many a Creole insists that the morning cup lengthens the life span, and travelers consider our coffee a wonder and a joy. How important then is the art of making good coffee! Of prime importance is fresh coffee; it must have a delightful fragrance when the package is opened. To retain this first aroma is our aim. Some Southerners like chicory in their coffee; this darkens the color and changes the flavor.*

Using a French drip pot, allow one tablespoon of coffee per cup of water. Pour into the grounds just enough boiling water to moisten well, and immediately put the top on and stop up the spout. Continue pouring slowly, a little boiling water at a time, until a delightful aroma escapes from the closed spout and tempts you to taste the rich, fragrant concoction that is café noir. Never boil coffee; set the pot in a pan of hot water to keep the coffee hot.

A word of caution about the necessity of cleanliness of the coffee pot. A bitter taste often results from the chemical action of the coffee creating a substance which clings to the interior of the pot. Hence, it requires more than ordinary care, or it may acquire a stale smell, as of an old pipe.

CAFÉ AU LAIT *is made by adding milk or cream just brought to the boiling point. Usually, equal parts of milk and coffee are used, though this is a matter of taste.*

EGGNOG I

Make One Week Before Serving:

4 eggs, separated	1 quart cream
¾ pint brandy	¾ cup granulated sugar
6 tablespoons rum	Nutmeg

Beat egg yolks. Add brandy and rum gradually (1 tablespoon at a time), while beating constantly. Add 1 pint of unwhipped cream and the well-beaten egg whites. Continue beating and add sugar and another pint of unwhipped cream. Sprinkle with nutmeg to taste. Shake in bottle before serving. Serves 10-12.

MRS. P. CHAUVIN WILKINSON

EGGNOG II

1 dozen eggs	1½ cups sugar
1 quart cream	1 pint whiskey

Separate eggs. Beat yolks and add sugar until creamy. Add whiskey slowly. Add whipped cream and stir well. Whip half of the whites (6) and add to the above mixture by folding them. Chill well. Serves 12-14.

MRS. RALPH PERLMAN

DANISH COFFEE

1½ squares chocolate
1 cup water
½ cup sugar
¼ cup instant coffee
¼ teaspoon salt
1 quart milk
⅓ cup chilled whipping cream

Chill bowl and beater; in medium sauce pan, mix chocolate, water, sugar, coffee and salt. Set over low heat, stirring until chocolate melts and comes to a boil; reduce heat and cook for 3 minutes, stirring occasionally. Remove from heat; stir constantly while adding milk. Return to heat until scalded, not boiled. Beat whipping cream in well chilled bowl until cream stands in peaks. Serve coffee piping hot, each serving topped with whipped cream. Serves 12-15.

Mrs. Prentice Bolin

ICED MINT CHOCOLATE

2 1-ounce squares chocolate
½ cup sugar
½ cup hot water
1 can (13 ounce) evaporated
   milk
¼ teaspoon vanilla
¼ teaspoon peppermint flavoring or 4 or 5 sprigs
   fresh mint
1 cup cracked ice

Cut chocolate into small pieces and place in blender; add sugar and hot water and blend about a minute, or stir over low heat until dissolved. Add other ingredients; place hand on cover of blender and blend another minute. Serve in tall glasses and garnish with whipped cream or ice cream. This makes 3 servings.

SOUTHERN MINT JULEP

4 sprigs fresh mint   1½ jigger bourbon whiskey
1 teaspoon sugar

Crush mint leaves and sugar in a 12-ounce glass. Fill with cracked ice and add whiskey. Stir until glass frosts. Decorate with sprig of mint.

Mrs. Henry Miller

MILK PUNCH

⅔ glass sweet milk
1 large tablespoon brandy
   or whiskey
Crushed ice
Nutmeg

Fill large glass ⅔ full of sweet milk. Add brandy or whiskey. Fill remainder of glass with crushed ice and pour into shaker, shaking until foamy. Sprinkle a pinch of grated nutmeg on top.

PINEAPPLE FIZZ

¾ cup Bacardi
1 egg white
¾ cup unsweetened pineapple
   juice
1½ cups crushed ice

Shake until frosted in shaker. Good ladies' drink.

Mrs. Prentice Bolin

EGG FLIP

1 egg
Sugar
1 tablespoon brandy

½ tablespoon rum
Hot milk
Pinch of grated nutmeg

Separate egg. Add sufficient sugar to the yolk to make it stiff. Beat egg white until stiff and add to yolk. Stir in the brandy and rum and fill remainder of glass with hot milk. Add sprinkling of nutmeg on top. Good for colds.

RUM PUNCH

2 quarts Bacardi rum
1 quart bourbon
1 quart unsweetened pine-
  apple juice

1 pint maraschino cherries
  and juice
6 oranges, cut in small pieces
6 lemons, cut in small pieces

Dilute with ice only

This makes 5 quarts. You can use 1 quart charged water or ginger ale.

The late MR. LEE HERZBERG
through MRS. RALPH PERLMAN

TRADER VIC'S SCORPION

6 ounces orange juice
4 ounces lemon juice
6 ounces light rum

1 ounce gin
1 ounce brandy
2 ounces orgeat syrup

Mix thoroughly and pour over cracked ice. Let stand 2 hours, add more ice and pour into champagne glasses. Garnish with a fresh flower. Serves 4.

TIPS FOR PUNCH

For very clear ice cubes, use boiled water in the ice trays.

Fancy ice cubes:

1. *Add a little green coloring to the water before freezing, for cool-looking effect.*

2. *Freeze cubes with curls of lemon or orange peel, maraschino cherries with stems intact, or sprigs of mint in the ice cubes.*

3. *Freeze left-over fruit juices or drinks in the cube trays to serve in iced tea or other fruit beverages.*

4. *Ice floats for holiday punches are made by freezing delicate flowers in various shaped containers.*

In making punches or fruit drinks, one may boil the rinds and use the juice remaining; it adds a nice flavor.

FROZEN FRUIT JUICE PUNCH

3 cans frozen lemonade
2 cans frozen orange juice
4 boxes frozen raspberries
2 cans frozen pineapple juice
2 cans frozen grapefruit juice

Dilute all frozen juices according to instructions on cans and combine. Crush frozen raspberries through food mill. Freeze ⅓ amount of raspberries to use in place of ice. Mix remaining ⅔ raspberries with above diluted juices. This makes 8 quarts punch.

MRS. W. R. EIDSON

PUNCH FOR A LARGE GROUP

4 cups sugar
2 cups water
2 cups strong tea
2 cups lemon juice
2½ cups orange juice
2 large cans pineapple juice
2 packages frozen strawberries (with juice)
3 gallons water
2 quarts ginger ale

Boil sugar and the 2 cups water together to make a syrup (about 10 minutes). Add tea, lemon juice, orange juice, and pineapple juice. Chill several hours, add the thawed strawberries (with juice), remaining water and ginger ale. Pour over block of ice or ice cubes. Serves 75, generously.

MRS. JOHN HOPPER

HOT SPICED PUNCH

1½ pints water
1 pint grape juice
1 lemon, sliced
1 teaspoon whole cloves
1 stick cinnamon bark
1 teaspoon whole allspice
¼-½ cup sugar

Combine and boil together several minutes. Serve steaming hot. Serves 12-14.

MRS. A. K. GORDON, SR.

RUSSIAN OR SPICED TEA

10 cups water
2 cups sugar
2 oranges, juice and rind
4 teaspoons tea
2 lemons, juice and rind
10 whole cloves
10 whole allspice

Boil together for 10 minutes, 8 cups water, sugar, lemon and orange rinds, cloves and spice tied in bag of cheesecloth. Pour 2 cups of boiling water over the tea; let stand 5 minutes. Add this to the first mixture. Strain through a thin cloth. If too strong, a little more water may be added. Serve very hot or very cold. Serves about 15.

MRS. THOMAS P. ROBERTS

"BOSTON CLUB" PUNCH

Juice of 9 dozen lemons
4 large fresh pineapples, cut
in small chunks, or 8 No. 2
cans pineapple chunks
3½ pounds sugar (7 cups)

3½ quarts white wine
3½ quarts good champagne
½ pint curaçao
10 boxes frozen strawberries
or fresh

Combine lemon juice, pineapple chunks, and sugar. Immediately before serving add remaining ingredients and pour over large chunks of ice. This makes 11 gallons and is a lovely punch for receptions.

Mrs. Ovide B. LaCour

SPARKLING CRANBERRY PUNCH

1 large can jellied cranberry
sauce
2¼ cups water
½ cup sugar

½ cup lemon juice
1 teaspoon almond extract
1½ cups ginger ale
Clove-studded lemon slices

Mint

Crush cranberry sauce in can with fork and empty into saucepan. Beat with rotary beater. Add water and beat until sauce is melted. Add sugar and cool. Stir in lemon juice, extract and 1 cup of ginger ale. Just before serving, dilute with remaining ½ ginger ale, and serve well iced in frosted glasses. Garnish with mint and clove-studded lemon circles. Serves 12 punch cups.

GUMBOS

AND

SOUPS

A Word About Gumbos:

Gumbo is an ORIGINAL *creation and a cherished possession in South Louisiana kitchens. The word "gumbo" comes from the Congo "quin-gombo" which means okra. It may be made with okra or with filé as a thickening agent. Filé is the powdered sassafras leaf made long ago by the Choctaw Indians. Whereas okra is cooked with the gumbo, filé is added* AFTER *the gumbo is removed from the heat. Never add filé while gumbo is cooking because boiling after the filé is added tends to make the gumbo stringy and unfit for use.*

Gumbo is a wonderful means of using leftovers: bits of ham or a ham-bone, turkey, duck or chicken carcass, sausage, seafoods or bacon. (When using a carcass or a hambone, boil the bones and use this stock in the gumbo.) Gumbo is subject to infinite variations; all these ingredients are interchangeable in the following recipes. The thickness of the gumbo depends on the amount of water. Gumbo is best served over mounds of hot rice in a large flat soup bowl.

BASIC GUMBO FILÉ

3 quarts water
1 onion, quartered
3 cloves garlic
½ bell pepper
3 tablespoons oil or bacon drippings

3 tablespoons flour
1½ teaspoons salt
Pepper
Oysters (½ pint and up)
Shrimp (⅔ pound and up)
1 teaspoon filé

Let vegetables simmer in water until they fall apart. Mash on plate, discarding pepper skin. Return pulp to water. Make dark roux of oil and flour, stirring constantly. Slowly stir in seasoned water, then salt and pepper. Cook 5 minutes. Add shrimp and cook 15 minutes; then add oysters and simmer 5 more minutes. Filé should be added after gumbo is removed from heat, just before serving. Allow to stand 5 minutes after stirring in filé. Serves 4.

The roux should be thicker for an oyster gumbo than one without because of the water exuded by oysters.

See Basic Roux in Meat Section. THE EDITORS

CHICKEN OKRA GUMBO

1 spring fryer (about 2 pounds)
1½ pounds fresh okra
1 fresh tomato, chopped
1 large onion, chopped
2 tablespoons shortening

3 tablespoons shortening or bacon drippings (from that used to fry chicken)
2 tablespoons flour
3 quarts water
Salt and pepper to taste

Cut up chicken; dredge with flour, salt, and pepper. Fry until brown. Fry okra with tomato and onion in the shortening. Make a roux in heavy skillet with grease from fried chicken and flour. Brown roux. Add fried chicken and the vegetables. Stir for a few minutes. Add water. Salt and pepper to taste. Cook for about 2 hours. Serves 6.

MRS. CHARLES HUSTMYRE

OKRA GUMBO

50 pods fresh okra, chopped
2 tablespoons cooking oil
1 3- to 4-pound chicken, cut up
Meat of 1 ham bone or 1 pound ham, chopped
1 No. 2 can tomatoes

1 large onion, diced
3 sprigs parsley, chopped
3 quarts boiling water
Salt to taste
Red pepper to taste
1 bay leaf

Wash, stem and cut okra into $\frac{1}{2}$-inch pieces. Fry until brown, being careful not to scorch. Season with salt and pepper. Do this with as little grease as possible. Put cooking oil into deep pot. When hot, add chicken and ham. Cover and let simmer about ten minutes. Chop tomatoes fine and save juice. Add the onion, parsley, and tomatoes to the cooking meat mixture, stirring frequently. Next add fried okra and juice of the tomatoes. Immediately add bay leaf and water which has been boiling. Let simmer for about an hour. Salt and pepper to taste. Serve hot over boiled rice. Makes about 4 quarts.

MRS. FRANK SAMUEL

SHRIMP GUMBO

2 pounds shrimp
2 tablespoons oil
2 tablespoons flour
3 cups okra, chopped or 1 tablespoon filé
2 onions, chopped
2 tablespoons oil

1 can tomatoes
2 quarts water
1 bay leaf
1 teaspoon salt
3 pods garlic (optional)
Red pepper (optional)

Peel shrimp uncooked and devein. Make roux (dark) of flour and oil. Add shrimp to this for a few minutes stirring constantly. Set aside. Smother okra and onions in oil. Add tomatoes when okra is nearly cooked. Then add water, bay leaf, garlic, salt, and pepper. Add shrimp and roux to this. Cover and cook slowly for 30 minutes.

If okra is not used, add gumbo filé after turning off heat.

Serve with rice. Serves 6 to 8.

SEAFOOD GUMBO

The same basic gumbo as for the shrimp may be used. In addition to the shrimp, add $\frac{1}{2}$ pint oysters and 1 can fresh or frozen crabmeat, which has been picked for shell. After adding oysters and crabmeat, cook slowly for about 15 minutes.

SOUPS

BORSCH

10 medium-sized beets,
    tops included
10 cups soup stock
  or 4 cans clear bouillon
    diluted with 2 cans water
  or 12 chicken bouillon cubes
    dissolved in 10 cups water

1 tablespoon lemon juice
1 tablespoon salt
½ teaspoon pepper
1 cup sour cream
¼ cup flour

Wash, peel, and slice beets thin, reserving fresh leaves. Place soup stock and beets in large pot; cover and bring to a boil. Reduce heat and simmer until beets are done. Add beet tops, chopped medium fine. Mix lemon juice, salt, pepper, and sour cream together. Blend in flour carefully, making certain all flour is moistened. A blender does a good job of this. Add a little of the hot beet mixture, stirring until well blended. Pour slowly into soup, stirring constantly. When mixture gets to steaming point, remove from heat. Do not allow mixture to boil. Serve at once. Serves 4 to 6.

MRS. CHESTER WILLIAMS

COLD TOMATO SOUP I

2 cups tomato juice or mixed
    vegetable juice
1 rib celery
¼ medium green pepper
2 medium carrots
1 medium tomato
½ cucumber

Salt
Tabasco
Pepper
Worcestershire sauce
½ lime or lemon, thinly
    sliced

Chop all vegetables to easy bite size. Add salt, pepper, Tabasco, Worcestershire sauce to taste. Slice lime or lemon very thin. Add. Chill thoroughly. Serve in bowls, place one of the lime or lemon slices in each bowl. Serves 2.

MRS. C. B. LUIKART, JR.

COLD TOMATO SOUP II

4 fresh ripe tomatoes,
    peeled and diced
1 medium onion, diced
2 tablespoons olive oil
1 tablespoon wine vinegar
Black pepper to taste

1½ cups water
1 clove garlic, mashed
1 cucumber, diced
2 teaspoons salt
2 teaspoons sugar

Mash and mix all ingredients except cucumber. An electric blender does a superb job. Let stand in refrigerator over night. Just before serving, add diced cucumber. Serves 4 to 6. *This is a refreshing soup for hot summer days.*

MRS. HUBERT F. BRENNAN

CRAWFISH BISQUE

(On River Road it's always Crawfish. In other areas, Crayfish)

18 pounds crawfish

Gravy:

1 cup fat	Salt and pepper to taste
1 cup flour	1 tablespoon Worcestershire
2 tablespoons tomato paste	sauce
3 medium onions	2 quarts water
4 ribs celery	2 quarts hot water
4 large cloves garlic	1 bay leaf
1 medium bell pepper	1 lemon sliced
½ crawfish fat	⅓ crawfish tails

Crawfish "heads"

Stuffing for heads:

⅔ cup butter or bacon fat	1 teaspoon thyme
2 ribs celery	Juice of 1 lemon
8 cloves garlic	1 tablespoon Worcestershire
½ bunch parsley	sauce
2 large onions	1 teaspoon monosodium
1 medium bell pepper	glutamate
⅔ crawfish tails	1 tablespoon salt
½ bunch green onion tops	1 box bread crumbs
1 teaspoon black pepper	½ crawfish fat
1 teaspoon red pepper	

Cook crawfish in almost boiling salted water for 20 minutes. Remove and drain. Peel tails and clean heads, saving any yellow fat that clings to them in a separate container. Save "head" shells to stuff. (These shells are actually the thorax or body.)

Gravy: Make a roux, stirring constantly until golden brown. Add tomato paste. Grind onions, celery, garlic and bell pepper. Cook in roux until tender. Add crawfish fat and seasonings. Slowly stir in 2 quarts water. Add 2 quarts hot water, stir and let boil up. Add bay leaf, lower heat and cook 30-40 minutes. Drop in lemon slices, crawfish tails, and stuffed heads 10 minutes before serving.

Stuffing: Grind celery, garlic, parsley, onions, and bell pepper and cook in fat until tender. Remove from heat. Grind crawfish tails and green onions to add to above. Stir in all seasonings, mixing well. Add bread crumbs (reserve ½ cup to roll heads in). Use crawfish fat and enough warm water to make stuffing the proper consistency for handling. Stuff heads, roll in bread crumbs, and bake in 400° oven for 20 minutes.

Place few stuffed heads in each soup bowl along with gravy mixture. Serve over rice. Serves 16.

MRS. HANSEN SCOBEE

CHICKEN BROTH

3- to 4-pound hen
3 to 4 quarts water
3 cups celery, chopped
1 large onion, stuck with a
clove
2 medium-sized carrots,
diced

6 sprigs parsley
2 sprigs thyme or ¼ tea-
spoon powdered thyme
1 tablespoon salt
¼ teaspoon pepper

Select an old hen or a stewing hen. Cover with water and let come to a boil. Cover tightly; simmer 3 or more hours. Add the vegetables; let boil 1 hour longer. Strain, remove fat and add seasoning to taste. Remove chicken from broth before it falls to pieces, and use for salads, croquettes, or creamed chicken. Serves 8 to 10.

Rice or noodles may be cooked in the broth to make chicken-rice or chicken-noodle soup.

MRS. DAVID T. HARVEY

CRÈME VICHYSSOISE

¼ cup sliced onion
2 tablespoons butter
2 cups thinly sliced potatoes
2 cups chicken broth
1½ teaspoon salt

1½ cups milk
1 cup breakfast cream
Worcestershire sauce, hot
sauce, celery salt to taste

Slightly brown onions in butter. Add potatoes, broth, and salt. Bring to boiling point. Cover and simmer for thirty minutes. Press through fine sieve, or mix in electric blender. Add milk; bring to boiling point. Cool. Add cream, Worcestershire sauce, hot sauce, and celery salt. Chill. Serve very cold and garnish with chopped chives. Additional zest may be obtained by adding about one tablespoon finely minced green onion when adding cream. Serves 6.

MRS. W. H. WRIGHT, JR.

FRENCH ONION SOUP

4 onions, preferably red
1 tablespoon olive oil
2 tablespoons butter
1 teaspoon sugar
Salt and cayenne pepper
to taste

1 quart chicken stock
Small rounds of French
bread, toasted
4 tablespoons grated Par-
mesan cheese

Cut onions rather small. Fry very slowly in oil and butter until soft and translucent. Add sugar, salt, and cayenne. Put all in casserole and add stock. After toasting French bread, float it on top of soup. Sprinkle cheese over all. Bake in oven for 20 minutes. Serves 4.

MRS. DAVID VAN GELDER

CRÈME VICHYSSOISE GLACÉE

5 leeks (white part), sliced
fine
1 medium onion, sliced fine
2 ounces sweet butter
5 medium potatoes, sliced
fine

1 quart chicken broth
1 tablespoon salt
2 cups milk
2 cups medium cream
1 cup heavy cream

Brown the leeks and the onion very lightly in the butter. Add potatoes, broth, and salt. Boil from 35 to 40 minutes. Crush and run through fine strainer or put in blender. Return to heat and add 2 cups milk and 2 cups medium cream. Season to taste and bring to a boil. Cool and then run through a very fine strainer. When soup is cold, add the heavy cream. Chill thoroughly before serving. Chopped chives may be added when serving. Serves 8.

Mrs. Lancaster Collens

OYSTER STEW

½ stick butter
1 tablespoon flour
1 small bunch green onions,
chopped
1 quart milk
1 rib celery

6 cloves
Salt
Red pepper
Worcestershire sauce
White pepper
3 dozen oysters and liquor

Make roux of flour and butter. Add white part of chopped onion and cook for short while. Heat milk separately; add to roux. Add green part of chopped onions, chopped celery, cloves, and seasoning. Cook slowly. When thickened, add oysters and liquor. Do not boil. Serve very hot. Remove cloves before serving. Serves 3.

The late Mrs. J. H. Bres,
through Mrs. Chauvin Wilkinson

OYSTER STEW

2 or 3 dozen small oysters
with liquor
6 small green onion, chopped
fine
1 rib celery, chopped fine
Few sprigs parsley, minced

1 quart milk
1 stick butter or oleo
Salt and pepper
Worcestershire sauce
8 rolled crackers

Strain oyster liquor and save. Pick oysters for shell. Cook chopped vegetables and oysters in oyster liquor until oysters are plump and edges begin to curl. Do not overcook. While oysters are cooking, simmer one quart milk and stick of butter in saucepan. Do not boil. Add oyster mixture to milk and butter. Simmer a few minutes. Add salt, pepper, and Worcestershire sauce to taste. Before serving, add rolled crackers. Serves 4.

Mrs. Willis N. Maddox

SPLIT PEA SOUP

1 large ham bone
1 pound split peas
3 quarts water
1 white onion
½ carrot, diced

Seasoning (salt, red and
  white pepper)
6 slices bacon (optional)
2 eggs, hard cooked
  (optional)

Place split peas and ham bone in cold water and let come to a rapid boil. Continue boiling until peas have dissolved. Turn heat low and add seasoning. Cook slowly for two and a half hours. Before serving put soup through strainer. Replace ham bits in soup, discarding bone, fat, etc. To serve, you may add a tablespoon crumbled bacon and chopped egg to each plate of soup after soup has been ladled. Serves 6.

The late Mrs. J. H. Bres,
through Mrs. Chauvin Wilkinson

TURTLE SOUP

3 pounds turtle meat
4 quarts water
3 tablespoons flour
2 tablespoons shortening
3 ribs celery, ground
3 onions, ground
6 pods garlic, ground
1 large green pepper, ground
3 heaping tablespoons whole

spice (tied in thin cloth)
2 lemons, sliced thin
4 tablespoons Worcestershire
  sauce
4 eggs, hard cooked
Salt and pepper to taste
1 tablespoon sherry per
  serving (optional)
Parsley (optional)

Boil turtle meat in water until tender. Remove scum which forms with spoon. Make roux using shortening and flour. Add ground celery, onions, garlic, and bell pepper.

Remove turtle meat from stock. Strain stock and add to roux. Bones may be removed from turtle meat. Add meat to stock. Add lemons, Worcestershire sauce, pepper, and salt.

Place bag of spices in soup. Simmer for one hour. Add 1 tablespoon sherry per serving shortly before serving, if desired. Garnish with sliced hard cooked eggs and parsley. Serves 10 to 12.

Mrs. Peter M. Wilbert
Plaquemine, La.

CREAM OF PEANUT SOUP

1 tablespoon butter
3 tablespoons peanut butter
1 teaspoon minced onion
2 tablespoons flour

2 cups scalded milk
or 2 cups milk and 1 cup
  chicken stock
Salt and pepper to taste

Cook onions in butter and peanut butter for 5 minutes. Add flour and stir until smooth. Add scalded milk. Season to taste. Cook in double boiler 20 minutes. Chopped peanuts can be added.

Mrs. Joe MacCurdy

VEGETABLE SOUP

2 pounds heavy beef brisket
or soup bone
1 large onion
2 teaspoons salt
2 ribs celery
1 large Irish potato
3 quarts water
1 can tomatoes
1 cup chopped cabbage

3 carrots, chopped
1 turnip, diced
2 ribs celery, chopped
½ onion, chopped
½ potato, chopped
6 sprigs parsley, minced
Pepper to taste (optional)
Spaghetti or macaroni
(optional)

In four-quart covered pot broil meat with salt, 2 whole ribs celery, whole onion, and whole potato very slowly for three hours or longer. Take soup meat from pot and remove meat from bone, chopping to bite size and discarding bone and fat. Mash the well cooked onion, potato, and celery through strainer. Return these ingredients and meat to liquid. Add tomatoes and other vegetables, cooking until vegetables are well done. One medium sized can of cooked vegetables may be used in place of fresh vegetables. A small amount of spaghetti or macaroni may be broken into soup during the last 20 minutes of cooking. Serves 10.

MRS. DUDLEY POPE

SALADS

FIVE BASIC GREEN SALAD DRESSINGS

There are literally hundreds of dressings for salads, but actually they are variations of the dressings of Escoffier, maestro of chefs. You may follow the recipe for any one dressing and add your own variation.

1. Oil Dressing—basis for French Dressing—three parts of oil to one of vinegar (or lemon juice), plus salt and pepper.

2. Cream Dressing—three parts of cream to one of vinegar, more salt and pepper than above oil dressing.

3. Egg Dressing—sieve hard-cooked egg yolks, mix with oil, vinegar, salt and pepper, using the whites sliced julienne fashion, chopped or sieved and sprinkled on the salad as garnish.

4. Bacon Dressing—hot bacon drippings replace the oil in the basic oil dressing. This is especially good on cabbage, spinach, or lettuce.

5. Mustard and Sweet Cream Dressing—one-third pint fresh cream mixed with one teaspoon dry mustard, the juice of a lemon, salt and pepper.

SALAD HINTS:

1. Always break lettuce in bite-size pieces; never cut it with a knife.

2. To mix your salad, place lettuces, greens and herbs in the salad bowl, shake dressing vigorously, pour over, toss the greens well with wooden fork and spoon. This tossing takes time, each leaf must be coated but not drenched with dressing.

3. Serve salad only in well chilled wooden bowls or on well chilled plates.

4. Salad dressing should be added to greens just before serving.

CELERY SEED DRESSING
(For Fruit Salad)

½ cup sugar	¼ grated onion
1 teaspoon dry mustard	⅓ cup vinegar
1 teaspoon salt	1 cup salad oil
1 teaspoon paprika	1 tablespoon celery seed
¼ teaspoon pepper	Red food coloring

To dry ingredients add a little vinegar, then add oil slowly, a little at a time, beating thoroughly after each addition. Then add remainder of vinegar and celery seed. Add a small amount of red food coloring to make the dressing a soft rose color. Will keep in a sealed jar in refrigerator. Good!

MRS. KENNETH SWARTWOOD

CREAMY FRENCH DRESSING

2 cups salad oil
2 tablespoons brown sugar
½ cup vinegar
3 tablespoons catsup
1 teaspoon salt

1 teaspoon paprika
⅛ teaspoon dry mustard
2 teaspoons grated onion or onion juice
½ egg white (unbeaten)

2 gloves garlic

Mix thoroughly all ingredients. Cut garlic and add last. Will keep in refrigerator. *Excellent. Delicious on tossed green salad.*

MRS. GEORGE SMALLING

MONKEY'S SALAD DRESSING

1½ cups salad oil
½ cup vinegar
6 tablespoons minced parsley
3 tablespoons minced green pepper
½ teaspoon red pepper

1 large onion (chopped)
1 tablespoon each of confectioner's sugar, and salt
1 teaspoon dry mustard
1 3-ounce package cream cheese

Put first eight ingredients into blender and blend for 1 minute. Break up cream cheese; add to above and blend again. This should be made at least one hour before using. Shake thoroughly. Use on green salad.

MRS. ROBERT BOWLUS

EGG SALAD DRESSING

5 hard cooked eggs
½ cup salad oil

¼ cup lemon juice
1 teaspoon salt

½ teaspoon pepper

Mash egg yolks in bowl. Add oil and mix well. Add lemon juice, salt and pepper. Break egg whites in small pieces and add. Stir well; serve on lettuce wedges.

MRS. FRED C. FREY, JR.

FRUIT DRESSING FOR FRUIT SALAD

Juice of 1 lemon
Juice of 1 orange
⅓ cup pineapple juice

½ cup sugar
⅛ teaspoon salt
3 eggs

1 teaspoon grated lemon rind

Measure lemon and orange juice into measuring cup. Add pineapple juice to make 1 cup of juice. Place in top of double boiler. Add sugar, salt, eggs, and grated rind and beat to blend. Cook over simmering water, stirring constantly until thickened. Cool and store covered. Thin with plain or whipped cream when ready to serve on fruit salads. Makes 1⅓ cups.

MRS. R. LOUIS MOSCHETTE

GREEN GODDESS SALAD DRESSING

1 clove garlic, crushed
2 tablespoons chopped an-
chovies (optional)
3 tablespoons chopped green
onion
1 tablespoon lemon juice

3 tablespoons tarragon wine
vinegar
½ cup sour cream
1 cup mayonnaise
⅓ cup chopped parsley
Salt and coarse black pepper

Mix in order given and chill. Makes 1 pint. Serves 8-12.

MRS. CLAY RICHMOND

OLD FASHIONED COOKED SALAD DRESSING

½ teaspoon mustard
1 teaspoon salt
¼ teaspoon paprika
1 tablespoon sugar

1½ tablespoons flour
1 egg
1 tablespoon butter
1 cup milk

¼ cup vinegar

Mix dry ingredients together in top of double boiler. Add well-beaten eggs to the milk and slowly mix the liquid into dry ingredients. Cook until mixture thickens. Remove from the fire and add butter; after mixture cools, add vinegar. Delicious poured over home grown lettuce. Add hard cooked egg, if desired.

MRS. THOMAS P. ROBERTS

ROQUEFORT CHEESE SALAD DRESSING

¼ cup wine vinegar
¾ cup oil
2 teaspoons salt
1 teaspoon black pepper
¾ teaspoon red pepper
1 teaspoon Worcestershire
sauce

1 teaspoon dry mustard
1 teaspoon salad herbs
1 teaspoon seasoning salt
1 clove garlic, pressed or
1 teaspoon garlic powder
¾ teaspoon hot sauce

½ pound Roquefort or Bleu cheese

Place all ingredients in blender and mix thoroughly. May be stored in refrigerator indefinitely. Dressing is salty and salad will need little, if any, salt. Serves 8.

MRS. ERNEST R. EANES, JR.

SENSATION SALAD DRESSING

½ pound finely ground
Romano cheese

1 pint salad oil
Juice of 2 lemons

Juice of 3 cloves of garlic

Shake all ingredients in a quart jar. Dressing will keep indefinitely in refrigerator. Especially good tossed with lettuce, water cress, and parsley leaves. Salt and pepper greens as desired before adding dressing.

MRS. JEAN FREY FRITCHIE

ROQUEFORT CHEESE DRESSING

2 tablespoons (heaping)
mayonnaise
2 tablespoons sweet cream
3 tablespoons Roquefort
cheese
Freshly ground pepper (to
taste)

3 tablespoons oil, half salad,
half olive
1 tablespoon white wine
vinegar
Crushed clove of garlic

Thin mayonnaise with cream; add cheese and blend well. Stir in oil, vinegar and pepper; mix well. Add garlic for flavor, but remove, if preferred, before pouring dressing over salad.

SWEET CREAM DRESSING

¼ cup cream
⅛ teaspoon ginger
¼ teaspoon curry

½ teaspoon salt
White pepper (to taste)
Juice of ½ lemon

Mix the cream with dry ingredients; add lemon juice slowly, mixing well. Good with fruit, fish, chicken, eggs, or lettuce salads.

MRS. MILTON WOMACK

THOUSAND ISLAND DRESSING

1 cup mayonnaise
¼ cup chili sauce
2 hard-cooked eggs, chopped
2 tablespoons chopped
pimiento
1 teaspoon grated onion

¼ teaspoon Worcestershire
sauce
1 tablespoon chopped stuffed
olives
Sweet pickles, chopped
(optional)

Combine ingredients. Serve on head of lettuce or on tomato salad.

PIQUANT MAYONNAISE

2 egg yolks or 1 whole egg
1 pint salad oil
1 teaspoon salt
¼ teaspoon red pepper
½ teaspoon black pepper
1 teaspoon mustard

½ teaspoon Worcestershire
sauce
¼ teaspoon hot sauce
2 tablespoons vinegar
3 tablespoons boiling water

Put egg yolks or whole egg into small mixing bowl; add all other ingredients except oil and water. Beat on medium speed until thoroughly mixed. Increase speed to medium high; slowly add salad oil, small amount at a time, until mayonnaise begins to thicken. Oil can then be added faster. When all oil is used, add boiling water and mix thoroughly. (Boiling water does away with the oily appearance.) Grated onion can be added if mayonnaise is to be used for sandwiches, potato salad, etc.

BLACK CHERRY SHERRY SALAD

2 packages cherry gelatin
1⅓ cups boiling water
1¾ cups juice from black
   Bing cherries

½ cup dry sherry wine
1½ cups seedless grapes
1 can Bing cherries
1 cup pecan meats

Dissolve gelatin in boiling water. Add juice and sherry wine to the gelatin mixture. Put in cool place and allow to slightly thicken. Lightly brush 8 or 10 molds, according to size, with salad oil and partly fill with grapes, cherries and nut meats. Finish filling molds with the liquid and set in refrigerator to congeal. Serves 8 or 10.

MRS. LEROY WARD III

SAUTERNES SALAD

1 cup water
1 package apple gelatin
1 cup green seedless grapes
1 small can crushed pineapple
   (reserve juice)

½ cup Sauterne wine and
   pineapple juice to make 1
   cup

Heat the water and dissolve gelatin. Add remaining ingredients and pour into individual molds. Unmold on lettuce; top with homemade mayonnaise. Serves 6 to 8.

MRS. DAVID W. THOMAS

COCA-COLA SALAD

(Delicious and perfect for Thanksgiving or Christmas)

1 package raspberry gelatin
1 package cherry gelatin
1 can seedless white cherries
1 large can crushed pineapple
1 cup pecans

1 8-ounce package cream
   cheese (frozen)
2 Coca-Colas (partially
   frozen)

Dissolve gelatin in juices (heated) from cherries and pineapple. Then add cokes, cherries, pineapple and nuts. Grate frozen cream cheese over top of molds (gives the appearance of snow). Place in refrigerator congeal. The "frozen" cokes make congealing faster. Serves 10.

MRS. MALCOLM SEVIER
Tallulah, La.

GREEN GAGE PLUM SALAD

1 package lime gelatin
1½ cups hot water
½ cup green gage plum juice
⅛ teaspoon salt
½ teaspoon vinegar

1 can green gage plums
   (pitted)
1 3-ounce package cream
   cheese

Dissolve gelatin in hot water; add plum juice, salt and vinegar; cool. Place plums in mold; pour half gelatin over plums; add remainder gelatin mixture to cream cheese and whip until light. Pour over plum mixture and chill several hours. Unmold on lettuce leaf. Serves 8.

MRS. HUGH A. NEAL

"EMERALD" SALAD

2 tablespoons gelatin
1 cup cold water
1 cup sugar
½ cup water
½ cup vinegar (scant)

1 medium size can pineapple, crushed, plus juice
1 cup nuts, finely chopped
1 cup sweet pickles, sliced thin
½ cup celery, chopped

Dash of onion juice, if desired

Dissolve gelatin in cold water and soak 5 minutes. Cook sugar, water and vinegar to a thin syrup. While hot, but not boiling, add gelatin and stir until dissolved. When it begins to set, add pineapple, nuts, pickles, celery and onion. Let set for 2 hours. Serve on lettuce with mayonnaise. Serves 12.

Mrs. George W. Garig

COTTAGE COMPOTE

(A Holiday Salad)

1 12-ounce box dry cottage cheese
1 large can evaporated milk
1 teaspoon almond flavoring
2 No. 2 cans fruit cocktail

2 envelopes gelatin
½ cup chopped celery
½ cup chopped pecans
1 4-ounce bottle maraschino cherries, chopped

Place cottage cheese in mixing bowl, gradually adding milk, beating at medium speed. Add almond flavoring. Drain liquid from cans of fruit cocktail. Dissolve gelatin in one half of liquid. Bring balance of liquid to boil and add gelatin to it. Add gelatin to cheese mixture, continue heating at high speed until fluffy. Fold in remaining ingredients. Spoon into 8" x 8" x 2" plan. Chill until firm. Serve in squares on lettuce. Garnish with green grapes and top with pink salad dressing. Serves 9.

Mrs. William R. McGehee

LIME GELATIN AND COTTAGE CHEESE SALAD

1 package lime gelatin
1 package lemon gelatin
2 cups boiling water
1 No. 2 can crushed pineapple, drained
1 carton cottage cheese

1 cup mayonnaise
1 can condensed milk
1 cup finely chopped nuts
2 heaping tablespoons horseradish
3 tablespoons lemon juice

¼ teaspoon salt

Dissolve the gelatin in hot water and let stand until cool; add pineapple. Blend cheese with mayonnaise until smooth and add to gelatin mixture. Add all other ingredients and stir until mixture begins to congeal. Pour into molds and place in refrigerator overnight. Serves 16.

Mrs. William Adams
Tallulah, La.

PINEAPPLE CHEESE SALAD

1 package gelatin
1 cup cold water
1 No. 2 can crushed pine-
  apple
1 heaping cup sugar

1 cup American cheese,
  grated
Salt to taste
Juice of 1 lemon
1 pint whipping cream,
  whipped

Dissolve gelatin in gold water. Cook pineapple with sugar; boil 10 or 15 minutes. Add cheese and a little salt to pineapple; then add gelatin and lemon juice. Let mixture stand until it cools and begins to jell. Fold whipped cream into gelatin mixture. Place in mold and slice when cold. Serves 8.

Mrs. M. E. Byrd, Sr.

PINEAPPLE CHERRY SALAD

1 small can crushed pine-
  apple
½ cup sugar
1 envelope gelatin

½ cup cold water
1 package soft cream cheese
½ pint whipping cream
½ cup chopped nuts

Small bottle red cherries

Drain juice from pineapple. Add to juice ½ cup sugar and let boil until syrupy. (Just a few minutes.) Dissolve gelatin in ½ cup cold water and add to warm syrup, stirring until completely dissolved. Mash cheese and add to pineapple. When syrup is cool, add cheese, pineapple, whipped cream, nuts, and cherries. Place in molds and chill.

Mrs. Millard E. Byrd, Jr.

RASPBERRY SALAD

1 10-ounce package marsh-
  mallows
1 package frozen raspberries

2 3-ounce packages cream
  cheese
⅔ cup mayonnaise

1 small can evaporated milk (chilled and whipped)

Melt marshmallows in double boiler with raspberries. Let cool; add cream cheese blended with mayonnaise. Add whipped milk to raspberry mixture. Place in tray and freeze. Unmold on lettuce leaves. Serves 12.

Mrs. William Adams
Tallulah, La.

FRUIT AND MARSHMALLOW SALAD
(Quickie)

1 small can crushed pine-
  apple
1 cup cherries (white or
  Bing), pitted
1 cup chopped pears

1 cup chopped peaches
2 medium sliced bananas
1½ or 2 cups miniature
  marshmallows
½ cup mayonnaise

¼ cup chopped nuts (optional)

Combine all fruits and marshmallows; mix lightly with mayonnaise. Chill several hours in refrigerator and serve in individual lettuce cup topped by ½ teaspoon mayonnaise, if preferred. Serves 8.

Mrs. Milton Womack

CRANBERRY SALAD I

2 boxes lemon gelatin
1 pint boiling water
1 cup cold water
¼ teaspoon salt

1 whole orange
3 cups raw cranberries
1 cup sugar
1 cup finely chopped apples

Dissolve the lemon gelatin in the boiling water; add the cold water and salt. Cool. Grind together the whole orange (including the rind) and cranberries. Add sugar and mix well. Then add apples. Combine with the gelatin and place in refrigerator in molds or in oblong pyrex plates. Serve on lettuce leaves and top with mayonnaise and a green cherry. This makes a pretty Christmas salad. Serves 8 to 10.

MRS. DON MCADAMS

CRANBERRY SALAD II

1 pound cranberries, ground
1 whole orange, ground
1½ cups sugar
2 packages cherry gelatin

2 cups warm water
1 cup chopped pecans
1 cup chopped marshmallows
1½ cups chopped celery

Let ground cranberries, orange and sugar mixture set overnight. Mix gelatin with warm water. When it starts to jell, add pecans, marshmallows, celery and cranberry mixture. Refrigerate until well set. Serve on lettuce leaf with mayonnaise. Serves 8 to 10.

MRS. PERCY ROBERTS, JR.

CRANBERRY SALAD III

2 cups raw cranberries
½ medium orange
Small can crushed pineapple
1 package raspberry gelatin

Sugar (1 cup), sweeten to taste
1 cup pecans

Wash and pick cranberries. Put cranberries and orange through food chopper alternately. Use rind of orange. Add pineapple, sugar and pecans. Use juices from drained pineapple, orange and cranberries to make 2 cups liquid for dissolving the gelatin. (Add water to make 2 cups, if necessary.) Make gelatin and add cranberry mixture. Serves 8.

MRS. JOE M. MACCURDY

MOLDED TUNA SALAD

2 6-ounce cans tuna
2 hard-cooked eggs, chopped
½ cup chopped stuffed olives
1 tablespoon minced onion
or chives

2 tablespoons plain gelatin
½ cup cold water
2 cups mayonnaise
Red pepper to taste

Lightly grease mold or individual molds with salad oil and turn to drain excess oil. Mince tuna with eggs, olives, and onion. Soften gelatin in cold water 5 minutes. Dissolve over hot water and add mayonnaise gradually, stirring constantly. Fold into fish mixture; turn into mold and chill until firm. Unmold on lettuce. Serves 8.

MRS. LEO SANCHEZ

CRABMEAT SALAD

3 tablespoons gelatin
⅔ cup cold water
1 tablespoon sugar
3 tablespoons flour
1 tablespoon dry mustard
3 egg yolks, beaten
1 whole egg, beaten
2¼ cups whole milk

½ cup Tarragon vinegar
3 tablespoons butter
4 cups fresh cooked flaked crabmeat
3 cups diced celery
½ cup diced pimento
¾ cup chopped green onions

Worcestershire sauce, salt and pepper, to taste

Dissolve gelatin in cold water. In double boiler cook until thick the following: sugar, flour, mustard, egg yolks, whole egg, milk, vinegar and butter. Add gelatin and remainder of ingredients. Chill and serve on lettuce leaf with homemade mayonnaise. Serves 14.

MRS. JOHN BARTON

SHRIMP SALAD

1 pound shrimp
1 large clove garlic
3 or 4 celery tops
2 celery ribs, finely chopped
1 hard cooked egg, finely chopped

1 sweet pickle, finely chopped or 1 teaspoon capers
2 tablespoons mayonnaise
Salt and pepper to taste

Boil shrimp in salty water, seasoned with the garlic and celery tops. Let water boil before adding shrimp. Boil shrimp for approximately 15 minutes. Peel and devein shrimp. Cut each shrimp into two or three pieces. Add celery, egg, pickle or capers, and mayonnaise. Mix thoroughly and add salt and red pepper to taste. Serve on lettuce leaves or stuffed into avocado halves or scraped out tomatoes. Serves 4 to 6.

MRS. LOUIS SELIG, SR.

EGG AND CHICKEN MOLD

1 envelope plain gelatin
½ cup cold water
1 teaspoon salt
1 tablespoon lemon juice
Dash hot sauce
¾ cup mayonnaise
1½ tablespoons grated onion
½ cup finely diced green peppers
¼ cup chopped pimento (optional)

4 hard cooked eggs, chopped
1 envelope plain gelatin
½ cup cold chicken stock (fat taken off)
1¼ cup hot chicken stock
½ teaspoon salt
1 tablespoon lemon juice
2 cups cooked chicken, diced
½ cup diced celery

Soften 1 envelope of gelatin in cold water. Dissolve over boiling water. Add 1 teaspoon salt, 1 tablespoon lemon juice, hot sauce, and cool. Add mayonnaise. Mix with onions, pimento, bell peppers and eggs. Let this mixture set. Then soften the remaining envelope of gelatin in the cold chicken stock. Dissolve gelatin mixture in hot chicken stock, and mix together remaining ingredients. Pour over the other mixture and refrigerate. Serves 9.

MRS. CLINTON COLEMAN

BEET SALAD

3 cups chopped beets
  (2 No. 2 cans)
½ cup vinegar
½ cup sugar
2 teaspoons powdered
  horseradish
1½ teaspoon salt

2 envelopes plain gelatin
½ cup cold water
¼ cup India relish
1½ cups diced celery
1½ tablespoons minced
  green onions

Drain beets, reserving all liquid. Place beets in vinegar and combine with dry ingredients; marinate until you boil beet liquor and add to gelatin, which has been swelled in cold water. Add other ingredients and place in greased mold. Serves 8 to 12.

MRS. WILLIAM R. SMITH

COLE SLAW

1 medium head cabbage,
  shredded
4 carrots, scraped and grated
1 cup mayonnaise

¼ cup light cream or milk
⅓ cup onions, finely minced
Salt and pepper to taste

Combine cabbage and carrots in large salad bowl and refrigerate. Mix together mayonnaise, cream or milk, and onion. Let stand in refrigerator at least 20 minutes. Pour dressing over vegetables, toss lightly, and season to taste. Refrigerate immediately. The colder the salad, the better it tastes. Serves 8.

MRS. FRANK McMAINS

JELLIED GAUCAMOLE SALAD

2 packages plain gelatin
1 cup cold water
2 cups boiling water
½ cup whole cooked shrimp
4 cups mashed avocado

¼ cup lemon juice
1 teaspoon salt (or more
  to taste)
Few drops Tabasco

Soften gelatin in cold water; dissolve in boiling water. Pour a little clear gelatin in the bottom of a mold, arrange shrimp in it and chill until firm. (Shrimp may be marinated in a French dressing for a few hours beforehand, then drained well.) Mash avocado with lemon juice; add seasonings and remaining gelatin and pour mixture on top of firm shrimp layer. Chill until firm. Unmold on serving dish and garnish with lettuce, tomato, and cucumber wedges. Serve with mayonnaise. Serves 10 to 12.

SUE BAKER
Times-Picayune Food Consultant

CUCUMBER SALAD

1 package lime gelatin
1 cup boiling water
½ cup chopped bell pepper
⅔ cup peeled, grated
  cucumber

½ cup minced parsley
1 cup cream cheese, drained
2 tablespoons onion juice
½ teaspoon salt
⅛ teaspoon white pepper
1 tablespoon horseradish

½ cup whipped evaporated milk

Dissolve gelatin in boiling water; let cool. Mix in all ingredients and lastly fold in whipped milk. Place in mold in refrigerator overnight. Serves 18 in small individual molds.

MRS. WILLIAM ADAMS
Tallulah, La.

SOUR CREAM CUCUMBERS

½ teaspoon salt
½ teaspoon sugar
½ teaspoon red pepper and
  cayenne
¼ cup garlic wine vinegar

1 cup sour cream
2 teaspoons chopped chives
  or 1 teaspoon grated onion
1 teaspoon celery seed

2 or 3 fresh cucumbers of medium size

Dissolve salt, sugar, and pepper in wine vinegar. Whip cream until smooth and stiff. Add chives and celery seeds. Slice cucumbers after scoring edges with fork tines. Combine with dressing and allow to stand in refrigerator for at least 2 hours before serving.

MRS. R. LOUIS MOSCHETTE
Home Economics Dept., LSU

MOLDED CARROT SALAD

1 package lemon gelatin
2 cups grated carrots

1 cup grated onion
2 cups finely chopped cabbage

1 cup finely chopped bell pepper

Prepare gelatin as directed on package, add all chopped ingredients and pour in individual molds. Serve on lettuce with mayonnaise. Serves 8 or 10.

MRS. JOHN FERGUSON

TOMATO ASPIC SUPREME

1 can tomato soup
1 12-ounce can V-8 juice
1 8-ounce package cream
  cheese
3 tablespoons gelatin
½ cup water
1 cup mayonnaise

¾ cup chopped bell pepper
¾ cup chopped celery
¼ cup chopped green onion
  tops
1 avocado, mashed or
  chopped
1 small onion, chopped

Heat soup and juice with cream cheese. Melt and beat lumps out. Dissolve gelatin in ½ cup water and add to soup mixture. Add salt and Tabasco or red pepper to taste. Stir in rest of ingredients and chill. Serves 12. Cooked shrimp or crabmeat may be added for a main dish.

MRS. FRED PARNELL, JR.

TOMATO SOUP SALAD
(Men like it)

2 cans tomato soup
1 soup can boiling water
1½ packages plain gelatin
½ cup cold water
1 cup chopped nuts

1 3-ounce package cream
  cheese
¾ cup chopped celery
3 tablespoons chili sauce
3 tablespoons mayonnaise

Combine first two ingredients. Dissolve gelatin in cold water and add to soup mixture. Add all other ingredients; pour into mold and refrigerate. Serve on lettuce leaves topped with home-made mayonnaise. Serves 8.

MRS. CHARLES PROSSER

SHRIMP TOMATO ASPIC

1½ envelopes of gelatin
¼ cup cold water
2 cups tomato juice
1 bay leaf
1 rib celery
¼ onion
Salt and pepper to taste
Lemon juice to taste

Worcestershire to taste
Dash of hot sauce
1 tablespoon minced parsley
¼ cup finely chopped celery
2 grated carrots
1½ cups shrimp (cut in
  pieces
Hard cooked eggs, sliced

Dissolve gelatin in cold water. Bring to boil and simmer slowly for 5 minutes the tomato juice, bay leaf, rib of celery and onion. Remove onion, bay leaf and celery and add dissolved gelatin. Mix well. Add salt, pepper, lemon juice, Worcestershire sauce and tabasco. Add minced parsley, chopped celery, carrots and shrimp. Pour a small portion into a large mold or individual molds and arrange slices of hard cooked eggs in bottom. Allow to jell. Then pour on rest. Place in refrigerator until firm. Turn out on lettuce leaves and top with home-made mayonnaise.

MRS. A. B. MOORE

ARTICHOKES IN ASPIC

1¾ cups tomato juice
1 envelope plain gelatin
1 tablespoon vinegar
1 teaspoon minced onion
½ teaspoon salt

Few drops Worcestershire
  sauce
1 hard cooked egg
3 cooked artichoke hearts
  (bottoms)
½ cup chopped celery
Salad greens

Mayonnaise

Heat 1½ cups tomato juice. Soften gelatin in remaining cold tomato juice and dissolve in hot juice. Blend in next four ingredients. Cool to consistency of unbeaten egg white. Slice egg and artichoke crosswise. In each of 6 individual molds, place a slice of egg and artichoke. Cover with thin layer of gelatin mixture. Chill. Chop remaining egg and artichokes and fold into rest of gelatin with celery. Turn into molds over firm layer and chill until firm. Unmold on salad greens and serve with mayonnaise. Serves 6.

PARISH LIBRARY PANTRY

AVOCADO SALAD WITH BLEU CHEESE DRESSING

Blend 1 triangle of bleu cheese into 1 cup French dressing. Add 1 large avocado, sliced. Keep refrigerated at least 4 hours. Mix lightly with hunks of green lettuce and ½ cup homemade mayonnaise. Serves 8.

MRS. JEAN FREY FRITCHIE

AVOCADO SALAD

2 packages gelatin	¼ cup sugar
½ cup cold water	1 small onion, grated
1 cup boiling water	1 teaspoon salt
½ cup lemon juice	3 or 4 avocados, mashed

Dissolve gelatin in cold water, then add boiling water and cool. Add lemon juice, sugar, onion, salt, and avocados. Place in greased (lightly) salad ring mold or individual molds and chill until firm. Unmold on lettuce. Serves 10 to 12.

MRS. TED DUNHAM, JR.

MARINATED GREEN BEANS

2 No. 2 cans of green beans	1 tablespoon salad oil
1 thinly sliced onion	1 tablespoon vinegar

Salt and pepper to taste

Mix. Let marinate several hours in refrigerator. Stir occasionally. Drain. Add sour cream sauce.

SOUR CREAM SAUCE

1 cup sour cream	2 teaspoons chopped chives
1 teaspoon lemon juice	½ cup mayonnaise
½ to 1 tablespoon horse-radish	¼ teaspoon dry mustard
	Grated onion, to taste

Combine all ingredients. Mix well and pour over green bean salad.

MRS. TED DUNHAM

SAVORY STRING BEAN SALAD

1 pound green beans (or No. 2 can)	1 onion, minced
6 tablespoons salad oil	4 hard cooked eggs, chopped
3 tablespoons vinegar	2 teaspoons vinegar
½ teaspoon salt and pepper	3 tablespoons mayonnaise
	1 teaspoon prepared mustard

4 strips bacon, sauteed

Cook beans. Cool and drain. Add next four ingredients and mix; cover and chill. Combine next four ingredients; cover and chill. When ready to serve, toss the crumbled bacon lightly with the beans. Heap in lettuce lined bowl and top with egg mixture. Serves 4 or 5.

MRS. CLAY RICHMOND

GREEN SALAD FOR SEVENTY PEOPLE

18 heads lettuce torn into bite-size pieces	8 bunches parsley, cut fine 4 quarts of salad dressing

Make salad dressing as follows: Grate 5 packages (6 ounce) Romano cheese and divide equally in four quart jars. Fill each jar with salad oil (this will take about 2 quarts). To each jar add pressed pods of garlic, 1½ teaspoons of salt and 4 tablespoons vinegar. More salt may be added, if needed. Make this dressing early in the day it is to be served. Toss with greens immediately before serving.

MRS. ROBERT BOWLUS

POTATO SALAD

5 medium sized red potatoes	¾ medium sized green pepper, chopped
2 hard cooked eggs	1 dill pickle, chopped
3 ribs celery, chopped	¾ cup mayonnaise
5 green onions (white part only), chopped	1 teaspoon prepared mustard

1 teaspoon Worcestershire sauce
1 tablespoon salt

Boil potatoes in salted water. Peel potatoes and shell eggs. Dice potatoes into small cubes. Mash eggs fine with fork. Mix mayonnaise, mustard and Worcestershire sauce with eggs. Add salt to taste. Mix all ingredients. Refrigerate immediately. Serves 6 to 8.

MRS. FRANK MIDDLETON

MARINATED VEGETABLES

2 No. 2 cans Blue Lake green beans	5 cloves garlic
1 No. 2 can shoe string beets	2 cups salad oil
2 large white onions, sliced thin and separated into rings	1 cup vinegar 2 tablespoons sugar Salt and pepper

Mix vegetables in a flat pan. Mix remaining ingredients and pour over vegetables. Put in refrigerator for 24 hours or longer before serving. Serve chilled. Serve as a salad or cold vegetable. Serves 12.

MOLDED VEGETABLE SALAD

1 box gelatin	3 3-ounce cakes cream cheese
½ cup cold water	1 bottle Durkee's dressing
1 large can petit pois peas	1 No. 2 can carrots, diced
1 large can asparagus, chopped	2 cups chopped celery

Dissolve gelatin in cold water. Heat liquid from peas and asparagus; add to gelatin. Blend cream cheese and Durkee's dressing until smooth; add to gelatin mixture. Add remaining ingredients; pour into mold. Serves 25.

MRS. WILLIAM ADAMS
Tallulah, La.

HOT BREADS

SOUTHERN BISCUITS

2 cups flour
1 tablespoon baking powder
2 teaspoons sugar

1 teaspoon salt
⅓ cup shortening
⅔ cup sweet milk

Sift dry ingredients into mixing bowl. Measure shortening and cut into flour mixture with pastry blender, two knives or blending fork, until mixture looks like "meal." Stir in almost all the milk. If dough does not seem pliable, add the remaining milk. Use enough milk to make a soft, puffy dough easy to roll out. Knead (fold dough over and press lightly with heel of hand about six times) on a lightly floured board (as lightly floured as you would powder your face). Too much handling makes tough biscuits. Roll or pat out ¼-inch thick for thin crusty biscuits and ½-inch for thick soft biscuits. Place on ungreased cookie sheet, close together for biscuits with soft sides, an inch apart for biscuits with crusty sides. Bake 10 to 12 minutes at 450°. Makes about 20 two-inch biscuits.

Triple this recipe when making biscuits for your freezer. For freezing, bake about 8 minutes at 450° (do not brown). Cool, freeze on cookie sheet and then put in bags.

EVELYN WILSFORD

CHEESE BISCUITS

1 pound American cheese
¼ pound butter
⅓ cup cool water
1½ cups flour

½ teaspoon salt
¼ teaspoon red pepper
½ teaspoon baking powder
¼ teaspoon paprika

Cream cheese and butter. Add water. Add dry ingredients sifted together. Let stand in refrigerator for two hours. Roll out thin, cut, and bake in 450° oven about 10 to 12 minutes. Makes about 20 small biscuits.

Cut smaller, these are good for cocktail parties and coffees.

MRS. D. C. JOHNSON
Lindsay, La.

BROWN BREAD

1 cup corn meal
1 cup whole wheat flour
1 cup white flour
1 teaspoon salt
1 teaspoon soda

1 teaspoon baking powder
¾ cup dark molasses
2 cups sour milk (or 1 teaspoon vinegar to cup of sweet milk)

1 cup raisins

Add corn meal and whole wheat flour to white flour that has been sifted with salt, soda, and baking powder. Add molasses, sour milk, and raisins. Beat thoroughly. Half fill three greased one-pound cans, cover with wax paper tightly and steam in pot with small amount of water for three hours. Remove wax paper after steaming and place in 450° oven for 5 minutes.

MRS. ROBERT BOWLUS

HOMEMADE BREAD

1 small can evaporated milk	1 tablespoon salt
1 cup water	½ cup warm water
⅓ stick oleo	2 packages yeast
5 heaping tablespoons sugar	7 cups flour

Scald milk and water together, add oleo, sugar, and salt. Let the milk mixture become lukewarm. Dissolve yeast in this lukewarm milk mixture, stirring until smooth.

Sift approximately 6 cups of flour into mixture. Use the seventh cup of flour on board in which to knead dough. Knead until smooth.

Grease large crock or bowl; butter dough and place in crock. Let rise for 1½ to 2 hours until double its size. Knead dough for second time about 15 minutes, then divide into four parts and place in baking pans (greased). Let rise again for 1½ hours. Bake in preheated 350° oven for 45 minutes. makes 4 small loaves.

MRS. HEIDEL BROWN

COFFEE RING

2 cups milk	2 packages yeast
½ cup sugar	1 cup melted butter
½ cup shortening	2 cups sugar
1 teaspoon salt	1½ tablespoons cinnamon
6 cups sifted flour	1 cup chopped pecans

Place milk, sugar, and shortening in saucepan. Scald milk. Remove from heat, add salt, and cool to lukewarm. Dissolve yeast in two tablespoons warm water and add to mixture. Beat in flour and knead. Let rise to double bulk and knead again.

Break dough into balls the size of a large marble. Dip into melted butter; then roll in sugar and cinnamon mixture and then in pecans. Place loosely in greased cake pan. Bake in 350° oven for 45 minutes. Turn pan upside down on cake plate and cool. (This allows any syrup in bottom of pan to pour over ring and hold it together.)

Each person breaks off a bite-size ball from ring.

Nice to serve in the living room with after-dinner coffee—no dessert plates necessary.

MRS. EDWARD WALL

DATE BREAD

½ pound dates	2 teaspoons soda
1½ cups boiling water	1 tablespoon melted butter
1 cup sugar	1 teaspoon vanilla
1 egg	1 cup nuts
2¾ cups flour	

Drop dates in boiling water and then allow to cool.

Combine sugar and egg. Add alternately the flour and the water off the dates. To the last cup of flour add the soda. Then add melted butter, vanilla, nuts and dates. Bake in 350° oven for one hour.

Using half brown and half white sugar will make the loaf more moist and help preserve it; it improves with age. This will also freeze well.

MRS. HUGH MIDDLETON

WHOLE WHEAT ROLLS OR BREAD

2 yeast cakes
¼ cup lukewarm water
1 teaspoon sugar
2 cups milk
½ cup sugar

2 tablespoons shortening
2 eggs
5 cups whole wheat flour
2 teaspoons salt

Soften yeast in water to which has been added 1 teaspoon sugar. Scald milk and pour over ½ cup sugar and shortening. Allow to cool and add beaten eggs. Mix in yeast. Add sifted flour and salt. Allow to rise once to double its size, then shape into rolls or loaves and bake in 400° oven for approximately 20 minutes.

MRS. HENRY WOOD
Danville, Va.

ITALIAN BREAD STICKS

2 cups sifted flour
1 teaspoon dry yeast dissolved in 3 tablespoons warm water
3 tablespoons melted butter

1 teaspoon sugar
1 teaspoon salt
¼ cup lukewarm milk
Sesame seeds

Place 1 cup flour in mixing bowl. Blend in yeast mixture. Knead until smooth. Put in floured bowl and cover with a damp cloth. Leave in a warm place until double in bulk.

Mix rest of ingredients into a smooth paste. Place on a floured board and add risen dough—knead until smooth and satiny. Put dough into a large floured bowl, cover and let rise to double in bulk. Turn and knead until it doesn't stick to unfloured board.

Divide into 24 parts. Shape each by rolling between hands—into a rope six to seven inches long. Place on buttered baking sheet one inch apart. Brush with milk and sprinkle with sesame seeds. Bake in 425° oven for 6 to 7 minutes.

MRS. ROY WEIL, JR.

CRANBERRY FRUIT BREAD

2 cups flour
1 cup sugar
1½ teaspoon baking powder
½ teaspoon soda
1 teaspoon salt
1 orange—juice and rind

1 egg, well beaten
2 tablespoons melted shortening
½ cup chopped nuts
2 cups raw cranberries, cut in halves

Sift dry ingredients. Combine juice and rind and add enough water for ¾ cup liquid. Add beaten egg and shortening. Pour over dry ingredients and mix until dampened. Add nuts and cranberries. Bake in loaf pan in 325° oven for 50 to 60 minutes. Cool before slicing.

MRS. WARREN JOHNSTON

CORN FRITTERS

2 eggs
1 cup milk
2 cups flour
3 teaspoons baking powder
1 teaspoon salt

1 teaspoon sugar
¼ teaspoon paprika
2 cups drained corn
2 tablespoons shortening

Beat eggs and stir in milk, flour, and other ingredients. Drop from spoon in deep fat and fry until brown. Serves 6 to 8.

MRS. U. S. HARGROVE

ICE BOX GINGERBREAD

1 cup shortening
1 cup sugar
3 whole eggs
1 cup dark syrup
1 cup sour milk
1¾ teaspoons soda

3 cups flour
2 teaspoons ginger
2 teaspoons cinnamon
1 teaspoon nutmeg
½ teaspoon salt

Cream sugar and shortening. Add eggs one at a time and beat thoroughly. Add syrup, milk, soda, and flour to which spices have been added. Let set in refrigerator for several hours before cooking. Pour in muffin tins and bake in 350° oven for about 12 minutes.

This mixture will keep for about a week in the refrigerator.

MRS. W. E. EDRINGTON

CRACKLING CORNBREAD

1½ cups corn meal
¼ cup flour
1 teaspoon soda
1 teaspoon salt

2 cups buttermilk
1 egg
1 cup finely cut cracklings or
crumbled crisp bacon

Sift together dry ingredients. Add buttermilk and egg, stirring until well mixed. Season cracklings with additional salt to taste and fold in last.

Pour batter into very hot, well greased iron skillet or muffin pan (12 muffins). Bake in 450° oven for about 25 minutes.

MRS. ANTHONY P. ACOSTA
Roseneath
Jackson, La.

CORNBREAD

⅔ cup oil or bacon drippings
2 eggs
2½ cups milk
2 cups corn meal

2 cups flour
2 tablespoons baking powder
3 teaspoons soda
1 teaspoon salt

Put oil in bowl; add eggs and beat until foamy. Add milk. Sift in dry ingredients. Put in greased pan and bake at 475° for 20 minutes.

Mrs. E. L. McGehee
Zachary, La.

DANISH PASTRY

1½ cups butter*
⅓ cup flour
2 packages yeast
¼ cup water
1 cup milk

¼ cup sugar
1 teaspoon salt
1 egg
4 cups flour

-----
* One-half margarine can be used.

Cream butter and ⅓ cup flour. Roll or pat between wax paper to 12″ x 6″ rectangle. Chill.

Dissolve yeast in ¼ cup water. Scald milk, sugar, and salt together. Cool to lukewarm. Add yeast and egg and beat. Stir in 4 cups flour. Knead one minute. Roll to 14-inch square. Place butter mixture on half the dough. Fold other half over and seal. Roll to 12″ x 20″ rectangle. Fold left end one-third over and then fold right end over (fold like you do a letter). Roll again to 12″ x 20″ rectangle. Repeat twice. Chill in 30 minutes. Divide into thirds. Roll each to 9 x 12 inches. Cut into 3-inch squares.

Blend together the following:

½ cup butter
½ cup nuts

½ cup sugar

Place 1 teaspoon of this mixture on each square. Fold over and pinch edges. Let rise 1 hour. Bake in 425° oven until golden brown (about 15 minutes. Glaze with confectioners' sugar glaze (powdered sugar and water). Makes a large quantity.

Mrs. Laurence Siegel

FLUFFY DUMPLINGS

1½ cups flour
⅔ teaspoon salt
4 teaspoons baking powder
1 egg

1 tablespoon melted shortening or oil
⅔ cup milk

Sift flour, salt, and baking powder into mixture of beaten eggs, shortening, and milk.

When ready to serve, drop by teaspoonfuls into boiling gravy (about 4 cupfuls), cover, and cook gently for 8 to 10 minutes or until done.

Mrs. Prentice Bolin

HOT CAKES A LA BELLE

3 cups milk
¼ cup cooking oil
4 eggs separated
2 tablespoons sugar

2 teaspoons salt
3 cups flour
4 teaspoons baking powder

Combine milk, oil, egg yolks, sugar, and salt. Lightly stir in flour and baking powder. Whip egg whites separately and slightly chop into the above ingredients. Do not fold in thoroughly—leave lumps of white. Use griddle that has been slightly greased once. This makes 48 medium cakes but can be cut in half successfully.

MRS. GEORGE M. SIMON, SR.

HOECAKES

Hoecakes as made at the "Big House"

2 cups flour
1 cup milk
1 teaspoon yeast

2 tablespoons butter
or 1 tablespoon lard

Mix ingredients well and knead. Roll out with rolling pin, cut criss-cross, like diamonds, with a knife and bake in oven.

Hoecakes as made in the "Cabin"

1 teaspoon lard
2 cups flour
1 teaspoon salt

Boiling water sufficient to make a batter

"These cakes may be baked on a griddle, just as you would a griddle cake, and served with butter. But the old Southern cooks always baked them on a hoe on hot coals in front of a wood fire, out in the open air, just before their cabin doors, or in their cabin before the roaring fire. Hence the name hoecake. The term hoecake, so extensively used by the field hands, was taken up by masters and mistresses and applied to the biscuit bread as described above." Picayune Creole Cook Book (1901)

MRS. ANTHONY P. ACOSTA
Roseneath
Jackson, La.

"PANAMA LIMITED" FRENCH TOAST

2 eggs
½ cup milk
3 cups shortening
Confectioners sugar

2 slices bread, cut 1½ inches thick, crusts trimmed, then cut diagonally to form triangular shaped pieces

Beat eggs well, then mix in the milk and beat again. Dip bread slices in egg and milk mixture. (It is not necessary to soak the bread, although this can be done according to preference.) Fry in hot shortening (about 3 cups of shortening in medium sized fry pan.) Brown on both sides. Drain the cooked toast. Sprinkle liberally with confectioners' sugar. Serve hot.

Simple but superb!

ILLINOIS CENTRAL RAILROAD

FRENCH MARKET DOUGHNUTS

1 cup milk
1/4 cup sugar
3/4 teaspoon salt
1/2 teaspoon nutmeg
1 package active dry or cake yeast

2 tablespoons lukewarm water
2 tablespoons salad oil
1 egg
3 1/2 cups sifted all-purpose flour

Sifted confectioners' sugar

Scald milk, add granulated sugar, salt, and nutmeg. Cool to lukewarm. Sprinkle or crumble yeast into warm water (use lukewarm water for cake yeast), stirring until yeast is dissolved.

To lukewarm milk mixture add oil, egg, dissolved yeast, blending with spoon. Add flour gradually, beating well. Cover with waxed paper, then clean towel, and let rise in warm place (about 85°F) until double in size.

Turn dough (it will be soft) on to well-floured surface; knead gently. Roll into 18" x 12" rectangle; cut into thirty-six 3" x 2" rectangles. Cover with clean towel and let rise 1/2 hour.

Fry a few doughnuts at a time in deep fat (375°F) until golden brown. Drain on crumpled paper towels. Drop doughnuts in brown paperbag, sprinkle with confectioners' sugar, and shake well until thoroughly coated. Serve piping hot.

MRS. W. E. ROBINSON, JR.

GOLDEN PUFFS

2 cups sifted flour
1/4 cup sugar
1 tablespoon baking powder
1 teaspoon salt

1 teaspoon nutmeg or mace
1/4 cup cooking oil
3/4 cup milk
1 egg

Mix all dry ingredients together. Then add cooking oil, milk, and egg. Mix thoroughly. Drop by small teaspoonful (too large does not cook thoroughly) into deep hot oil (375°F). Fry about 3 minutes or until golden brown. Drain on absorbent paper. Roll warm puffs in cinnamon-sugar or confectioners' sugar. Makes about three dozen. The batter may be kept in refrigerator several days.

These are delicious for a morning coffee.

MRS. W. E. ROBINSON, JR.

LOST BREAD ("PAIN PERDU")

2 eggs
1/2 cup sugar

1/4 teaspoon cinnamon
4 to 6 slices bread (stale)

Beat eggs, sugar, and cinnamon together. Dip bread in mixture and fry on buttered griddle.

MRS. EDWARD WALL

HUSH PUPPIES

1 cup cornmeal	1 egg
1 teaspoon baking powder	¾ cup milk
1 teaspoon salt	Dash of red pepper
1 teaspoon sugar	Chopped green onion tops
1 cup flour	1 tablespoon grated onion

Sift dry ingredients into bowl. Beat egg, add milk, and add this to cornmeal mixture. Add onion and red pepper. Drop by spoonful in hot deep fat (375°F) and fry until brown. Should you like a lot of crust, these may be patted flat. This makes approximately two dozen.

While there is a great deal of speculation as to the origin of hush puppies, there should be no speculation on the tastiness of these.

MRS. ROBERT BOWLUS

HERB AND BACON ROLLS

1 package yeast, dry or compressed	½ cup shortening
¼ cup lukewarm water	¼ teaspoon each: thyme, mace, rosemary or oregano
1 cup milk	2 eggs
¼ cup sugar	3¼ cup flour
½ teaspoon salt	½ cup crumbled, cooked bacon or minced ham
½ teaspoon garlic and celery salts	

Soften yeast in lukewarm water. Scald milk, add sugar, salt, and shortening. Cool to lukewarm. Add flour mixed with herbs and beat well. Add eggs and softened yeast. Beat until smooth. Add bacon or ham. Cover and let rise until bubbly, about 1 hour.

Prepare small muffin pans by putting ½ teaspoon of melted butter and poppy or caraway seeds in bottom. When dough is light, stir down, fill muffin pans half full, and let rise until double in size. Bake in 425° oven until golden brown.

MRS. R. LOUIS MOSCHETTE
Home Economics Department, LSU

BUTTER HORN ROLLS

2 packages yeast	1 teaspoon salt
1 cup warm water	6 cups flour
½ cup sugar	1 cup melted butter
3 eggs, well beaten	

Dissolve yeast in warm water. Add sugar, salt and 1½ cups flour, stirring well. Let rise 25 minutes. Add melted butter, eggs and remaining flour. Roll out and cut into small wedge shaped pieces. Roll up wedges by rolling large end first, roll in melted butter, and place in pan with rolled end on underneath side. Let rise again for 30 minutes. Bake in 450° oven for 15-20 minutes. Will make about 48 medium sized rolls. *There is nothing better!*

MRS. HUGH A. NEAL

ONION SHORTCAKE

2 cups flour
4 teaspoons baking powder
½ teaspoon salt
4 tablespoons shortening
½ to ⅔ cup milk

2 tablespoons butter
2½ cups sliced onions
1 egg
½ cup top milk
1 teaspoon salt

Sift together flour, baking powder, and ½ teaspoon salt. Cut in shortening. Add milk and knead dough slightly. Flatten in a greased casserole.

Melt butter in a skillet; add onions and brown. Cool and spread over dough.

Beat egg, milk, and salt and pour over onions. Bake in a 400° oven for 15-20 minutes. *Good with roast beef, and also nice when you have no gravy.*

Mrs. D. C. Johnston
Lindsay, La.

SPOONBREAD

1 cup milk
1 cup water
1 cup cornmeal

1 teaspoon salt
2 eggs
2 tablespoons baking powder

1 tablespoon butter

Place milk and water in saucepan. Add cornmeal and salt. Cook 5 minutes. Add beaten egg yolks, baking powder, butter, and stiffly beaten egg whites. Pour in greased casserole and bake in 425° oven for 40 minutes. Serves 6.

Mrs. Edward Percy
Ellerslie Plantation
St. Francisville, La.

ROSETTES OR TIMBALE CASES

1 teaspoon sugar
¼ teaspoon salt

1½ cups sifted flour
2 eggs, beaten

1 cup milk

Mix and sift dry ingredients. Add beaten egg to milk. Combine mixtures and beat until smooth—the consistency of thick cream.

Timbales: a regular timbale iron must be used. Heat shortening to 365°. Use enough shortening to cover the top of your timbale form. Heat iron in shortening about 30 seconds. Remove, drain, and dip in batter to top of form. Fry until golden brown. Drain, slip timbale off form and proceed again.

Timbales may be used like pastry shells for tuna fish, creamed chicken, green peas, etc. Makes about 18.

Rosettes: A rosette iron must be used. Follow above procedure for frying. Delicious when sprinkled with confectioners' sugar. They may be reheated in a warm oven. Makes 42 to 48.

Mrs. W. E. Bingham

CHEESE WAFFLES

2 cups sifted flour
2 tablespoons sugar
1 teaspoon salt
1 tablespoon baking powder
3 eggs, separated

2 cups milk
7 tablespoons melted
  shortening
¾ cup grated American
  cheese

Sift flour, sugar, salt, and baking powder. Beat egg yolks until light in a separate bowl. Add milk, shortening, and cheese. Add dry ingredients. Beat egg whites until stiff but not dry; fold into batter. Bake in waffle iron. Serve with tart jelly or chicken livers. Makes 6 waffles.

MRS. THOMAS PUGH, II

VEGETABLES

TIPS FOR VEGETABLES

Add sugar to fresh green vegetables before cooking. This improves the flavor.

Soak dry beans overnight to shorten cooking time.

Chicken bouillon cubes mixed with hot water may be used in place of chicken stock for vegetable casseroles.

Finely rolled cheese crackers may be used in place of bread crumbs to cover vegetables. This changes the flavor.

To add appetizing color to vegetable casseroles sprinkle liberally with paprika.

Add hot water to vegetables when cooking to keep the vegetables from being tough.

STUFFED ARTICHOKES

1 artichoke
½ cup bread crumbs
½ cup grated Romano
  cheese

4 cloves garlic, finely
  chopped
¼ cup oil
Salt and pepper to taste

Parsley to taste

Mix together bread crumbs, Romano cheese, garlic, parsley and salt and pepper, by rubbing in hands. Cut top and bottom from artichoke and turn upside down and mash slightly to open leaves. Fill each leaf from outside in by using the top of each leaf. Then pour oil over stuffed piece. Steam in covered pot in a little water 45 minutes or longer. Done when leaf pulls off easily.

MRS. H. B. HARRINGTON

ASPARAGUS AMANDINE

2 303 cans green asparagus
  spears, drained
1 can cream of mushroom
  soup
½ cup water drained from
  asparagus

½ teaspoon salt
¼ teaspoon pepper
1 cup American grated
  cheese
1 cup bread crumbs
4 tablespoons butter

½ cup blanched almonds

Lay asparagus in oblong casserole, pour over the mushroom soup, mixed with water, salt and pepper. Sprinkle with grated cheese. Melt butter, add bread crumbs and sprinkle over grated cheese. Dot with whole almonds. Bake 45 minutes in 300° oven. Serves 8.

MRS. WILLIAM R. MCGEHEE

ASPARAGUS AND CREAM SAUCE CASSEROLE

2 tablespoons oleo
2 tablespoons flour
1 cup milk
¼ cup grated cheese
½ cup chopped celery
1 teaspoon onion juice

½ teaspoon Worcestershire
  sauce
Salt and pepper to taste
3 eggs, hard cooked and
  chopped
½ can pimento, chopped
1 No. 2 can green asparagus

Buttered bread crumbs

Make white sauce by melting oleo, adding flour, and slowly adding milk, stirring constantly. Cook and stir slowly until it thickens. Add cheese, celery, onion juice, Worcestershire sauce, salt, pepper, eggs, and pimento to white sauce. Drain asparagus and add to mixture. Pour in casserole and top with buttered bread crumbs. Bake in 350° oven for 15-20 minutes, until hot and bread crumbs are browned. Serves 6-8.

Mrs. Millard E. Byrd, Jr.

GREEN BEANS WITH ALMONDS

2 cans Blue Lake variety
  green beans
3 teaspoons dill seed
2 slices bacon
6 tablespoons butter or
  margarine
6 tablespoons flour
½ cup milk

1 cup bean juice
3 tablespoons grated onion
1 teaspoon mei yen seasoning
1 teaspoon cracked java
  pepper
3 dashes Tabasco
Salt to taste
1 cup slivered almonds

Cook beans with dill seeds and bacon over low heat for 30 minutes. Let sit overnight. In a saucepan melt butter, add flour, milk and bean juice. Add other seasoning. In a buttered casserole place a layer of beans, then a layer of sauce until all is used. Sprinkle slivered almonds over top and bake for 30 minutes at 350°. Serves 10.

Mrs. S. G. Henry, Jr.

GREEN BEANS A LA PEGGY

1 303 can Blue Lake variety
  green beans
1 tablespoon bacon drippings
1 clove garlic

1 small onion
¼ stick butter
¼ cup broken pecan pieces
¼ cup bread crumbs

Sauté chopped onions and garlic in bacon drippings. Add drained green beans and ½ can of water. Cook in saucepan over low heat for one hour. Make the topping from melted butter, bread crumbs and pecans, stirring constantly over low heat. Put in serving dish and sprinkle topping over heated beans, but the topping does not need to be hot when served. Serves 4. *This topping is also good with other vegetables.*

Mrs. C. Lenton Sartain

STRING BEAN CASSEROLE

1 8-ounce can mushrooms
1 medium onion, chopped
1 stick butter
¼ cup flour
2 cups warm milk
1 cup light cream
¾ pound sharp cheddar cheese
⅛ teaspoon Tabasco
2 teaspoons soy sauce
1 teaspoon salt
1 teaspoon monosodium glutamate
5 packages frozen green beans
1 5-ounce can water chestnuts, sliced and drained
¾ cup almonds, sliced

Sauté mushrooms and onions in butter. Add flour, milk, cream, cheese, Tabasco, soy sauce, salt, monosodium glutamate. Simmer until cheese melts. Cook green beans. Mix with sauce. Add water chestnuts. Pour into 2 casseroles and top with almonds. Bake at 375° for 20 minutes. Serves 12-15.

Mrs. Sanders Cazedessus

STRING BEANS AND MOCK HOLLANDAISE SAUCE

1 medium size onion, chopped
1 tablespoon paprika
1 tablespoon bacon drippings
Salt and pepper to taste
¼ pod garlic, if desired
Several bits of ham, if available
1 303 can whole stringless green beans

Sauté onion, garlic and paprika in drippings. Add ham and string beans and about ½ of the juice from the can of beans. Simmer on very low heat approximately 15 minutes. If the beans seem too dry, add a little of the remaining juice from the can. When ready to serve, pour about ⅔ cup Mock Hollandaise sauce (see Index) in center. Serves 4.

Mrs. P. Chauvin Wilkinson

GREEN BEANS HORSERADISH

2 303 cans whole green beans
1 large onion, sliced
Several bits of ham, bacon or salt meat
1 cup mayonnaise
2 hard cooked eggs, chopped
1 heaping tablespoon horseradish
1 teaspoon Worcestershire sauce
Salt to taste
Pepper to taste
Garlic salt to taste
Celery salt to taste
Onion salt to taste
1½ teaspoons parsley flakes
1 lemon, juiced

Cook beans with meat and sliced onion for 1 hour or more. Blend mayonnaise with remaining ingredients and set aside at room temperature. When beans are ready to serve, drain and spoon mayonnaise mixture over beans. Serves 8. *These are excellent, left over, cold. The green beans are so different.*

Mrs. William R. Smith

STRING BEANS WITH TOMATOES

1 green pepper, finely chopped
1 medium onion, finely chopped
4 strips of bacon, cut in pieces
2 cups drained tomatoes
2 cups drained string beans

1 teaspoon Worcestershire sauce
¼ cup mayonnaise
½ teaspoon salt
Dash of pepper
Dash of cayenne
1 small can sliced mushrooms

½ cup buttered bread crumbs

Cook peppers, onion and bacon together for 5 to 8 minutes. Drain excess fat from bacon. Add drained tomatoes, chop and mix well and simmer 5 minutes. Add beans, mayonnaise and seasonings. Blend thoroughly but do not cook. Add mushrooms. Place in greased casserole. Cover with bread crumbs, dot with butter, bake uncovered in 350° oven for 20 minutes. Serves 6.

MRS. NEWELL C. DUNN

SWEET SOUR BEANS

1 No. 2 can green beans, drained
3 slices bacon

½ cup vinegar
½ cup sugar

Fry bacon crisp. Crumble and set aside. Into the skillet with bacon drippings, put the vinegar and sugar. Add drained beans. Simmer 25 minutes, turning occasionally. When ready to serve, top with bacon. These reheat well. Serves 4.

MRS. LAURENCE SIEGEL

SOUTHERN BAKED BEANS

3 No. 2½ cans pork and beans
1 large onion, chopped
6 cloves of garlic, chopped fine

4 tablespoons mustard seeds
2 tablespoons brown sugar
½ bottle chili sauce
¼ bottle tomato catsup
¼ cup molasses

¼ cup water

Mix all ingredients together and cook slowly in 250° oven for about 4 hours. Serves 12.

MRS. HUGH B. O'CONNOR

LOUISIANA RED BEANS AND RICE

1 cup red beans, washed and drained
3 cups of water
1 clove of garlic, chopped

1 rib celery, chopped
2 tablespoons parsley, chopped
1 large bay leaf, crushed

1 medium onion, chopped

Cook beans in water. Season with salt and bacon drippings, ham or other seasoning meat. Cook for 1½ to 2 hours. Add onion, garlic, celery, and bay leaf. Continue to cook over low heat for ½ to 1 hour. If beans become too dry, add heated water. 2 tablespoons of sugar improve the whole effect. Serve on mounds of rice. Serves 4. *A Louisiana treat!*

MRS. LEWIS C. PETERS

SOUTH LOUISIANA RED BEANS

1 pound red kidney beans
Ham bone with generous
    amount of meat
1 pound pepperoni, sliced

1 bay leaf
Dash red pepper
Cumin powder to taste
1 large onion, chopped

1 clove garlic, chopped

Wash and pick over beans. Cover in cold water and soak overnight. Cook pepperoni, onions, and garlic until slightly browned. Add beans and water in which they have been soaked, then ham bone and more water to cover, bay leaf, red pepper and cumin powder to taste. Cook slowly for several hours. Serves 8. *Cornbread goes well with red beans.*

MRS. BILL ANDRE

NAVY BEANS

2 cups navy beans
6 cups cold water
1 medium onion, chopped
¼ cup chopped parsley

3 tablespoons sugar
2 cloves garlic, chopped
½ pound salt pork, cubed
    (or left over ham)

1½ teaspoons salt

Wash and pick over beans. Combine all ingredients in a large covered saucepan. Cook for 2½ to 3 hours. Serves 8. *Slice baked ham and serve as a main course.*

SOUTHERN BLACK-EYED PEAS

1 1-pound package dried
    black-eyed peas
2 quarts water
1 onion, chopped

¼ green pepper, chopped
1 rib celery, chopped
Ham bone, piece of salt pork,
    or several slices of bacon

Salt and pepper to taste

Wash the peas; soak them overnight, or at least five to six hours in fresh, cold water. Drain off soaking water; put peas in a large pot containing at least 2 quarts of water. Add onions, green pepper, celery, and ham bone or bacon. Season to taste with salt and pepper. Cook about 2 hours or until peas are tender enough to mash easily. Add water as needed while cooking.

GOLDEN BROCCOLI

2 packages frozen broccoli
2 teaspoons salt
2 tablespoons lemon juice

Pepper to taste
1 10-ounce can cream of
    chicken soup

½ cup grated cheddar cheese

Cook broccoli in salted water as directed on package until tender. Drain. Place broccoli in shallow serving dish. Sprinkle with lemon juice, pepper and cover with soup. Sprinkle cheese on top and place under broiler for 10 minutes or until cheese is melted and bubbly. Serves 8.

MRS. M. S. CADWALLADER

BROCCOLI CASSEROLE

2 large onions, chopped
1 stick butter
6 packages chopped broccoli
4 cups cream of mushroom
  soup
3 packages garlic cheese

2 teaspoons monosodium
  glutamate
1 large can mushrooms
1 cup chopped blanched
  almonds
1 cup bread crumbs

Sauté onions in butter. Add broccoli and cook until tender. Add mushroom soup, cheese, monosodium glutamate, mushrooms, and ¾ cup almonds. Pour in largest casserole available or in 2 casseroles. Sprinkle rest of almonds and bread crumbs on top. Bake in 300° oven until bubbly. Serves 18.

Mrs. J. Burton LeBlanc, Jr.

BAKED CAULIFLOWER

1 head of cauliflower
2 tablespoons butter
2 tablespoons flour
1 cup milk
½ teaspoon salt
¼ teaspoon pepper

2 tablespoons chopped
  pimento
½ cup green onions, chopped
¼ cup buttered bread
  crumbs
1 tablespoon grated cheese

Cook the whole cauliflower in boiling salt water for about 20 minutes. Drain and place in baking dish. Melt butter in small skillet. Add flour and stir until blended. Gradually add milk, stirring until smooth and thick. Add salt, pepper, pimento and green onions. Blend. Pour over cauliflower. Sprinkle with bread crumbs and grated cheese. Bake in 375° oven for 20 minutes or until slightly browned. Serves 4 to 6.

Mrs. J. D. Aymond, Jr.

CORN PUDDING

2 tablespoons butter
2 tablespoons salad oil
½ onion, chopped fine
1 cup whole kernel corn,
  canned or fresh

Salt and pepper to taste
1 tablespoon sugar
3 eggs, separated
½ cup cheddar cheese

Heat butter and salad oil in skillet. Sauté onion, add corn, sugar, salt and pepper. Cool and add cheese and well beaten egg yolks. Fold in stiffly beaten egg whites. Pour in well greased 9″ x 11″ casserole and set in pan of hot water. Bake in 350° oven for 1 hour. Serve at once. Serves 4. *This is good served with pork.*

Mrs. G. C. Harris
Ada, Oklahoma

CABBAGE WITH CREAM

1 medium size head of   ½ cup breakfast cream
   cabbage   1 cup grated sharp cheese

Remove heart from cabbage and outer leaves. Cut in sections and boil about 10 minutes or until tender. Drain well and place in casserole. Add cream and sprinkle cheese on top. Bake in 350° oven about 20 minutes or until top is brown and nearly all the liquid is gone. Serves 4.

MRS. EUGENE R. McCRORY

CELERY AND BRUSSELS SPROUTS

2 cups sliced celery   ½ package smoked processed
2 cups Brussels sprouts   cheese
1 303 can cream of celery   ¼ cup sherry
   soup

Cook vegetables separately in boiling salted water only until tender. Drain carefully. Save ¾ cup water from celery. To water from celery add cream of celery soup. Stir until smooth. Add cheese broken into small pieces and heat to the boiling point. Do not boil. Add sherry and drained vegetables. Season with additional salt, black pepper and 2 tablespoons of butter of desired. Serves 4-6.

MRS. R. LOUIS MOSCHETTE

CELERY AND MUSHROOMS

3 cups celery, cut crosswise   1 4-ounce can sliced mush-
   stalk in ¼ inch thick cres-   rooms, stems and pieces
   cent pieces   1 teaspoon soy sauce
1 cup boiling water   ½ can almonds, toasted and
1 cube chicken bouillon   slivered
         Black pepper to taste

Cook celery until tender in water in which bouillon cube has been dissolved. Drain. Sauté mushrooms in butter for 3 to 5 minutes. Season with pepper and soy sauce. Add to cooked celery. Pour into serving dish and top with slivered almonds. Serves 4-6.

MRS. R. LOUIS MOSCHETTE

BAKED CUSHAW

1 medium cushaw   1 teaspoon vanilla
2 eggs   ½ pound butter
2 cups sugar   ½ teaspoon baking powder
2 tablespoons flour   Nutmeg to taste

Cut cushaw in pieces, scrape out seed, and boil until tender. Remove peeling. Mix cushaw with the rest of ingredients. Place in baking dish and bake in 350° oven until brown on top.

MRS. EDWARD WALL

BAKED EGGPLANT

1 eggplant
¼ stick butter or bacon
   drippings
2 tablespoons flour
⅔ cup milk

1 cup sharp cheese
1 cup cracker crumbs
1 cup tomatoes
2 eggs, separated
Pinch of salt

Peel and dice eggplant. Cook in a little water until tender over low heat. Make a cream sauce with butter or drippings, flour and milk. Add cheese and melt over low heat. Drain eggplant and mash it. Add cracker crumbs, tomatoes, beaten egg yolks and salt. Mix together with the cream sauce and fold in beaten egg whites and bake at 350° for 30 minutes. Serve at once. Serves 6.

MRS. U. S. HARGROVE

DEVILED EGGPLANT

1 medium eggplant
2 tablespoons bacon drip-
   pings
1 medium onion, chopped
2 cloves garlic, chopped

¼ bell pepper, optional
4 slices dry bread
1 cup shrimp, oysters, ham,
   or any other meat
Salt and pepper to taste

Peel eggplant and boil in salted water until tender. Drain. Sauté onion, garlic and chopped bell pepper in bacon drippings. Remove from heat and add eggplant. Soak bread in water, squeeze out excess and add to other mixture. Add fish or other meat at this point. Place in casserole, top with bread crumbs and bake at 350° for ½ hour. Serves 6.

MRS. HANSON E. SCOBEE

EGGPLANT SUPREME

1 large eggplant
1 small bell pepper
2 ribs celery
1 large onion
½ stick butter

1 teaspoon Worcestershire
   sauce
1 dash hot sauce
1 cup sharp cheese, grated
1 cup ripe olives, chopped

Cracker crumbs

Cut up peeled eggplant and steam in a little water on low heat until tender. Sauté celery, onion, and bell pepper in butter. Add cooked eggplant. Add Worcestershire sauce and hot sauce, stir. Now add cheese and olives. Taste before adding any salt, for the cheese is salty. Put in baking dish and cover with cracker crumbs. Bake 30 minutes in 375° oven. Serves 6.

MRS. WILLIAM R. SMITH

GARLIC CHEESE GRITS

1 cup grits, uncooked	1 stick butter or oleo
4 cups water	1 roll garlic cheese
1 tablespoon salt	½ pound sharp cheese

2 tablespoons Worcestershire sauce

Cook the grits in the salted water. When cooked add the butter, garlic cheese, sharp cheese and Worcestershire sauce. Stir until the butter and cheese have melted. Put in greased casserole, and sprinkle with paprika. Bake in preheated 350° oven for 15 to 20 minutes. Serves 8 to 10. *Use as main supper dish or starch.*

MRS. J. L. HOCHENEDEL

GRITS SOUFFLÉ

2 cups grits	4 egg yolks, beaten well
8 cups water	4 egg whites, beaten stiff
1 package garlic cheese	1 teaspoon salt
1 stick butter	Cracker or dry bread crumbs

Cook grits in salted water. When cooked add cheese, butter and egg yolk. Stir until cheese and butter have melted. Fold in egg whites, Put in greased casserole. Sprinkle with crumbs. Bake in 350° over for 45 minutes.

MRS. C. D. BALDRIDGE, JR.

BAKED MIRLITONS (VEGETABLE PEARS)

3 vegetable pears, peeled	2 tablespoons cooking oil
1 pound ground pork	4 slices dry toast or stale
3 medium onions, chopped	bread
4 cloves garlic, pressed	Salt and pepper to taste

Cut pears in half lengthwise; remove seed in center. Boil pears until tender. Scoop out vegetable pear, reserving shell for stuffing. Fry onions, garlic and meat to a light brown. Add 1 cup of water, cook slowly. Add the drained, mashed or cut up vegetable pears. Add the toast or stale bread that has been soaked in water and squeezed out. Season to taste and fill shells or put in casserole. Cover with crumbs. Dot with butter and bake in 350° oven until crumbs brown, about 30 minutes.

MRS. P. CHAUVIN WILKINSON

COLD MIRLITON SALAD

4 small mirlitons	Your favorite French Dressing

Cut mirlitons in half; pare and remove center seed. Boil until tender in salted water. Cool; marinate several hours in French dressing in the refrigerator. Place two halves per serving on crisp lettuce leaves. Company touch: cream cheese in cavities sprinkled with paprika. Serves 4.

MRS. KENNETH C. LANDRY

STUFFED MIRLITONS

4 large mirlitons (vegetable pears)
1 large or 2 small onions, chopped
1 large garlic clove, optional
½ cup chopped celery
3 tablespoons shortening
¾ pound fresh cooked shrimp, cleaned
½ cup grated sharp cheese
¼ cup buttered bread crumbs
½ teaspoon monosodium glutamate
Salt and pepper to taste

Parboil mirlitons until almost tender. Cut in half and scoop out meat. Set aside and sauté onion and garlic in a heavy skillet until transparent. Add celery and cook until tender. Mash mirlitons, mix with shrimp, monosodium glutamate, cheese, and mixture in skillet. Fill shells, cover with additional cheese and bread crumbs and bake in moderate oven 350° until crumbs are browned.

MRS. CHARLES DUCHEIN, JR.

FRENCH LETTUCE

3 tablespoons butter
2 tablespoons flour
1 cup chicken stock or bouillon cube
2 medium size heads lettuce
1 cup sour cream
1 tablespoon cider vinegar
2 tablespoons washed capers
Salt and pepper to taste

Melt the butter in a heavy skillet. Stir in flour. Blend over low heat, stirring constantly until it bubbles. Stir in chicken stock and stir constantly until smooth. Season to taste with salt and pepper. Shred 2 heads lettuce and add to sauce. Scald sour cream with cider vinegar. Add washed capers. Cover tightly and let simmer gently 15 minutes. Serves 6 to 8.

MRS. E. R. STRAHAN

BAKED LIMA BEANS

1 pound big dried lima beans
1 cup melted butter
1 cup sour cream
2 tablespoons molasses
2 teaspoons dry mustard

Soak beans over-night. Cook lima beans in salted water with cover until done. Mix rest of ingredients and pour beans in covered casserole. Place slice of ham or canadian bacon on top if desired. Bake at 300° for 1½ hours. Serves 8.

MRS. NEWELL DUNN

MUSHROOMS AND SOUR CREAM

1 pound fresh mushrooms
1 small onion, sliced
¼ cup margarine
1 cup sour cream
1 tablespoon sherry
1 teaspoon salt
Pepper to taste

Wash and halve mushrooms if large. Sauté onion in melted margarine until limp. Add mushrooms, cover and cook slowly 5 minutes. Add cream, sherry, and seasonings. Simmer until thoroughly heated. Serves 8.

MRS. E. R. STRAHAN

MUSTARD OR TURNIP GREENS

2 to 3 bunches of turnip
  tops or mustard greens
          Salt and pepper to taste

1 large onion, chopped
½ pound salt pork or bacon

Stem and pick the greens; wash several times. Put greens in large pot; the water on the leaves from washing is sufficient; do not add any. Add salt pork, onion, and seasonings; cook slowly, until meat and greens are tender.

Serve the greens with hot, buttered cornbread. Just for the sake of information, the liquid in the greens is the famous "pot likker," and with the family folks, the cornbread is often surreptitiously dunked therein.

MRS. KENNETH LANDRY

PEAS SCOVILLE

1 cup small pearl onions, or
  ½ cup chopped shallots
2 cups shelled peas (green)
½ pound small white mush-
  rooms

Lemon juice
4 tablespoons olive oil
Salt and pepper to taste

Put onions in cold water, bring to a boil and drain. Blanche peas in the same way. Wash the mushrooms in lemon juice and water. Cut in slices and sauté in the hot olive oil. Add the peas, onions, salt and pepper. Cover with the lid and cook over slow heat for 10 to 15 minutes, stirring occasionally until the peas are soft but not mushy. Serve in one quart casserole. Serves 4.

MRS. O. R. MENTON

CANDIED YAMS

4 medium size sweet
  potatoes
1 cup sugar
Dash of salt
1 teaspoon cinnamon or
  nutmeg

¾ stick butter
2 slices lemon
1 tablespoon flour
¼ cup water

Peel and cut potatoes as for thick french fries. Place in 8″ x 12″ x 2″ baking dish. Cover potatoes with sugar and salt. Sprinkle cinnamon or nutmeg over the sugar. More can be used. Cover with pieces of butter. Twist slices of lemon over this and place peel in with potatoes. Sift flour evenly over potatoes. Add water to mixture so it may be barely seen. Bake in 400° oven for 1 hour or until potatoes are done and sugar and butter have made a thick syrup about the consistency of molasses. Baste potatoes frequently with syrup. Serves 4 to 6. *Marvelous—a southern treat.*

MRS. I. P. COLLIER

NOODLE CASSEROLE

¼ cup butter
1 large can sliced mushrooms
¼ cup finely chopped onions
¼ cup finely sliced blanched
  almonds
1 clove garlic, minced or

¼ teaspoon garlic puree
1 tablespoon lemon juice
1 can condensed onion soup
1 4-ounce package fine
  noodles

Melt butter. Add mushrooms, onion, almonds, garlic, and lemon juice. Sauté gently about 10 minutes. Stir in undiluted soup and bring to a boil. Add the noodles; reduce the heat, cover and simmer about 5 minutes. This is very good served with vineyard chicken. Serves 4.

MRS. RODNEY G. COCO

BAKED ONIONS

12 medium size fresh onions
1 3¾-ounce bag potato chips
½ pound Wisconsin mild
  cheese

2 cans cream of mushroom
  soup
½ cup milk
⅛ teaspoon cayenne pepper

In a 9″ x 13″ buttered casserole place alternate layers of thinly sliced onions, crushed potato chips and grated cheese. Pour mushroom soup and milk over the top of the onion mixture and it will cook through. Sprinkle cayenne pepper over the top and bake 1 hour at 350°. *This is good with barbecue.*

MRS. JAMES H. SIMPSON, JR.

STUFFED ONIONS

4 large yellow onions
1 pound ground chuck
1 or 2 tomatoes
Few drops of Worcestershire
  sauce
¼ teaspoon tarragon
¼ teaspoon oregano

¼ teaspoon marjoram
¼ teaspoon parsley
2 ribs celery, chopped
1 egg
¼ teaspoon basil
Salt and pepper to taste

Peel onion, scoop out middle, leaving 3 or 4 layers thick. Boil in salted water for about 5 minutes. Mix beef, egg, chopped tomatoes, and seasonings until well blended. Stuff in onion shells which have drained. Sprinkle each stuffed shell with a pinch of basil and a few drops of Worcestershire sauce. Top each with a pat of butter. Bake in individual casseroles in 350° oven for 45 minutes to 1 hour.

MRS. PERCY ROBERTS, JR.

BAKED POTATOES WITH SOUR CREAM

6 medium baked potatoes,
   steaming hot
1 pint commercial sour cream
1 wedge of chive cream
   cheese (optional)

1 teaspoon celery salt
½ bunch green onions,
   chopped
At least ½ pound bacon, fried
   crisp and crumbled

Dash hot sauce

Mix softened cream cheese, sour cream, and celery salt together until smooth. A mixer helps. Serve this in one container, the chopped onions in another, the bacon in another at the table. Pats of butter make it even better. *This is "la pièce de résistance" for any meal!*

CRAB STUFFED POTATOES

4 medium Idaho potatoes
1 6½ ounce can crab meat
½ cup butter
½ cup light cream
1 teaspoon salt

4 teaspoons grated onion
1 cup sharp yellow cheese,
   grated
½ teaspoon paprika

Scrub potatoes well; dry thoroughly. Put in oven and bake at 325° until you can pierce with fork. Cut the baked potatoes lengthwise and scoop out potato and whip with butter, cream, salt, pepper, onion and cheese. With a fork mix in crab meat and refill the potato shells. Sprinkle with paprika and reheat in very hot oven about 15 minutes. These freeze nicely.

MRS. CHARLES D. NUNN

GERMAN FRIED POTATOES

¼ cup bacon drippings
4 potatoes peeled and sliced

1 medium onion, sliced
½ cup water

Salt and pepper to taste

Heat drippings in iron skillet. Add sliced potatoes, turning until light brown. Add sliced onions; cook for about five minutes longer. Add salt and pepper. Pour water over potatoes and cover immediately with tight fitting lid. Reduce heat to low; let steam, turning potatoes occasionally. When tender remove from skillet. Serves 4.

MRS. ROBERT SLOWEY

POTATO AND MUSHROOM CASSEROLE

4 large or 6 medium potatoes
Chopped green onion
Chopped bell pepper

1 4-ounce can mushrooms,
   drained
½ cup milk

1 can cream of mushroom soup

Parboil potatoes for about 10 minutes. Cut in rather large pieces. Put 1 layer of potatoes; salt; sprinkle with onions and bell peppers; sprinkle with mushrooms. Repeat layers. After all ingredients are used, dilute can of soup with milk and pour over all. Top with buttered bread crumbs. Bake at 350° for 30-40 minutes. A little marjoram can be added. Serves 6.

MRS. EDWARD O. WARMACK

ITALIAN POTATOES

14 or 15 large red potatoes
½ cup chopped parsley
½ cup chopped green onion
3 large pods garlic, sliced thin
1 heaping teaspoon salt
½ teaspoon dry mustard

1 scant tablespoon sugar
1 tablespoon Worcestershire
sauce
1 8-ounce bottle pure olive oil
About 4 ounces tarragon
vinegar

Boil potatoes. When done peel and cut in 1 inch chunk size pieces. Sprinkle parsley and green onion over potatoes. Make sauce from rest of ingredients; strain so that there will be no garlic pieces in sauce; pour over potatoes. Stir well. Let stand all day. (At least four hours or longer.) Stir every hour. Do not refrigerate. Serves about 16. *These are marvelous!*

MRS. COOPER SPENGLER

BAKED SWEET POTATOES WITH MARSHMALLOWS

8 medium size sweet
potatoes
1 cup milk
1 teaspoon vanilla
3 tablespoons sugar

½ stick butter
¼ teaspoon cinnamon
Few dashes of nutmeg
1 tablespoon orange juice
Marshmallows

Bake sweet potatoes in 350° oven until done. Peel hot potatoes and put through ricer until mashed. Scald milk and add vanilla, sugar and butter. To potatoes add cinnamon, nutmeg and orange juice. Stir. Add milk mixture to potatoes, a layer of marshmallows, remaining potatoes and bake at 350° until very hot. Add a top layer of marshmallows and brown. Serves 8 to 10.

MRS. A. J. NOLAND

DIRTY RICE

4 pounds raw rice
4 pounds red onions
¼ cup shortening or bacon
drippings
2 packages frozen gizzards
and livers

Salt to taste
5 cloves garlic
3 bunches green onions
2 pods red pepper
¼ bunch parsley
9 cups water

Cook rice until almost done. Cut up red onions very fine and brown in shortening. Cut up giblets and put in with onions and cook until brown. Add garlic cut very fine. Chop green onions with tops and parsley, and add to the mixture along with salt and red pepper and water. Pour over cooked rice. When the water is absorbed, put in a large baking pan. Dot with butter and brown in 350° oven for 15 minutes, if desired. Serves 30-40.

MRS. MATT G. SMITH

BROWNED RICE

1 medium size onion, chopped
1 stick oleo or butter
1 cup rice, uncooked

1 can consommé
1 can mushrooms
1 cup water

Sauté onion in butter in heavy skillet. Remove onions, add rice to remaining butter. Very slowly let uncooked rice brown, moving the rice constantly. Mix with onions and other ingredients. Bake in 9" x 13" uncovered casserole in 350° oven, stirring occasionally while it cooks. Serves 4.

MRS. MARY LOU WOODSIDE

RICE PILAFF

2 tablespoons chicken fat,
    butter or shortening
1 onion, ground
2 cloves garlic, ground
1 bay leaf

1 cup rice, raw
1 teaspoon salt
1 1-inch slice bell pepper
1½ cups hot chicken broth
    or consommé

1½ cups hot water

Melt fat in heavy saucepan; add onions, garlic and bay leaf. Cook gently for 5 minutes or until lightly browned. Add rice and salt. Stir. Add all other ingredients. Stir and bring to a boil; taste and season. Cover and simmer for 5 minutes. Place in 375° preheated oven and bake uncovered for 30 minutes. Remove bay leaf and bell pepper from mixture when cooked. Serves 6.

MRS. W. AMISS KEAN

BAKED WILD RICE

2 cups uncooked wild rice
1 No. 2 can tomatoes
1 teaspoon butter
½ pound sharp cheese,
    grated

12 stuffed olives
2 large cans whole mush-
    rooms
Salt and pepper to taste

Rub a 9" x 13" baking dish with butter. Add all ingredients, and mix well. Cook in 350° oven for 1½ hours. If desired, put extra cheese on top and brown. Serves 12. *Delicious!*

MRS. CALVIN L. SIMPSON II

WILD RICE AMANDINE CASSEROLE

2 cups wild rice or 1 cup wild
    rice and 1 cup long grain
    white rice
½ cup olive oil
2 tablespoons chopped onions
2 tablespoons chopped chives
1 teaspoon chopped shallots

3 tablespoons chopped green
    pepper
4½ cups hot chicken broth,
    or bouillon
¾ cup almonds, blanched and
    slivered
Salt and pepper to taste

Wash and drain rice. Sauté vegetables in olive oil. When limp, stir in rice until golden color. Stir in chicken broth. Salt and pepper to taste. Add almonds and turn mixture into casserole. Bake covered in 250° oven for 1¼ hours or until done. Serves 12.

MRS. NEWELL DUNN

SPINACH MADELEINE

2 packages frozen chopped
  spinach
4 tablespoons butter
2 tablespoons flour
2 tablespoons chopped onion
½ cup evaporated milk
½ cup vegetable liquor
½ teaspoon black pepper
¾ teaspoon celery salt
¾ teaspoon garlic salt
Salt to taste
6 ounce roll of Jalapenos
  cheese
1 teaspoon Worcestershire
  sauce
Red pepper to taste

Cook spinach according to directions on package. Drain and reserve liquor. Melt butter in saucepan over low heat. Add flour, stirring until blended and smooth, but not brown. Add onion and cook until soft but not brown. Add liquid slowly, stirring constantly to avoid lumps. Cook until smooth and thick; continue stirring. Add seasonings and cheese which has been cut into small pieces. Stir until melted. Combine with cooked spinach. This may be served immediately or put into a casserole and topped with buttered bread crumbs. The flavor is improved if the latter is done and kept in refrigerator overnight. This may also be frozen. Serves 5 to 6. *So different.*

MRS. WILLIAM G. REYMOND

SPINACH WITH SOUR CREAM

1 package frozen chopped
  spinach
1 tablespoon grated onion
2 eggs
½ cup sour cream
1 cup grated Parmesan
  cheese
1 tablespoon flour
2 tablespoons butter
Salt and pepper to taste

Cook frozen spinach in small amount of water with onion until thawed. Beat eggs, and mix rest of ingredients with spinach and onions and bake in greased casserole for 25 to 30 minutes in 350° oven or until center is set. Do not overcook as it will separate. Serves 4.

MRS. WILLIAM BAILEY SMITH

BAKED SQUASH RING

3 cups summer squash
¼ cup melted butter
¼ cup milk
3 eggs, well beaten
1 teaspoon salt
⅛ teaspoon white pepper or
  dash hot sauce
¼ cup buttered bread crumbs
1 tablespoon minced onion
A pinch of fine herbs

Wash and dice unpeeled squash. Cook in a small amount of water uncovered until tender. Force through a good mill or sieve. Add other ingredients. Blend well. Turn into a 1½ quart well buttered ring mold. Set ring in a pan of hot water and bake at 350° for 45 minutes or until inserted knife comes out clean. Serves 4 or 5.

MRS. WILLIAM R. SMITH

SQUASH SOUFFLÉ

6 medium white squash	1 small bunch green onions
2 slices French bread	Salt to taste
½ cup milk	Pepper to taste
1 egg	Bread crumbs

Peel and cut squash in medium sized pieces. Boil in unsalted water until tender. Drain and mash well. Soak two large pieces of French bread in milk. When well soaked, blend into the squash. Add one egg and beat well into the mixture. Add onions, salt and pepper to taste. Bake in greased casserole for 35 minutes at 350°. Sprinkle with bread crumbs and dots of butter before baking if desired. Serves 6.

THE LATE MRS. J. H. BRES
from
MRS. P. CHAUVIN WILKINSON

STUFFED WHITE SQUASH

4 white summer squash	4 tablespoons tomato paste
1 large or 2 medium onions	1 cup cracker crumbs
1 bud garlic	2 tablespoons chopped fresh
2 slices white bread	parsley or flakes
1 egg	4 tablespoons butter

Salt and pepper to taste

Boil squash in salted water until tender. Brown chopped onion and garlic in half mixture of bacon drippings and butter. Wring bread in ice water and chop fine. Add to onion and garlic mixture and cook a few minutes, stirring frequently. Scoop squash out of shells and chop fine. Add to cooking mixture and cook a few more minutes stirring frequently. Beat egg and add very carefully, making sure egg does not come in contact with skillet. Cook a few minutes and add tomato paste. Just before removing from heat, add chopped parsley. This mixture can be either stuffed in shells or put into casserole. Cover with cracker crumbs and small dots of butter. Bake in 350° oven until crumbs are brown. Serves 6.

ESTHER CHISHOLM

TOMATO AND APPLE CASSEROLE

1 No. 2 can quartered apples	½ cup sugar
1 No. 2 can tomatoes (not	4 tablespoons oleo or butter
whole)	3 slices toasted bread
(do not use all the juice)	Nutmeg, salt

Make alternating layers of apples and tomatoes. Season with a little salt and nutmeg. Sprinkle sugar on top, then top with toast crumbs. Dot with butter and bake at 350° for 45 minutes. Use 1 quart casserole. Serves 4 to 6.

MRS. LEROY WARD III

BAKED OR STUFFED TOMATOES

3 tablespoons butter	1 No. 2 can of tomatoes
1 large onion, minced	1 teaspoon minced parsley
1 rib celery, minced	1½ cups bread crumbs

Cooked shrimp, can of deviled ham, or diced ham

Melt butter in iron skillet with onion and celery and cook over low heat until onions are clear. Add tomatoes and bring to a boil. Boil about two minutes. Add bread crumbs (saving some to sprinkle over top) and stir well. Add parsley and meat, if desired. Turn into a one quart casserole and dot with butter and slices of bacon. Sprinkle top with bread crumbs. Bake at 350° until the top is brown. Serves 4. This same mixture may also be used with fresh tomatoes as a stuffing.

MRS. ROBERT J. STONE

HOT STUFFED TOMATOES

8 medium size tomatoes, firm but ripe	1½ cups bread crumbs
6 green onions, chopped fine	1 tablespoon Worcestershire
3 tablespoons butter	A pinch of thyme
3 tablespoons parsley, chopped	Salt and pepper to taste

Dip the tomatoes in boiling water to easily remove skins. Hollow center of each tomato leaving the stem end for the bottom. Save pulp. Lightly salt inside of each tomato. Sauté onions in butter; add chopped parsley, cut up tomato pulp. Add bread crumbs and seasonings to mixture. If too dry add a little tomato juice. Stuff mixture in tomatoes. Sprinkle more bread crumbs on top of each one and add a dot of butter on top of each. Place in baking dish and add just a little water to keep tomatoes from sticking. Bake at 400° for 25 to 30 minutes or until crumbs are slightly brown and the tomato looks tender. Serves 8.

MRS. ASHER WHITLEY

VEGETABLES VINAIGRETTE

2 packages frozen broccoli spears or Frenched green beans	1 tablespoon brown sugar
	1 tablespoon chopped onion
¾ cup salad oil	¼ cup red wine vinegar
	¼ cup sweet pickle relish

¼ cup Brazil nuts

Cook frozen vegetables as directed on package. Drain. Combine all other ingredients and heat. Do not boil. Pour over vegetables and serve. Sauce can be made a day before and refrigerated until time to heat and serve. Serves 8. Chopped almonds may be used if Brazil nuts are not available.

MRS. RODNEY G. COCO

VEGETABLES GALORE

3 carrots, sliced thin
2 potatoes, diced
Fresh green beans
Fresh eggplant, cubed
Frozen limas (½ package)
Frozen peas (½ package)
½ small cauliflower
3 medium summer squash
½ small cabbage
2 ribs celery, chopped

½ green pepper, chopped
1 No. 303 can tomatoes
½ cup seedless green grapes, optional
2 cloves garlic, mashed to a pulp
Salt and pepper to taste
½ cup olive oil
1 stick butter
2 onions, chopped

1 bouillon cube in ½ cup water

Layer all vegetables in a *very large* skillet in same order. Pour over ½ cup boiling olive oil. Sauté the two onions in butter until golden brown. Add bouillon cube in water. Pour over top of vegetables. Cook 30 minutes uncovered. Serves 12 or more.

MRS. R. W. RIEDEL
Houston, Texas

WHITE SAUCES

Kind	Butter	Flour	Salt	Pepper	Milk
Thin	3 Tblsps.	2 Tblsps.	1 tsp.	¼ tsp.	2 cups
Medium	4 Tblsps.	4 Tblsps.	1 tsp.	¼ tsp.	2 cups
Thick	6 Tblsps.	8 Tblsps.	1 tsp.	¼ tsp.	2 cups

Melt butter over low heat; add flour, salt and pepper; stir until well blended. Remove from heat. Gradually stir in milk and return to heat. Cook, stirring constantly until thick and smooth. Makes 2 cups.

Variations to White Sauce:

SOUR CREAM SAUCE

Using proportions for thin white sauce, substitute 2 cups thick sour cream for the milk; when sauce is thick, add 1½ tablespoons lemon juice.

CHEESE SAUCE

Using proportions for thin white sauce, add 2 cups grated cheese and ½ teaspoon Worcestershire sauce to thickened white sauce. Stir over low heat until cheese is melted.

SAUCE FOR GREEN BEANS OR SPINACH

2 cups mayonnaise
Small onion, chopped fine
1 teaspoon prepared mustard
½ cup olive oil
Dash of hot sauce

1 teaspoon Worcestershire sauce
4-6 eggs, hard cooked, grated or mashed
Add salt, if needed

Mix in order given and serve on green beans or spinach. Half the recipe serves for family use.

MRS. GLENN S. DARSEY

HOLLANDAISE (NEVER FAIL)

¾ cup water
Salt, red pepper, and paprika
  to taste

Juice of 1 lemon
1 tablespoon cornstarch
2 egg yolks, beaten

2 tablespoons butter

Heat water in top of double boiler. Add salt, red pepper, paprika and lemon juice. Dissolve cornstarch in a little cold water. Add to above mixture, stirring constantly. When mixture is slightly thickened, remove from over hot water. Add the beaten egg yolks and one tablespoon butter. Stir in thoroughly; place over hot water again until thickened. Add another tablespoon of butter before serving.

Note: Too high a temperature, too long cooking or too long standing over heat before serving may make Hollandaise curdle. It can be made smooth again by very slowly adding 1 tablespoon of boiling water, beating with a rotary beater. If sauce cannot be served immediately, it should preferably be made in advance and allowed to cool; then reheated over hot, not boiling, water for 5 minutes.

MRS. WILLIAM A. NICHOLS

MOCK HOLLANDAISE SAUCE

½ cup mayonnaise
Juice of ½ lemon
½ teaspoon onion purée

¼ teaspoon prepared
  mustard
Worcestershire sauce to taste

Mix all ingredients well in a small bowl; let stand several hours over the warm part of the top of the stove. When warm, pour over hot string beans. Do not cook.

MRS. P. CHAUVIN WILKINSON

SAUCE FOR BROCCOLI

2 tablespoons butter
2 tablespoons olive oil
1½ teaspoons Worcestershire
  sauce

Salt and pepper taste
1 teaspoon mustard
1 tablespoon vinegar
Red pepper to taste

Mix all ingredients and heat until butter melts. Pour over cooked broccoli just before serving.

MRS. HENRY VOORHIES

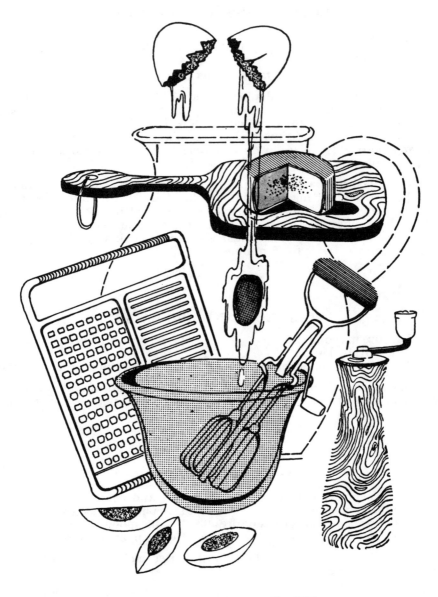

Cheese and Eggs

ANCHOVY AND EGGS

2 cans filet of anchovies (cut small)
1 dozen hard cooked eggs (cut coarsely)
2 teaspoons chopped parsley
Paprika to taste

½ tablespoon Worcestershire sauce
¾ cup mayonnaise
Red pepper to taste
Salt to taste

Mix ingredients and serve on round crackers.

MRS. CARROLL S. MAYER, SR.

EGGS BENEDICT

4 slices toast (crust removed)
4 thin slices fried ham

4 eggs
Hollandaise sauce

Cut ham slices the same size as toast, and place ham on top of toast. On top of each, place a poached egg and cover with Hollandaise sauce. Serve at once.

EGGS ST. DENIS

¾ cup chopped lean ham
4 tablespoons chopped green onion
1 tablespoon chopped, cooked liver
2 tablespoons chopped mushrooms

2 tablespoons butter
Dash white wine or lemon juice
6 eggs
6 slices toast
6 slices boiled ham
Salt and pepper to taste

Make sauce (1½ cups) by cooking chopped ham, green onion, liver, mushrooms together in butter. Add wine or lemon juice. Break each egg into a saucer. Then, slide eggs into deep grease (not too hot). Keep turning egg over with perforated turner to keep eggs round and to get whites to cover yolks. Fry only 2 to 3 at a time. Have slices of toasted, buttered bread ready. Place a slice of ham and an egg on each slice of toast. Pour sauce over. If preferred, instead of the above sauce cooked in butter, you can make a sauce with a roux foundation (browning equal amounts of flour and butter), using green onions, mushrooms, green peppers and seasonings.

MRS. GEORGE HILL

SCRAMBLED EGGS DELICIOUS

1 onion, chopped fine
2 tablespoons butter
½ cup sliced mushrooms

6 eggs
2 tablespoons water
Pinch marjoram
Salt and pepper to taste

Cook onion in butter until golden brown. Add mushrooms and sauté for a few minutes. Break eggs into bowl and add 2 tablespoons water. Beat lightly. Pour egg mixture over onions and mushrooms, sprinkle with pinch marjoram, salt, and pepper and scramble slowly. Serves 4.

MRS. FRED PARNELL

OLIVE EGG SPREAD

1 whole egg
5 egg yolks
A little less than ¼ cup
   white vinegar
2 tablespoons butter
2 tablespoons Durkees
   dressing

Large bottle of stuffed olives
2 tablespoons chopped
   parsley
4 green onions (tops only)
Salt to taste

Beat eggs thoroughly. Heat vinegar to boiling point, (add 1 teaspoon of water before heating to cut vinegar.) Pour boiling vinegar into eggs, beating constantly. Place in sauce pan over heat and stir until it thickens. Remove and add lump of butter; then add Durkees dressing, chopped olives, green onions, and chopped parsley, red pepper sauce and salt to taste. Do not leave out the Durkees!

Mrs. Asher Whitley

PUFFY OMELET

4 eggs, separated
½ teaspoon salt

¼ cup cream or milk
Dash pepper
1 teaspoon butter

Beat egg whites until they will hold a point. Beat yolks with seasonings until thick and lemon colored. Add cream. Fold egg yolk mixture into egg whites. Pour into hot buttered skillet. Reduce heat and cook until bottom is golden brown. Run under broiler to brown top and finish cooking.

Mrs. M. S. Cadwallader

SPANISH OMELET

½ cup chopped green onions
1 small green pepper,
   chopped fine
2 tablespoons butter

1 No. 1 can tomatoes
2 pimentos, cut fine
6 large olives, chopped
Salt and pepper to taste

Sauté onions and peppers in butter. Add tomatoes and cook until moisture has nearly evaporated. Add chopped olives and seasonings and cook a few minutes. Pour a few spoonfuls of this sauce in center of Puffy Omelet. Then fold omelet and pour the reminder of sauce over top.

Mrs. M. S. Cadwallader

EGGS AND MUSHROOMS

4 toast rounds
2 tablespoons butter
4 poached eggs

1 4-ounce can sliced mushrooms
Cheese sauce

Place toast rounds in buttered baking dish. Cover with sliced mushrooms, sautéed in butter. Place poached egg on each toast round and cover all with hot cheese sauce. Sprinkle with grated cheese and place in oven at 375° until cheese on top is melted. Serve at once. Serves 4.

SUNDAY NIGHT QUICKIE

4 eggs   1 can undiluted chicken
                                        noodle soup

Beat eggs slightly; add soup and beat again together. Pour into buttered skillet and scramble. Serve hot on toast. Serves 2 or 3.

MRS. J. H. BENTON

TOAD IN HOLE

1 egg   1 slice bread
3 tablespoons butter

Cut a circle out of center of bread slice. Fry bread in butter until brown and crisp on one side. Turn over and break egg into circle. Fry over low heat for 5 minutes.

MRS. D. S. MILLER

CHEESE SAUCE

3 tablespoons butter   ⅛ teaspoon pepper
3 tablespoons flour   ¼ teaspoon dry mustard
¼ teaspoon salt   ½ cup sharp cheese
                1 cup milk

Melt butter and add flour and seasonings making a paste. Slowly, add milk and stir until thick. Add cheese and stir until melted.

MRS. COMPTON HUMMEL

CHEESE DELIGHTS

½ pound sharp American   2 cups chopped pecans
    cheese, grated   2 cups sifted flour
½ pound butter or oleo   Salt to taste
                Pepper to taste

Soften butter to room temperature and mix with cheese. Add flour, pecans, and salt. Bake about 15 minutes at 350° in small patties.

MRS. NELSON BOURGEOIS

CHEESE AND CRABMEAT

1 pound processed cheese   1 10-ounce can tomatoes and
1 pound fresh crabmeat   green chilis

Melt cheese in top of double boiler and add tomatoes and chilis; add crabmeat and mix well. Serve hot on toast rounds.

MRS. ROLAND CALDWELL

CHEESE MOLD

1½ pounds American cheese
3 cloves garlic
¼ pound blanched almonds
1 small onion
1 envelope plain gelatin

¼ cup cold water
1 cup hot water
1 tablespoon Worcestershire
  sauce
1 teaspoon hot sauce

Parsley and paprika

Put in food grinder the cheese, garlic, almonds and onions. Swell gelatin in ¼ cup cold water and add 1 cup hot water. Cool to lukewarm. Add gelatin mixture to cheese mixture and stir in hot sauce and Worcestershire sauce. Place in ring mold and let chill until firm. Sprinkle parsley around, and paprika over the top. Serve with triangle crackers.

MRS. STANFORD BARDWELL

CHEESE SOUFFLÉ

2 tablespoons butter
2 tablespoons flour
1½ cups milk
½ teaspoon salt

1½ cups grated cheese
1 cup cold boiled rice
3 beaten egg yolks
3 stiffly beaten egg whites

Dash of Tabasco (optional)

Make a cream sauce by melting butter over low heat and blending in flour. When smooth, add milk slowly and stir constantly. Add salt and grated cheese. Turn off heat and add rice. Let this cool and then add egg yolks and fold in beaten egg whites. Place in greased casserole dish and bake in 325° oven for 45 minutes. Serves 6.

MRS. J. N. OGDEN

CHEESE SANDWICH SPREAD

1 pound American cheese
  (cut up)
1 small can evaporated milk
1 small can pimento, drained
  and crushed

1 teaspoon Worcestershire
  sauce
Salt to taste
Pepper to taste
3 eggs, well beaten

Put milk and cheese in double boiler and cook until melted. Turn off heat and add the eggs, sauce, pimento, pepper and salt. Beat well with a rotary egg beater. This makes about 1½ pints. It may be put in refrigerator and kept for several days.

MRS. THOMAS P. ROBERTS

MEXICAN CASSEROLE

4 cans enchiladas
1 can corn
1 large bottle stuffed olives

1 pound sharp American
  cheese (cut in small pieces)
Plenty salt and red pepper

Mix all ingredients and bake in moderate oven for 1½ hours. Good served with ham or chicken. Serves 12.

MRS. HARRY L. HAGAN

ROQUEFORT AND COTTAGE CHEESE SPREAD

1 cup creamed cottage cheese
¼ pound Roquefort or bleu
   cheese
¼ cup evaporated milk or
   thin cream

¼ small onion
1 teaspoon Worcestershire
   sauce
Few drops green vegetable
   coloring (optional)

Have cheese at room temperature. Place cottage cheese in blender container. Crumble in Roquefort or bleu cheese. Add evaporated milk or cream, onion, and Worcestershire sauce. Cover container and blend on high speed. Stop and start blender and scrape down sides of container as needed. Add vegetable coloring a drop at a time, and blend after each addition until desired color is obtained. Chill thoroughly before serving. Yields about 1½ cups.

EVELYN WILSFORD

BAKED CHEESE SANDWICHES

12 slices white bread
6 slices sharp American
   cheese

Butter
4 eggs
1½ cups milk

1 can cream of mushroom soup

Cut crusts off bread; spread with butter. Place slice of cheese between two slices of bread. This makes six cheese sandwiches. Place sandwiches side by side in flat baking dish. In separate dish, beat eggs with milk. Pour this mixture over sandwiches and place in refrigerator over night, or allow to stand one hour before baking. Bake ½ hour at 350° Serve with heated cream of mushroom soup slightly diluted with milk.

MRS. J. BURTON LeBLANC

SHRIMP RABBIT (RAREBIT)

4 tablespoons butter
½ onion, chopped
2 tablespoons green pepper,
   chopped
1 pound raw shrimp, cleaned
1 tablespoon flour

½ cup milk
½ pound American cheese,
   grated
1 teaspoon Worcestershire
   sauce
⅛ teaspoon dry mustard

Salt and pepper

Sauté onion and green pepper in the 2 tablespoons butter. Add shrimp and cook until they turn pink. In separate sauce pan, melt rest of butter and add flour. Stir until smooth. Add milk, gradually, and then add cheese, Worcestershire sauce, mustard, salt and pepper. Stir this mixture until cheese melts. Add shrimp and green pepper and onion. Heat and serve on toast. Serves four.

WELSH RABBIT (RAREBIT)

3 tablespoons butter
2 tablespoons flour
1 cup milk
¼ teaspoon salt
⅛ teaspoon pepper

½ teaspoon dry mustard
1 teaspoon Worcestershire
    sauce
1 cup sharp American cheese

In the top of double boiler melt butter and add flour to make a smooth paste. Add milk gradually and stir constantly. After mixture thickens and cooks about ten minutes, lower heat and add cup of grated cheese, salt, pepper, Worcestershire sauce and mustard. Stir until cheese melts and mixture is smooth. Serve immediately on toast or crackers.

WOODCOCK

1 large can tomatoes
¾ pound American cheese
1 teaspoon Worcestershire sauce

2 eggs
1 teaspoon dry mustard

Cook tomatoes for five minutes. Grate cheese and add slowly to tomatoes until well blended. Beat eggs and add mustard. Remove tomatoes from heat and slowly add egg mixture. Add Worcestershire sauce. Serve on crackers or toasted bread.

MRS. PAULINE O'BRION HART

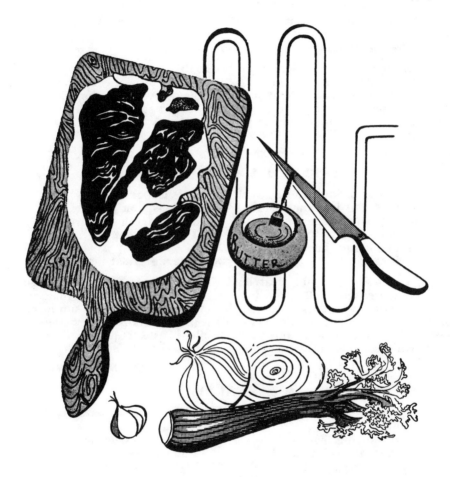

MEAT

FIRST YOU MAKE A ROUX

"First, you make a Roux!" How very often we have all heard "good French cooks" begin to share a recipe with just those words! And the roux is certainly the foundation of many sauces and gravies.

2 tablespoons butter, shortening or bacon drippings	**2 tablespoons flour**

Melt the butter, shortening or bacon drippings in thick pot or skillet. Add the flour and stir constantly until *dark* brown, being careful not to burn. If there is the slightest indication of over-browning, dispose of the roux and start over. Even a slightly burned sauce will ruin a savory dish. To this basic roux, add seasoning and stock to make various sauces and gravies.

THE EDITORS

BEEF KABOBS DELUXE

2 pounds sirloin tip or chuck roast, cut in 2-inch cubes	**1 teaspoon salt**
¼ cup soy sauce	**½ teaspoon pepper**
½ cup salad oil	**1 pint fresh mushrooms**
¼ cup lemon juice or vinegar	**1 large onion or**
	1 large green pepper

If chuck is used, add meat tenderizer as directed on package. Combine soy sauce, salad oil, lemon juice, salt and pepper, and marinate meat in refrigerator 3-4 hours or overnight. Alternate meat with mushrooms, piece of onion or pepper on skewer of rotisserie. Individual skewers may also be used and cook kabobs under broiler. Baste frequently with marinade while cooking. Broil to desired doneness—20-30 minutes.

EVELYN WILSFORD

JAMBALAYA

1½ pounds sausage or cubed beef	**2 tablespoons parsley, chopped**
3 tablespoons bacon drippings, if beef is used	**2 cloves garlic, minced**
Salt and pepper beef	**2 cups rice**
3 tablespoons flour	**2½ cups water**
2 medium onions, chopped	**¾ teaspoon red pepper**
1 bunch green onions, chopped	**2 teaspoons salt**

Brown meat in bacon drippings; remove, and add flour. Use a heavy black pot and brown flour to a dark roux. Add onions, parsley, and garlic. Cook until soft, then add water and rice, salt and pepper, and browned meat. When it comes to a boil, lower heat to lowest point and cook for about 1 hour, covered tightly. When rice is done, remove lid and let cook for a few minutes until rice dries a little. Serves 6-8.

MRS. W. R. SMITH

HAIGAYAN KABOB

4 large squares of heavy-duty
  aluminum foil
2 pounds lamb shoulder, cut
  in 4 pieces
2 green peppers, halved
2 tomatoes, halved
1 onion, quartered
1 medium eggplant,
  quartererd
1 potato, quartered
Salt and pepper to taste

Place in center of each square of foil: 1 piece of lamb, ½ tomato, ½ pepper, ¼ onion, ¼ eggplant, ¼ potato, salt and pepper. Fold each unit into a compact package and place side by side in roasting pan. Bake in 350° oven for 2½ to 3 hours. Do not turn packages, do not use water. To serve, leave in individual packages. Serves 4.

MRS. DONALD A. DRAUGHON

CITY CHICKEN

8 skewers
1½ pounds veal, cubed
1 pound lean pork, cubed
2 eggs
Salt and pepper
Cracker crumbs

Put meat on skewers, alternating veal and pork. Roll them in cracker crumbs and egg seasoned with salt and pepper. Brown in fat in skillet. Bake in 300° oven for about 1 hour, with lid on skillet. After they are cooked, remove lid and let cook for 10-15 minutes longer, until a little dry. Serves 6 or 8.

MRS. PAUL DIETZEL
MRS. W. R. SMITH

OLD FASHIONED HASH

2 pounds top round steak,
  cubed
6 tablespoons olive oil
3 tablespoons flour
2 large onions, chopped
2 buds garlic, crushed
½ cup celery, chopped
1 can. beef gravy
2 teaspoons Worcestershire
  sauce
1 teaspoon monosodium
  glutamate
Dash of thyme
Dash of oregano (optional)
1 bay leaf
¼ cup dry red wine
Salt and pepper to taste
1 teaspoon soy sauce
½ bunch parsley
Mushrooms (optional)

Brown meat in 3 tablespoons olive oil until golden. Remove from heavy dutch oven, add 3 more tablespoons oil, and brown flour. Add onions, garlic, and celery, and cook until transparent. Return meat to gravy; add remaining ingredients except parsley, and simmer until tender. When ready to serve, sprinkle with chopped parsley. Carrots and diced potatoes may be added to this toward the last of the cooking if desired. Mushrooms are optional. Serves 8.

MRS. CHARLES DUCHEIN, JR.

NOODLE CASSEROLE

1 pound cubed veal
1 pound cubed lean pork
2 onions, chopped
Butter, enough to saute
   meat, onions, pepper
¼ green pepper, chopped

1 can mushroom soup
½ pound noodles, cooked
½ pound yellow cheese,
   grated
½ can pimento
2 cups sour cream

Fry meat, green pepper, and onions in butter, until tender. Combine with all remaining ingredients except sour cream. Spread sour cream over the top. Bake at 300° for 2 hours in 9″ x 13″ baking dish. Serves 10.

Mrs. Robert Donald

DAUBE GLACÉE

10 pounds boneless chuck
   roast
1 can consommé
6 large onions
Pinch thyme
3 or 4 bay leaves
2 or 3 cloves garlic

Salt, pepper, cayenne pepper
   to taste
4 ounces sherry or Madeira
   wine
1 package gelatin to each
   pint of liquid

Rub meat with salt and pepper, and brown in fat. Place meat in large pot. Add water and consommé to cover (less liquid, if pressure cooked). Add onions, thyme, bay leaves, garlic, salt, pepper. Simmer 5-7 hours, or until meat is tender. Remove meat; strain stock. Add sherry or wine to stock. Bring to boil and remove from fire. To stock add gelatin, already softened in small quantity of water. Place meat in mold (vegetable crisper, or other large enamel pan, suggested). Pour hot stock and gelatin over meat. Skim off grease as it rises to top. Mold in refrigerator until congealed. Serve cold, unmolding in lukewarm water. *Place on platter and garnish with parsley, tomato wedges, green pepper rings, etc. Serves at least 20.*

Mrs. Thomas B. Pugh, II

CHOW MEIN

½ pound pork, diced
¾ pound veal, diced
½ pound beef, diced
6 tablespoons soy sauce
1 cup water
1 large bunch celery (cut
   in ½-inch pieces)
1 large onion, chopped

2 tablespoons cornstarch
¼ cup water
1 10½-ounce can water
   chestnuts
1 No. 2 can bean sprouts,
   drained
1 2-ounce can mushrooms
Salt and pepper

Brown meats in hot fat. Add soy sauce and cup of water. Simmer 2 minutes. Add celery and onion. Simmer 1½ hours. Blend cornstarch and water. Stir into meat mixture. Add chestnuts, bean sprouts, and mushrooms. Heat through. Season to taste with salt and pepper. Serve this over chow mein noodles and rice. Serves 8.

Mrs. J. M. Cadwallader

MARINATED BEEF ROAST

4 or 5 pounds eye round beef
1 tablespoon meat tenderizer
3 cups white wine
¾ cup salad oil
1 tablespoon salt
1 teaspoon rosemary

Pinch of sage
Pinch of thyme
1 tablespoon black pepper
2 onions
2 tablespoons melted butter
1 teaspoon celery seeds

Pierce surface of the roast in many places with a fork or skewer and sprinkle with meat tenderizer. Put beef in a deep bowl and pour -in marinade mixture of wine, salad oil, salt, rosemary, sage, thyme, pepper, and sliced onions. Cover bowl and let meat stand for 24 hours in refrigerator, turning occasionally to flavor and tenderize all areas. At the end of marinating time, drain meat (save marinade) and insert spit through center. Combine 2 cups of marinade, melted butter (or margarine) and celery seed. Baste meat frequently with this mixture. Roast in an electric rotisserie for about 1 hour and 20 minutes or until meat thermometer registers desired degree of doneness. Follow manufacturer's directions for using rotisserie. Serves 6-8.

POT ROAST IN RED WINE

Small pot roast <u>or</u>

1½ pounds beef, cubed
1 large white onion, sliced
Red wine to cover
4 tablespoons fat
4 tablespoons flour

½ cup hot water
2 beef bouillon cubes
½ teaspoon garlic puree
½ teaspoon rosemary
½ teaspoon ground thyme
Salt and pepper to taste

4 large carrots

Marinate the meat overnight in red wine to cover, to which is added the onion. Remove meat from marinade, drain onion rings and save with the wine. Brown meat in fat. Remove meat. Make a roux by adding the flour to the fat and stirring until it is dark brown. Add onion rings. Cook until soft. Add wine from marinade. Add ½ cup hot water in which 2 beef bouillon cubes have been dissolved. (More water may be added if necessary). Season with garlic purée, rosemary, ground thyme, salt and pepper. Put beef back in gravy. Add carrots which have been scraped and cut into chunks. Simmer tightly covered for at least 3 hours or until meat is well cooked. Serve over Sour Cream Noodles.

MRS. FRANK JORDAN

SOUR CREAM NOODLES

1 8-ounce package noodles
½ pint commercial sour
cream

¾ cup grated Parmesan
cheese

Cook noodles according to directions on package. Drain; rinse with cold water. Mix noodles and sour cream. Add ½ cup cheese. Put into casserole. Sprinkle top lightly with ¼ cup more Parmesan cheese. Bake about an hour at 225°.

MRS. FRANK JORDAN

BEEF STROGANOFF

2 large onions, chopped
Shortening, enough to saute
    onions and meat
2 pounds lean round steak
    (heavy beef), slivered*
1½ cups tomato juice
2 bay leaves, broken
2 teaspoons soy sauce
2 tablespoons Worcestershire
    sauce

Dash of Tabasco
Salt, pepper and paprika
2 cloves garlic, minced
5 tablespoons flour
2 small cans mushrooms
    (save juice)
1 pint sour cream
2 cans fried onions
    (for garnish)

Sauté onions in shortening. Pour into deep pot. Sauté slivered beef and pour into pot. Add tomato juice, seasoning and sauces. Let bubble up and cook slowly about 30 minutes, until meat is tender but not falling apart. Taste meat for tenderness and don't over cook. Set aside until ready to serve. (The preceding can be done the day before, as it takes time to sliver meat, especially when doubling the recipe). When ready to serve, heat tomato-meat mixture and thicken with flour mixed with the juice from the canned mushrooms. Add mushrooms and sour cream. Serve on rice and top with crisp, canned fried onions. Serves 6.

* To sliver: take hard frozen meat and slice in thin pieces while still frozen.

MRS. J. H. BENTON

HAM LOAF

3 pounds uncooked ham,
    ground fine
1 pound lean uncooked pork,
    ground fine
2 eggs

½ cup brown·sugar
½ cup bread crumbs
½ cup milk
4 pineapple slices
Maraschino cherries

Grind ham and pork sauce together. Combine eggs, sugar, bread crumbs, milk in electric mixer and mix well. Work in meat with hands. Shape into loaf and decorate top with half pineapple slices and cherries. Bake in baking dish 300° for 2½ hours or longer, basting often with ½ cup of the pineapple juice. Serves 12.

MRS. VERNON PORTER

HAM ON PINEAPPLE

1 cup cooked ground ham
1 teaspoon prepared mustard

2 tablespoons mayonnaise
4 pineapple slices

To ham add mustard and mayonnaise. Shape in four patties. Place on top of pineapple slices. Bake in a hot oven 400° for 10 minutes. Serves 4.

MRS. C. B. LUIKART, JR.

BAKED CROWN OF HAM

3 eggs
¾ cup milk
3 cups soft bread crumbs
½ cup claret
2 teaspoons Worcestershire
    sauce
⅓ cup minced onion
⅛ teaspoon pepper

2 pounds ground smoked ham
2 pounds ground veal
    shoulder
½ cup currant jelly
2 red apples
2 tablespoons fat or salad oil
Parsley

Beat eggs; add milk and crumbs; let stand 10 minutes. Add claret, Worcestershire sauce, onion and pepper. Add ham and veal; mix well. Pack in greased tube pan, 10″ in diameter. Bake in moderate oven 350° for 2 hours. Unmold in shallow pan. Spread top and sides with jelly. Bake in moderate oven 350° for 30 minutes. Cut apples in eighths; sauté on both sides in fat or salad oil. Serves 8-10. *Place meat on platter; garnish with apples, parsley and Browned Butter Hominy.*

MRS. R. LOUIS MOSCHETTE

BAKED HAM AND CORN CASSEROLE

3 tablespoons butter
3 tablespoons flour
1½ cups milk
½ teaspoon dry mustard
¼ teaspoon Worcestershire
    sauce
¼ teaspoon salt
⅛ teaspoon pepper

1 No. 2 can whole corn
    or
1 package frozen corn
1 small onion chopped
¼ cup green pepper, chopped
2 cups cooked ham, cubed
½ cup grated cheese (or
    more)
Bread crumbs

Mike a white sauce of butter, flour, and milk. Add mustard, Worcestershire sauce, salt, and pepper. Add corn, onion, green pepper, and ham. Pour in a 2-quart casserole. Top with bread crumbs and cheese. Bake at 375° for 25 minutes. Serves 6. *A very good way to use the last of a ham.*

MRS. LENTON SARTAIN

RAISIN SAUCE FOR HAM

½ cup brown sugar
½ tablespoon dry mustard
½ tablespoon flour
½ tablespoon salt
⅛ teaspoon pepper

¼ teaspoon cloves
Few grains of mace, nutmeg
    and cinnamon
¼ to ½ cup seedless raisins
¼ cup vinegar

1½ cups water

Mix dry ingredients. Add raisins, vinegar and water. Cook to a syrup. Serve hot. May be reheated.

MRS. KENNETH SWARTWOOD

STUFFING FOR BAKED HAM

This recipe belonged to Patrick Henry's mother. It is better when stuffed into ham but can be baked in greased loaf pan if desired. Have your butcher remove bone from $\frac{1}{2}$ a ham and stuff the hole with the following:

⅓ cup vinegar	1 tablespoon dry mustard or
2 eggs	prepared mustard
1 medium onion, chopped	½ cup white sugar
1 cup bread crumbs	Red pepper to taste
2 tablespoons celery seed	Black pepper to taste

Dash of sage may be added, if desired

Mix above ingredients all together. After stuffing ham and tying it together with cord, bake in your usual way. This is pretty for a buffet supper as the dressing is a mustard color, and it is nice to be able to cut the ham all the way through. If baked separately, bake at about 300° in greased tin until firm but not hard. Let cool and slice and serve on platter with ham.

MRS. ASHER WHITLEY

ROAST LEG OF LAMB

Stick lamb with tiny bits of celery and garlic. Rub well with lemon juice. Sprinkle with salt and pepper. Place on rack (very important to keep all lamb cuts out of own drippings for that is why it may have a strong, objectionable flavor). Place 2 or 3 strips of bacon across lamb leg, lay several slices of lemon on top. Bake on rack in open pan in 300° to 350° oven about 2 hours or until well done. When cooked, drain off drippings. Remove rack, put lamb leg down in pan. Pour the following sauce over lamb.

6 tablespoons melted butter	2 tablespoons Worcestershire
Juice of 3 lemons	sauce

Little water

Heat with meat. Instead of the above sauce, you may use your own favorite mint sauce.

MRS. P. CHAUVIN WILKINSON

MEXICAN CASSEROLE

1 can tamales	¼ pound cubed cheese, sharp
1 can chili (no beans)	Cheddar
1 bag corn chips, medium	1 small onion, chopped

Break tamales. Layer ingredients in 1-quart casserole. Put juice of tamales over all. Bake about $\frac{1}{2}$ hour at 350°. Serves 4.

MRS. WILLIAM R. SMITH

MEXICAN CASSEROLE

1½ pounds bacon, fried then
  crumbled
1 tablespoon flour
2 cups canned or fresh
  tomatoes

Salt and pepper, to taste
1 teaspoon chili powder
1 No. 2 can hominy (2½
  cups)
1 medium onion, chopped
¼ pound mild cheese, grated

Fry the bacon (cured pork loin with no waste and very little shrinkage). Add flour, tomatoes, and seasonings. Brown hominy and onion in hot bacon grease; add to bacon mixture. Place in bacon-greased casserole; sprinkle with cheese. Bake in moderate oven for 30 minutes. Serves 6 generously.

MRS. GEORGE HILL

CORN CASSEROLE

2 tablespoons butter
1 medium onion, chopped
¼ bell pepper, chopped
2 green onions, chopped if
  desired

1 rib celery, chopped
1 can whole kernel or
  creamed corn
Salt and pepper to taste
1 can hot tamales
Chili powder

Sauté seasonings in butter. Add corn and cook slowly a few minutes, stirring frequently. Add salt and pepper to taste. Arrange mixture in a 1½ quart casserole, alternating layers of corn and sliced hot tamales. Sprinkle each layer with chili powder. Bake in 350° oven until brown. Serves 4. *Good to serve with barbecue.*

MRS. L. J. PERSAC, JR.

MEXICAN DINNER
ENCHILADAS

Tortillas
½ cup fat
½ teaspoon chili powder
1 onion, chopped

½ teaspoon salt
1 large can chili
⅔ cup cheese, grated

Heat tortillas in melted fat to which chili powder has been added. Drain liquid from can of chili. Spread tortillas with chili; sprinkle onion and cheese and roll tortilla. Place in flat baking dish and put remainder of chili, cheese and onion on top. Place in 300° oven to heat and serve at once. Serves 4.

CHALUPAS

Tortillas
1 cup mashed kidney beans
1 can tomatoes

1 cup cheese, grated
½ cup onion, chopped
Guacamole Salad

Drop tortillas in deep fat, and using large ladle, hold down center in order to form a cupped tortilla. Drain and cover bottom of tortilla with mashed beans; then layer of tomato, onion and top with cheese. Place in 300° oven until heated thoroughly. Top with a spoonful of Guacamole. Serves 4.

GUACAMOLE SALAD

Avocado (soft)   Lemon juice
Small onion, minced   Mayonnaise
                    Salt and pepper

Mash avocado, add lemon juice, onion, salt and pepper to taste. Mix in a bit of mayonnaise. Top on chalupas or serve with tomato and lettuce. Serves 4.

Mrs. J. W. Cole

TAMALE PIE

1 pound round steak, cut in   3 tablespoons chili powder
  cubes (ground meat can be   1½ cup yellow corn meal
  used)   3 eggs
2 cloves garlic, minced   1 cup milk
2 onions, chopped   1½ teaspoon salt
1 cup salad oil   Pepper to taste
1 can niblet corn   1 jar stuffed olives
1 can tomatoes   3 tablespoons butter

Cook meat, garlic, and onions in oil about 15 minutes. Add corn, tomatoes, chili powder dissolved in a little water. Cook about 15 minutes more, stirring constantly. Add yellow corn meal, well beaten eggs, milk, salt, pepper, stuffed olives and butter. Cook 15 minutes; then pour into a 2-quart casserole and bake about 1 hour at 350°. Serves 8.

Mrs. Robert Lyle

LEMON PORK CHOPS

3 or 4 very thick pork chops   1 lemon, sliced
Salt and pepper to taste   1 bell pepper, sliced
1 large onion, sliced   2 cups tomato juice

Sear chops on both sides until brown in skillet with no grease. When chops are brown on both sides, turn, add sliced ingredients. Add tomato juice. A little more salt and pepper may be needed. Turn heat to simmer and cook covered for 1 hour.

Mrs. W. C. Boyd

PORK CHOPS AND APPLESAUCE

6 pork chops   ¼ teaspoon cinnamon
1 large can applesauce   ¼ teaspoon nutmeg
½ cup sherry wine   Salt and pepper to taste

Brown chops in skillet. Remove to baking dish. Mix applesauce, spices and sherry. Spoon ½ of this mixture on chops. Bake 20 minutes in 350° oven, turn chops and spoon on remainder of sauce. Return to oven for another 20 minutes. *Good!*

Mrs. Richard A. Roberts

PORK CHOP CASSEROLE

4 pork chops	1 bell pepper, sliced
¾ cup rice	1 onion, sliced
1 tomato, sliced	1 can beef bouillon

Place raw rice in bottom of casserole. Brown pork chops in skillet, then arrange on top of rice. Or remove chops from skillet, put rice in bottom, then replace chops. Place slice of onion, tomato, and pepper ring on top of each pork chop. Pour can of beef bouillon over this. Cover casserole and bake in oven at 375° for about an hour. Add water if needed. *This is a casserole dish that can be prepared ahead of time and then put in oven when ready for it. It may also be simmered on top of stove, covered, for about 30 minutes or until rice is tender.*

Mrs. R. W. Scheffy

VEAL CUTLETS WITH WINE

4 veal cutlets	1 3-ounce can mushrooms
4 tablespoons butter	¼ cup white wine
¼ cup water	

Brown mushrooms in butter, melted in large skillet. Pound cutlets thin, pounding in seasoned flour as you do. Brown cutlets in skillet with mushrooms. Then, add the wine and water. Cover; simmer for 20 minutes. The wine and water will be absorbed when done. Serves 4.

Mrs. McVey Graham

VEAL POCKET

7 pounds veal pocket (cut off shoulder)
Salt, pepper and garlic salt

Filling

2 pounds ground beef chuck	4 green onions, chopped
3 eggs	6 sprigs parsley, chopped
1 cup bread crumbs	Salt and pepper to taste
1 onion, chopped	¼ cup Worcestershire sauce
8 cloves garlic, crushed	¼ cup dry red wine

Rub inside of pocket with salt, pepper, and garlic salt. *Filling*: Combine all ingredients for filling. If mixture is not very moist, add a little more wine or another egg. Stuff into veal pocket; close with skewers. Salt and pepper entire veal pocket. Rub with bacon drippings or oil. Place in shallow baking pan. Cover pocket with bacon strips. Bake uncovered in a 350° oven at least 3 hours so that filling is thoroughly cooked. Remove pocket from oven; give it a chance to set before slicing in ½ inch slices. Serves 12.

Mrs. Naven O. Couvillon

VEAL PAPRIKA

¼ cup tissue-thin sliced
   onions
3 tablespoons butter
1 pound veal cutlets
¼ cup flour

1 teaspoon salt
⅛ teaspoon pepper
1½ cup chicken stock
¾ cup sour cream
1 teaspoon paprika

Saute onions in butter; remove. Brown cutlets that have been turned in seasoned flour. Add stock and onions, and simmer covered for 1 hour. Add sour cream and paprika and heat until blended.

Mrs. Jim Smith

VEAL SCALLOPINI

1½ pounds ground beef
½ cup grated Italian cheese
   (Romano)
3 eggs
1 cup bread crumbs
Salt and pepper
2 tablespoons parsley, finely
   chopped

½ teaspoon garlic puree
½ teaspoon oregano
6 cans tomato sauce
1 can tomato paste
1 pound veal round (½"
   thick, cut in 1" squares)
1 large can mushrooms
6 bell peppers, finely chopped

Garlic salt

Mix ground beef, cheese, eggs, bread crumbs, salt, pepper, parsley, oregano, and garlic puree in large mixing bowl. Form into small balls. Brown in small amount of fat. Brown tomato paste in small amount of fat; add to meat balls. Add tomato sauce to above. Brown the veal pieces in small amount of fat; brown the drained mushrooms in small amount of fat. Mix with above. Sprinkle top with black pepper, garlic salt, and oregano. Cook 20 minutes. Then cook 1¼ hours over slow fire, stirring every ten minutes. Half cook the bell peppers in a little fat; add to above and cook 15 minutes more. Add water to thin if necessary. Serve as spaghetti sauce. Serves 6-8.

Mrs. Roland Selig

VEAL SCALLOPINI

2 pounds veal shoulder
½ cup flour
1 onion
1 clove garlic
¼ cup fat

1 cup sliced mushrooms
1 teaspoon salt
1 teaspoon sugar
1 can tomato soup
1 can water

Pepper, to taste

Cut veal in 2-inch squares. Dredge with flour. Mince onion and garlic. Cook veal, onion, and garlic in fat until veal is browned. Add remaining ingredients (to can of soup, add water as directed). Turn into casserole. Cover. Bake in moderate oven (350°) for 2 hours. Serves 6.

Mrs. Sara Matter

GROUND MEAT DISHES

STUFFED HAMBURGERS

1 pound hamburger meat	Stuffed green olives, chopped
Tomato catsup	Sharp cheese, grated
Salt and pepper	

Make four patties out of hamburger meat, salt and pepper; spread with catsup, sprinkle equal amounts of chopped olives and cheese. Fold pattie over and pinch edge together in shape of $\frac{1}{2}$ circle. Broil very slowly in oven and serve with some of sauce which remains after cooking. Spoon sauce over burger. Serves 4.

MRS. W. T. BAYNARD

BEANS SUPREME

2 pounds ground beef	1 can (1 pound, 13 ounce)
¼ cup bacon drippings	pork and beans
1 large onion, chopped	1 can (16 ounce) red beans
½ green pepper, chopped	1½ teaspoons salt
1 can (4 ounce) mushrooms	Dash of cayenne pepper
1 can (16 ounce) stewed	1 tablespoon Worcestershire
tomatoes	sauce
1 can tomato soup (undi-	1½ cups sharp cheese, grated
luted)	

Brown meat in drippings in heavy skillet; add onions, green pepper, and mushrooms. Cook until vegetables are lightly browned. Add tomatoes, soup, beans, salt and Worcestershire sauce. Put in a $2\frac{1}{2}$ quart casserole. Top with grated cheese and bake at 350° for about 1 hour. Serves 10-12.

MRS. H. PAYNE BREAZEALE

EGGPLANT AND GROUND MEAT CASSEROLE

1 pound ground beef	½ to 1 teaspoon oregano
2 tablespoons salad oil	1 tablespoon Parmesan
1 medium eggplant	cheese
⅓ cup flour	1 cup grated Cheddar cheese
¼ cup olive oil	1 teaspoon salt
2 cans tomato sauce or	Pepper to taste
2 cups homemade sauce	

Shape ground beef into thick patties. Season to taste with salt and pepper. Brown in hot oil. Slice eggplant into thick slices (do not remove skin). Season with salt and pepper, coat with flour, and brown in olive oil. Place cooked eggplant slices in shallow baking dish. Top each with browned meat patties. Cover with tomato sauce. Sprinkle oregano and Parmesan cheese over it all. Top with the grated Cheddar cheese. Bake at 300° for 35 minutes. Serves 6.

MRS. FRANK JORDAN

CABBAGE ROLLS

1 large head of cabbage
1 pound ground beef
1 pound ground pork
1 tablespoon butter
1 tablespoon salt

½ teaspoon black pepper
2 small onions, minced
1 clove garlic, minced
1 cup cooked rice
1 No. 2 can tomatoes

Gently pull off eight large cabbage leaves from the head. Simmer in 1″ boiling water, covered, for 5 minutes. Drain and lay out for filling. Combine ground beef and pork. Saute in butter until brown. Add salt, pepper, onions, garlic and rice. Fill leaves with mixture, using ⅛ of it for each. Roll up each, folding ends to center. Secure with toothpick. Place in greased skillet. Add tomatoes, cover and simmer for 45 minutes. Or may be cooked in oven at 350° for 45 minutes. Remove toothpicks. Serves 4. *Serve with cornbread sticks, baked potatoes and green beans and onion ring salad.*

MRS. FREDERICK P. HOLLIER

STUFFED BELL PEPPERS

6 medium sized bell peppers
2 tablespoons bacon drippings
1 pound ground veal
4 slices bread, soaked in
   water

2 strips bacon, fried and
   chopped
2 ribs celery, chopped
1 medium sized onion,
   minced

Brown veal in bacon drippings. Add minced onion, celery, bacon, salt and pepper to taste. Cook 10 minutes. Add bread and simmer 30 minutes. When cooked, stuff into cleaned peppers. Sprinkle top with bread crumbs and a bit of butter. Place in baking pan in small amount of water and bake in oven at 450°, until peppers are done. Serves 6.

MRS. C. A. HUSTMYRE

BAKED LASAGNA

1 pound ground beef
1 clove garlic, minced
1 tablespoon parsley flakes
1 tablespoon basil
1½ teaspoons salt
2 cups tomatoes
2 6-ounce cans tomato paste
1 10-ounce package lasagna
   noodles

2 12-ounce cartons large curd
   cream-style cottage cheese
2 beaten eggs
2 teaspoons salt
½ teaspoon pepper
2 tablespoons parsley flakes
½ cup Parmesan cheese
1 pound Mozzarella cheese

Brown meat slowly. Add next 6 ingredients to meat. Simmer uncovered until thick, 45 minutes to 1 hour, stirring occasionally. Cook noodles until tender; drain; rinse in cold water. For lasagna, combine cottage cheese with next 5 ingredients. Place ½ noodles in 13″x9″x2″ baking dish; spread ½ of cheese mixture over noodles; add ½ Mozzarella cheese and ½ meat mixture. Repeat layers. Bake at 375° for 30 minutes. Serves 6-8.

MRS. LOUIS MCHARDY

ITALIAN PIZZA PIE

3 tablespoons olive oil
2 cups onions, sliced
2 cloves garlic, minced
1 can tomato paste
2 cups water
1 teaspoon salt

1 teaspoon oregano
1 box roll mix
½ to ¾ pound just cooked
    hamburger meat
Romano cheese, grated
Mozarella cheese, slivered

Saute the onions and garlic in the olive oil. When clear, add tomato paste, water, salt and oregano. Simmer 25 minutes. Allow the roll mix to rise once, but not after rolling out. Roll mix will cover two 9″ or 10″ pie pans and one 7″ pan. Divide sauce on pies. Sprinkle hamburger meat on them. Then sprinkle Romano cheese over meat. Lay slices of Mozzarella cheese on top. Sprinkle oregano over each pie. Bake at 400° for 20 minutes or until dough browns and the rest is bubbly. Freezes perfectly. Serves. 8.

MRS. LAURENCE SIEGEL

GROUND BEEF, CORN AND TOMATO PIE

2 tablespoons fat
1 clove garlic, minced
1 onion, chopped
1 pound ground beef
2 cups canned tomatoes
2 cups canned corn

4 tablespoons butter
5 tablespoons flour
1 teaspoon brown sugar
½ teaspoon chili powder
1 teaspoon salt
¼ teaspoon paprika

Pie crust, biscuits or slices of buttered bread

Melt fat and sauté garlic and onion; stir in ground meat and brown. Add tomatoes and corn. Melt butter; stir in flour. Add these ingredients to the meat mixture; stir and cook until boiling. Season with sugar, chili powder, salt and paprika. Place in a greased, oven-proof dish. Top with pie crust, biscuits or slices of buttered bread. Place in a hot oven of 425° until the top is done, about 20 minutes. Serves 6.

MRS. CHARLES SHRADER

MEAT PIE À LA LU

1 pound ground beef
2 tablespoons fat
1 medium onion
1 clove garlic, minced
1 large carrot, grated
½ to ⅔ cup celery, chopped

1 can cream of mushroom
    soup
½ to ⅔ cup Romano or Parmesan cheese, grated
Salt, black pepper, pinch red
    pepper
Pinch oregano, cumin, and
    marjoram (optional)

Brown meat in fat (lightly); add onions, garlic, celery, carrots; cook slightly. Add soup, cheese, and seasonings. Thin with milk, if necessary. Line casserole with pie crust, reserving enough crust for the top. Put above mixture in pie crust and bake at 350° for about 30 minutes or until crust is desired shade of brown. Serves 4-6.

MRS. JAMES LAROCHE

CHILI CON CARNE

2 pounds ground round steak
2 tablespoons butter
2 green peppers
1 or 2 onions, sliced
2 cans kidney beans

1 can tomatoes or tomato
   soup
2 or more tablespoons chili
   powder
Salt and pepper to taste

Brown meat in butter. Add peppers and onions, cooking until onions are soft. Add beans, tomatoes and seasoning. Simmer 30 minutes. *Serve while hot on toast, crackers or just plain.*

MRS. A. K. GORDON, SR.

PIZZA

Crust

2 packages dry yeast
2 cups warm water
2 teaspoons sugar

2 teaspoons salt
¼ cup olive oil
7 cups flour

Stir yeast into water until dissolved; add sugar, salt, olive oil. Add 4 cups flour, beat until smooth; then add 3 cups flour. Mix well, use your hands for this. Turn out on board and knead well. Let this rise until double in bulk (about 1 hour). Punch down and roll out very thin into 4 large pizza pans.

Filling

2 cans Italian style tomatoes
1 teaspoon basil
1 teaspoon oregano
Salt and red pepper
Anchovies or mushrooms

Italian sausage or lightly
   browned ground meat
Mozzarella cheese
Parmesan cheese, grated
½ cup olive oil

Mash tomatoes, spread on dough. Sprinkle with basil, oregano, salt and pepper. Spread with anchovies or mushrooms, Italian sausage, or ground meat. Top with thinly sliced Mozzarella cheese and Parmesan cheese and olive oil. Cook at 400° for about 25 minutes. Serve hot.

MRS. P. E. ROBERTS, JR.

QUICK BEEF STROGANOFF

½ cup onion, minced
¼ cup butter
1 pound round steak, ground
1 clove garlic, minced
2 tablespoons flour
2 teaspoons salt
¼ teaspoon pepper

¼ teaspoon monosodium
   glutamate
¼ teaspoon paprika
1 medium can mushrooms
1 can cream of chicken soup
1 cup sour cream
½ cup chopped chives

Brown onion and steak in butter. Add the next 7 ingredients and sauté for 5 minutes. Add chicken soup, undiluted and simmer for 10 minutes. Stir in sour cream. This can be served over rice, noodles, potatoes or toast and garnished with chopped chives. Serves 4-6.

MEAT BALLS AND RICE IN CONSOMMÉ

1 pound ground meat
1 teaspoon salt
⅛ teaspoon pepper
¼ cup green pepper, chopped

2 tablespoons celery and
leaves, chopped
1 small onion, chopped
⅔ cup rice
1 can condensed consommé

1 can water

Mix ground meat, salt and pepper, and shape into 12 balls. Brown slowly on all sides in skillet, using a small amount of fat, if necessary. Add green pepper, celery and onion, and cook 5 minutes longer. Add rice, consommé and water. Bring to boil; cover, and simmer gently, stirring occasionally, for 20 minutes or until rice is tender and liquid is absorbed. Serves 4.

NOTE: If desired, 3 bouillon cubes dissolved in 3 cups of hot water may be substituted for the canned consommé.

MRS. HUGH MIDDLETON

QUICK ITALIAN RICE

1 cup minute rice
1 tablespoon butter
1 pound ground chuck
½ medium sized onion,
chopped

1 clove garlic, finely chopped
¼ teaspoon salt
¼ teaspoon sugar
Pepper to taste
1 cup tomato juice

Brown rice in butter, stirring constantly. Remove from skillet. Brown meat, onion and garlic in same skillet. Add rice to mixture, seasonings and tomato juice. Cover and let simmer until rice absorbs tomato juice, about 5-10 minutes. Serves 4-6.

MRS. DONALD HALLMAN

HAMBURGER SKILLET DISH

1 cup uncooked rice
2 tablespoons shortening or
bacon drippings
1 pound ground meat
¼ cup onion, chopped
¼ cup celery, chopped

1 No. 2 can tomatoes
2 teaspoons salt
Pepper
1 teaspoon sugar
1 cup bouillon
1 teaspoon Worcestershire
sauce

Brown rice slowly in hot fat in a heavy skillet, stirring frequently. Add ground meat, onion and celery. Brown well. Add tomatoes and other ingredients. Cover and simmer until rice is tender, about 45 minutes. Serves 4-6.

MRS. R. W. SCHEFFY

SAUSAGE AND RICE CASSEROLE

1 pound bulk sausage
1 cup onion, chopped
1 clove garlic, chopped
1 cup celery, chopped

1 green pepper, chopped
1 cup rice, uncooked
1 can cream of mushroom
  soup
2 cans cream of chicken soup

Brown sausage in frying pan and pour off grease. Add chopped onion, garlic, celery and green pepper to sausage and simmer until tender. Wash rice and add to mixture in pyrex baking dish along with the soups. Bake 1½ hours at 350°, stirring occasionally. Serves 6.

Mrs. J. H. Benton

ZATONI (FOR A LARGE GROUP)

2 green peppers, chopped
4 onions, chopped
4 cloves garlic, crushed
¼ cup salad oil
4 cans tomato soup
2 cans tomato paste
Salt, at least 4 teaspoons
Pepper to taste

2 cans whole kernel corn
Juice of 1 lime
2 cans (large) mushrooms,
  drained; save juice
2 12-ounce packages spaghetti
4 pounds ground beef, lean
1½ pounds American cheese,
  mild

Sauté peppers, onions and garlic in salad oil. Add tomato soup and paste. Season to taste with salt and pepper. Let simmer. Add corn, juice of lime, and mushrooms. Boil spaghetti; drain. Simmer meat in mushroom juice. Place in layers in largest casserole you can get your hands on or in 2 large casseroles. Sprinkle each layer with grated cheese. Bake until heated through at 350°. Cover to heat. Serves 30.

Mrs. Claude D. Smith
Jackson, Mississippi

BAKED CHILI SPAGHETTI

1 package spaghetti
¾ pound ground round steak
2 tablespoons chili powder
  (mixed in meat)
2 medium onions, chopped
1 green pepper, chopped
Bacon drippings
1 can tomatoes
1 medium can chopped mushrooms

1 tablespoon Worcestershire
  sauce
8 shakes hot sauce
3 tablespoons chili powder
  (mixed in sauce)
Salt and pepper
½ pound sharp cheese,
  grated
Catsup

½ cup buttered bread crumbs

Cook spaghetti in boiling water for 20 minutes, or until tender. Brown onion, pepper and seasoned meat in bacon drippings. Mix with tomatoes, mushrooms, Worcestershire sauce, hot sauce, chili, salt, pepper and most of the cheese. Add cooked spaghetti, mix well. Place in buttered baking dish, top with rest of cheese, catsup and crumbs. Bake in oven at 350° for 30-45 minutes. Can be mixed beforehand and kept in refrigerator.

Mrs. Benton Harelson

MEAT

ITALIAN DELIGHT

1½ pounds ground beef	1 can creamed corn
3 large onions, chopped	2 cans tomato soup
3 cloves garlic, minced	3 soup cans water
1 stick butter	Salt and pepper
1 can sliced mushrooms	1 8-ounce package vermicelli (uncooked)

Sauté meat, onions, and garlic in the butter. Add mushrooms, corn and soup with water. Add vermicelli. Start at 350° oven for 30 minutes. Then turn oven to 200° for 1½ hours or until like baked spaghetti. Serves 8-10.

MRS. CHARLES BEADLES

SPAGHETTI CASSEROLE

¼ cup bacon drippings	1 sprig thyme
1 pound ground beef	1 teaspoon salt
1 large onion, minced	Dash cayenne pepper
1 green pepper, chopped	2 cans tomato sauce
1 rib celery, chopped	2 cups cooked spaghetti
1 clove garlic, minced	1 large can mushrooms
1 bay leaf	¾ cup sharp cheese, grated

Melt ½ the above amount of bacon drippings in a skillet and brown ground beef in it. Remove to a bowl. Add remaining bacon drippings and sauté onion, green pepper, celery and garlic until onion is slightly browned. Add bay leaf, thyme, seasonings, tomato sauce, and browned meat, and simmer slowly for 1 to 1½ hours. A little water may be added if sauce becomes too thick. Stir occasionally to prevent scorching. Meanwhile, cook spaghetti in boiling, salted water, until tender. Drain. When meat and sauce are done, combine with spaghetti and mushrooms in a casserole, and top with the grated cheese. Cover and bake in oven at 350° for 30 minutes. Remove cover for the last 10 minutes of baking to brown slightly. *Makes a good meal with a green salad, French bread and dessert.*

MRS. WYLIE BARROW

MEAT SAUCE FOR SPAGHETTI

2 tablespoons bacon drippings or margarine	2 teaspoons salt
	½ teaspoon black pepper
1 cup onions, diced	Cayenne to taste
1 cup celery, chopped	¼ teaspoon thyme
1 cup green pepper, chopped	2 bay leaves
1 pound ground beef or veal	½ cup tomato paste
2 cups tomato juice	

Brown onions, celery and green pepper in margarine. Add meat and fry until meat turns from red to brown. Add remaining ingredients and cook on low heat for at least 1 hour. Mix with boiled, salted spaghetti (⅔ pound). Serve topped with Parmesan cheese. Serves 6.

MRS. KENNETH LANDRY

HOLIDAY MEAT LOAF

1 cup bread crumbs
1 cup milk
3 eggs
1 pound lean beef, finely ground
1 pound ham, finely ground
2 ounces salt pork, finely ground

1 pound lean veal, finely ground
3 teaspoons salt
½ teaspoon black pepper
½ teaspoon marjoram
½ teaspoon thyme
2 medium onions, chopped finely

Soak bread crumbs in milk. Mix all ingredients, including soaked bread crumbs, thoroughly. Shape into a loaf in a flat baking pan. Bake for 2 hours and 15 minutes at 350°. While baking, baste with the following mixture:

¾ cup brown sugar
2 teaspoons dry mustard

2 tablespoons vinegar
¾ cup water

NOTE: This may be garnished with bits of canned fruit after the first basting. Mix basting ingredients and bring to a boil before using to baste. Small amounts of water may be added if necessary. This meat loaf serves 12.

MRS. HUBERT F. BRENNAN

COMPANY MEAT LOAF

½ cup bell pepper, chopped
1 clove garlic, minced
2 onions, chopped
½ cup celery, chopped
1 cup bread crumbs
1 pound veal, ground
1 pound beef, ground
2 eggs
½ cup milk

Salt to taste
Pepper to taste
1 can cream of mushroom soup
3 tablespoons Worcestershire sauce
3 tablespoons horseradish
⅔ cup tomato catsup
Parsley

Add bell pepper, garlic, onions, celery, bread crumbs to ground meats. Work in eggs and milk along with salt and pepper. Shape and put in loaf pan. Bake at 325° for 45 minutes. Mix soup, Worcestershire sauce, horseradish and catsup, and put on top of loaf. Bake 30 minutes longer. Sprinkle with parsley before serving. Serves 8.

MRS. J. EMORY ADAMS

MEAT LOAF WITH SWEET SOUR SAUCE

2 pounds ground meat
½ cup onion, finely chopped
½ cup celery, finely chopped
2 cloves garlic, finely chopped

2½ teaspoons salt
1 teaspoon dry mustard
2 beaten eggs
¼ cup bell pepper, minced

Cracker crumbs or bread soaked in warm milk if desired for filler

Mix lightly the above ingredients, form into loaf, and bake at 325° for 30 minutes before adding the following sauce:

½ cup tomato sauce
1 cup water

2 tablespoons brown sugar or molasses

2 tablespoons vinegar

Mix together sauce ingredients and pour over meat loaf in oven. Con·tinue baking 1½ hours longer, basting occasionally. Serves 6.

Mrs. Gerald Byars

JANE'S SPECIAL

¼ cup olive oil
1 pound ground beef
1 large onion, finely chopped
½ pound fresh mushrooms
(or more), sliced

1 pound fresh raw spinach
(washed, trimmed and
chopped)
Salt and pepper
2 beaten eggs

Note: Instead of fresh mushrooms, you may use 1 large can of stems and pieces.

Heat olive oil in a heavy skillet. Sauté beef and onion in hot oil until beef is brown and onion is tender. Add mushrooms and sauté until tender. Add spinach, salt and pepper, and sauté lightly, turning constantly with a fork. Add the well beaten eggs and continue turning with the fork until eggs are set and evenly distributed throughout the mixture. *Serve as a one-dish meal with plenty of crusty French or Italian bread and a good dry red wine, if desired.* Serves 4.

Mrs. David Van Gelder

QUICK BROWN SAUCE

3 tablespoons butter or bacon
drippings
3 tablespoons flour
2 cans beef consommé or
bouillon

1 teaspoon soy sauce
1 teaspoon monosodium
glutamate
Garlic salt to taste
Pepper to taste

Make a roux of bacon drippings and flour. Gradually add consommé and bring to a gentle boil. Reduce heat and simmer approximately 30 minutes. Skim off fat and strain through a sieve. If a seal of fat is used, the brown sauce may be kept in the refrigerator about three weeks. If the seal of fat is not used, remove the sauce from the refrigerator every four or five days. Boil it; cool it; and return it to refrigerator. *This sauce may be kept in the freezer indefinitely.*

BROWN SAUCE

⅔ cup beef suet (or ⅔ cup
   beef or pork drippings)
2 cups diced carrots
2 onions, coarsely chopped
⅔ cup flour
2 ribs celery, coarsely
   chopped
4 sprigs parsley, chopped
2 cloves garlic, crushed
½ teaspoon thyme
4 peppercorns

2 bay leaves
3 cups red wine
1 teaspoon salt
1 teaspoon seasoning salt
1 teaspoon monosodium
   glutamate
1 teaspoon soy sauce
3 cups beef consommé (or 3
   bouillon cubes melted in 3
   cups boiling water)
2 cups canned tomatoes (or 6
   fresh tomatoes)

Melt suet or drippings in heavy Dutch oven. Cook carrots and onions until onions turn yellow. Add flour and stir constantly until dark brown, being careful not to burn. Add all ingredients, except tomatoes; bring to boil, skimming off fat as it rises to surface and stirring occasionally. Add tomatoes or tomato sauce and simmer approximately 30 minutes. Strain through a sieve. Cool sauce and store in refrigerator with a seal of melted fat until needed. Yield—about 4 cups. *May be kept 3 weeks. Good for ragouts, braised steaks, ribs, Chateaubriand—any meat or game.*

Mrs. Charles Duchein, Jr.

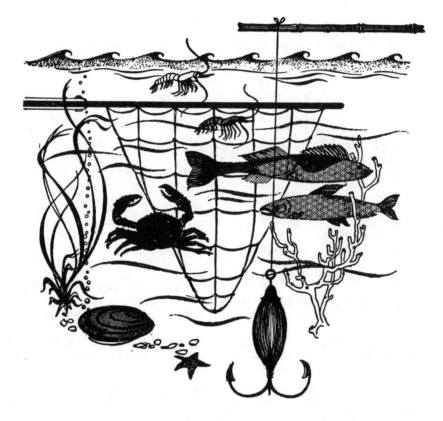

SEAFOOD

SEAFOOD

Seafoods par excellence—a superabundance is ours in "River Road" country—the perfection and variety of which is unsurpassed! From the waters of the Gulf of Mexico come the famous salt-water varieties—the red fish and red snapper, the flounder and the pompano, the speckled trout and the Spanish mackerel. The rivers and bayous of Louisiana offer fresh water varieties such as the bass and the sac-a-lait. To enhance our culinary advantage from a seafood standpoint there are such delicacies as the lake and river shrimp, the hard-shell and the soft-shell crabs, the oysters, the crawfish and the famous green turtle. These can be had for the fishing!

BOUILLABAISSE
À LA NOUVELLE ORLEANS

("Bouillir"—to boil; "baisse"—stop)

Thackeray once said of the Creole Bouillabaisse: "In New Orleans you can eat a Bouillabaisse, the likes of which was never eaten in Marseille or Paris." The reason for this New Orleans triumph is two matchless fish from the waters of the Gulf of Mexico—the red snapper and the red fish. Use equal parts of each.

4 pounds fish filets	2 onions, chopped fine
Salt and pepper	⅔ cup sherry wine
3 sprigs thyme, minced very fine	2 cups tomato pulp
3 sprigs parsley, minced very fine	½ lemon, cut in very thin slices
3 bay leaves, minced very fine	1 pint fish stock or boiling water
3 cloves garlic, minced very fine	Salt, pepper and cayenne to taste
6 allspice, ground, very fine	Pinch of saffron, chopped fine
2 tablespoons olive oil or butter	Buttered toast slices or rice

(To make the fish stock, boil the head of the red snapper and red fish in 1½ quarts of water containing one sliced lemon and a herb bouquet of thyme, bayleaf and parsley. When reduced to *one pint*, remove the fish head and herb bouquet; strain the stock and reserve.)

Rub each slice of the fish with salt and pepper and then with the mixture of minced herbs, garlic, and allspice. The fish must be permeated by the herbs, garlic, and spice to assure the success of this dish. Heat oil or butter in a very large pan—so large that fish filets will not overlap. Add onion to heated oil. Lay fish slice by slice into the pan; cover and let étouffée, or smother, about 10 minutes, turning once, so that each side may be partially cooked. Remove fish filets. Add wine and stir well. Add tomato, lemon, and fish stock or water. Season with salt, pepper and cayenne. Let mixture boil until it is reduced almost one-half. Add fish filets; cook about 5 minutes longer. Add a little hot sauce to the pinch of saffron to dissolve it. Spread saffron over top of fish. Place fish on toast or rice; pour sauce over fish and serve immediately.

COURTBOUILLON

5 pound red snapper
1 cup water
Salt and pepper
1 cup bacon drippings
1 large onion, chopped
1 bell pepper, chopped
6 stalks celery, chopped
1 can tomato paste
1 can water
1 cup either red or white dry
  wine

Salt, black pepper and red
  pepper to taste
¼ cup Worcestershire sauce
Small bunch green onions,
  chopped
Small bunch parsley, chopped
6 bay leaves
Good size pinch sweet basil
¼ teaspoon oregano

Cut the thick fine meaty part of the red snapper into two inch squares and set aside. Cook the remainder of the fish—the head, bones and small bits of meat thereon—in 1 cup of seasoned water to make fish stock. Remove head and bones; reserve stock containing small bits of meat.

GRAVY: In an iron pot, sauté the onion, celery and bell pepper in the bacon drippings very, very slowly until vegetables appear almost congealed, but not browned. Add tomato paste, can of water and the cooled fish stock, containing bits of fish. Add the wine and remainder of seasonings. Add garlic and herbs. Cook two hours at very low temperature. Then add the squares of red snapper which form the individual servings. Cook *only* 20 minutes after adding squares of fish. Serve over hot rice. Serves 6 to 8.

This Courtbouillon may also be used as an hors d'oeuvre and served in a chafing dish. In this case, cut up the whole fish and add to the 1 cup of seasoned water to make stock. Then debone fish and add to gravy, as directed above. Cook to a consistency for spooning over crackers.

MRS. NAVEN O. COUVILLON

FISH COURTBOUILLON

3 pounds catfish steaks
½ cup salad oil
2 onions, minced

1 clove garlic, minced
1 can tomato sauce
Lemon slices

Bring oil to medium heat. Add alternate layers of fish, sprinkled with salt and black pepper, onions and garlic, lemon slices and tomato sauce. Add no water. Cover. Simmer for 1 hour. A small amount of water may be added toward end of cooking time if necessary for more gravy. Serves 4. *Serve on mounds of rice, along with tossed green salad and French bread.*

MRS. FREDERICK HOLLIER

CRABS

To BOIL CRABS: *Crabs are boiled in seasoned water (as for shrimp) using plenty of salt, and enough water to cover. They should cook about 20 to 25 minutes. Adding 2 tablespoons of vinegar to the water makes crabs easier to pick.*

To CLEAN SOFT SHELL CRABS: *Lift and bend back tapering points on crab's back. Remove the spongy substance underneath. Remove eyes and "sand bags" behind eyes. Remove long narrow "apron" on front of crab which begins in center of crab and ends in a point.*

CHINESE CRAB CASSEROLE

1 can cream of mushroom
   soup
¾ cup sherry, optional
1 pound fresh crab meat
½ cup walnuts, coarsely
   chopped
1 small can water chestnuts
½ cup finely chopped onions

1 cup sliced celery
Dash Worcestershire sauce
1 small can sliced mushrooms
1 No. 303 can Chinese
   noodles
1 cup potato chips, bread, or
   cracker crumbs

Mix soup and sherry. Combine other ingredients, except noodles, and add to soup mixture. Add noodles at the very last in two quart casserole. Sprinkle crumbs on top just before baking in 350° oven for 30 minutes. Serves 12.

MRS. ROBERT DONALD

CRAB MEAT CASSEROLE

5 tablespoons butter
3 tablespoons flour
2 cups milk
2 tablespoons minced onion
½ teaspoon celery salt
1 tablespoon grated orange
   rind, optional
1 tablespoon minced parsley
1 tablespoon minced green
   pepper

1 pimento, minced
2 tablespoons sherry
1 egg, beaten
Dash of hot sauce
1 teaspoon salt
Dash of black pepper
1 pound fresh crab meat
Bread crumbs
1 tablespoon butter

Make white sauce of butter, flour and milk; then add next six ingredients. Remove from heat. Add sherry. Add little hot sauce to egg; then add egg to rest of sauce. Add hot sauce, salt, pepper and crab meat. Put in 1½ quart casserole—sprinkle top with bread crumbs mixed with 1 tablespoon melted butter. Bake in a 350° oven 15 to 20 minutes. Serves 6 to 8.

MRS. LENTON SARTAIN

DEVILED CRABS

12 hard shelled crabs or
   1 13-ounce can crab meat
   (2⅔ cups)
4 tablespoons butter
2 tablespoons flour
1 tablespoon minced parsley
2 teaspoons lemon juice

1 teaspoon prepared mustard
½ teaspoon bottled horse-
   radish
1½ teaspoons salt
1 cup milk
2 hard cooked eggs, minced
½ cup soft bread crumbs

2 tablespoons melted butter

Flake the crab meat. Melt 4 tablespoons butter in a double boiler; stir in flour; add parsley, lemon juice, mustard, horseradish, salt, pepper and milk. Heat, stirring until thickened. Add crab meat and minced eggs. Fill the crab shells or ramekins with this mixture. Sprinkle with the bread crumbs which have been combined with 2 tablespoons melted butter and bake in a moderately hot oven 400° for 10 minutes. Serves 6.

MRS. LAURANCE W. BROOKS

CRABMEAT RAVIGOTE

1 pound lump crab meat   Hollandaise Sauce
1 bunch chopped green onions (using only green ends)

Make Hollandaise Sauce as follows:

½ cup butter   4 egg yolks, slightly beaten
2 tablespoons flour   2 tablespoons vinegar
1 cup milk   2 tablespoons lemon juice
                ½ teaspoon salt

Make a white sauce in top of a double boiler by blending melted butter, flour and milk. When blended pour over beaten egg yolks. Put mixture back in double boiler, stirring constantly until thick. Remove from heat and add vinegar, lemon juice, salt and chopped green onions. This makes a medium thick Hollandaise and must be served immediately. Put a serving of crab meat in individual casseroles, and pour sauce to cover on top of crab meat. Serves 6 to 8.

MRS. WILLIAM T. BAYNARD

CRAB MEAT AND MUSHROOMS IN WINE SAUCE

1 pound fresh crab meat   2 tablespoons flour
¼ pound fresh mushrooms,   ½ cup milk
  sliced, or 1 large can of   ½ cup white wine
  mushrooms (stems and   ½ teaspoon dry mustard
  pieces)   ¼ teaspoon dry tarragon
2 tablespoons butter (to   Salt to taste
  sauté fresh mushrooms)   Pepper to taste
2 tablespoons butter   Hot sauce to taste
                ¾ cup bread crumbs

Pull crab meat apart and remove stiff membranes. Sauté mushrooms in butter. (If mushrooms are not fresh add later.) Make a cream sauce blending melted butter, flour and milk, wine, mustard, tarragon, salt, pepper and hot sauce. Cook 2 or 3 minutes, then add crab meat and mushrooms. Place in casserole; sprinkle top with bread crumbs and dot with butter. Bake at 350° for 30 minutes uncovered. Cover before serving. Serves 4. This can be made with shrimp, or crab meat and shrimp.

MRS. J. BURTON LEBLANC

CRABMEAT MORNAY

1 stick butter   ½ pound grated Swiss cheese
1 small bunch green onions,   1 tablespoon sherry wine
  chopped   Red pepper to taste
½ cup finely chopped parsley   Salt to taste
2 tablespoons flour   1 pound white crab meat
1 pint breakfast cream

Melt butter in heavy pot and sauté onions and parsley. Blend in flour, cream, and cheese, until cheese is melted. Add other ingredients and gently fold in crab meat. *This may be served in a chafing dish with Melba toast or in patty shells.*

MRS. CHARLES CAPLINGER

CRAB AND ARTICHOKE CASSEROLE

3 tablespoons butter
3 tablespoons flour
1½ cups milk
1 teaspoon salt
⅛ teaspoon pepper
½ teaspoon Worcestershire
  sauce
⅓ cup Parmesan cheese

Dry mustard to taste
Hot sauce to taste
4 hard-cooked eggs, chopped
1 pound can artichoke hearts
  (bottoms)
2 cups crab meat
¼ cup or more Parmesan
  cheese

Make white sauce by melting butter, adding flour, and gradually adding milk, stirring constantly. Season with salt, pepper, Worcestershire sauce, cheese, mustard, hot sauce. Add eggs, artichoke hearts, and crab meat. Pour into 1½ quart casserole. Sprinkle top with ¼ cup or more Parmesan cheese. Bake at 350° for 30 minutes. Serves 4 to 6—6 for luncheon, 4 for dinner—men like it! If you use frozen artichoke hearts, use 1 package and defrost before using. A pound can of fresh crab meat is enough. This may be cooked at a slower heat for a longer period, but it must be watched or it will dry out.

MRS. JOHN GORDON
MRS. LENTON SARTAIN

CRABMEAT TECHE

1 large bell pepper, chopped
2 large white onions, chopped
6 ribs celery, chopped
1 large can mushrooms
  (stems and pieces)
3 cloves garlic (through
  press)
4 tablespoons bacon drip-
  pings
6 slices dry toast
1½-2 cans chicken broth
1 tablespoon Worcestershire
  sauce

1 teaspoon salt
½ teaspoon black pepper,
  freshly ground if possible
½ teaspoon celery salt
1 teaspoon oregano
  (pounded)
Dash hot sauce
¾ cup chopped parsley
1 pound can white lump crab
  meat*
¾ cup cracker crumbs
3 tablespoons butter
Dash of paprika

* Equivalent amount of canned Alaska King crabmeat may be substituted.

Sauté onions, bell pepper, celery, mushrooms and garlic in bacon drippings until tender. Add crumbled toast which has been soaked in ½ of chicken broth. Add seasoning and simmer in skillet until well blended. Add parsley and second half of chicken broth, to moisten. Finally, add crab meat, blend thoroughly, and turn into buttered casserole. Cover with cracker crumbs, dot with butter and sprinkle with paprika. Bake in 350° oven for 20 minutes. If casserole is made ahead and refrigerated, bake 45 minutes to 1 hour. Serves 8.

MRS. ROY DABADIE

To Boil Crawfish: *Boil exactly as shrimp, but boil a little longer— about 20 minutes. If preparing for Crawfish Bisque, scald the crawfish, but do not boil. They are cleaned by removing head, tail and body shell. The body shell is what is used in Crawfish Bisque for the stuffing, referred to as the "head."*

CRAWFISH ÉTOUFFÉE

30 pounds crawfish	1 pimento
1 cup shortening	Hot sauce to taste
Crawfish fat	Salt and pepper to taste
1 stalk celery	1 teaspoon monosodium
6 medium onions	glutamate
4 cloves garlic	4 teaspoons Worcestershire
1 bell pepper	sauce
1 cup green onion tops	Crawfish tails

Cook 30 pounds crawfish in almost boiling water for 20 minutes; remove and drain. Peel tails, saving any yellow fat that clings to tail or head in a separate container. Grind vegetables and cook in shortening until tender. Add seasonings and blend well. Add crawfish tails and cook about 15 or 20 minutes (do not overcook). Turn off heat and let stand 30 minutes until seasoning blends. Serve on rice. When reheating, use double boiler. Makes 8 quarts or 30 servings.

Mrs. Hansen Scobee

LOBSTER RARA AVIS

1 pound rock lobster tails	2 tablespoons lemon juice (or
½ stick butter	enough to give tart flavor)
¼ cup chopped onion	½ teaspoon black pepper
¼ pound fresh mushrooms,	1 teaspoon Worcestershire
sliced	sauce
1 teaspoon salt (or to taste)	

Remove raw lobster tails from shells, cut into 1-inch square pieces. Melt butter in skillet. Sauté chopped onion and sliced mushrooms over medium heat until onion is soft but not brown. Add lobster meat and cook, stirring occasionally, until meat is opaque. Do not overcook. Add lemon juice, salt, pepper and Worcestershire. Serve over crisp toast strips. Serves 2 or 3. Shrimp may be substituted for lobster. Canned mushrooms may be used, although flavor is not as good. Do not spare lemon juice and Worcestershire. Red pepper may be added if you like.

Mrs. W. G. Reymond

OYSTERS FITZPATRICK

2 dozen oyster shells	Hot sauce
3 dozen oysters	8 strips bacon
1 clove of garlic	Catsup

Rub well dried out oyster shells with clove of garlic. Put a drop of hot sauce in shell, add one large or 2 small oysters, top with 1 inch piece of bacon, and add dash of catsup. Broil 15 minutes in 350° oven. Serves 2, using one dozen oysters apiece.

Dr. Elizabeth Faust

ÉCREVISSE DE MER CONGELÉE
(Congealed Lobster Salad)

2 envelopes plain gelatin
½ cup cold water
1 cup tomato juice
½ cup tomato sauce
Juice of one large lemon
1 tablespoon Worcestershire
  sauce
¼ cup white wine
2 tablespoons prepared horseradish

1 large onion, chopped fine
½ cup finely chopped celery
¼ cup green pepper
2 green onions, chopped
Parsley
2 cloves garlic, grated
Salt, red and black pepper to
  taste
1 medium can lobster, or
  2 cups boiled crayfish

Soften gelatin in ½ cup cold water. Heat tomato juice; then add hot tomato juice to softened gelatin. Add remaining ingredients, except the lobster. Break lobster into medium sized pieces; add to mixture. Pour into well buttered mold. Chill and serve with Horseradish Sauce.

HORSERADISH SAUCE

¾ cup mayonnaise
4 tablespoons horseradish
1 tablespoon Worcestershire
  sauce

⅓ cup lemon juice
Salt and pepper to taste
Chopped parsley

Mix all ingredients and serve over salad.

MRS. NAVEN O. COUVILLON

OYSTER-ARTICHOKE RAMEKINS

Makes 3 ramekins:
3 artichokes (burr)
3 tablespoons butter
1½ tablespoons flour
¾ teaspoon salt
¾ teaspoon pepper
¼ teaspoon hot sauce
2 tablespoons paprika
½ teaspoon thyme

2 dozen oysters and oyster
  liquor
1 tablespoon chopped pimento
1 clove garlic (through
  press), optional
¾ cup bread or cracker
  crumbs
1 ounce sherry

Boil artichokes until very tender—1½ hours at least. Scrape leaves and mash hearts. Brown flour in butter, add seasoning, oyster water, and artichoke mixture. Broil oysters in a little butter until they curl. Mix all ingredients, adding sherry last. Place mixture in ramekins, top with crumbs and dot with butter. Sprinkle with paprika. Heat in hot oven, 450°, 10 minutes or until crumbs are brown.

Variation: 6 ground artichokes may be used rather than burr, when in season. Mushrooms may be added if desired. Serves 4 to 6.

MRS. ROY DABADIE

OYSTERS BIENVILLE I

48 oysters
2 pounds cooked shrimp
2 cans (No. 1) mushrooms
1 pod garlic (or 5 cloves)
1 large onion
1½ cups milk
1½ cups chicken broth or
fish stock

½ pound butter (1 cup)
½ cup cream
½ demitasse cup absinthe
(or any white wine)
4 tablespoons flour
1 pound cheese, grated
(Sharp American)

Dice fine the shrimp, mushrooms, garlic and onion. Mix and simmer milk, broth, butter, cream, wine and flour. Add chopped ingredients and simmer slowly 15 minutes. (This is best and easiest done in a blender, and then simmered.) Put oysters in shells on rock salt and run under hot broiler for 2 minutes. Drain water off oysters. Pour sauce on each oyster and run under broiler for 2 minutes. Add grated cheese, bread crumbs and paprika. Brown under broiler. Serve hot. Serves 4 at 1 dozen apiece.

MRS. JACK REITZELL

OYSTERS BIENVILLE II

¼ cup butter
3 tablespoons flour
1 clove garlic, minced
1 tablespoon onion juice
1 tablespoon Worcestershire
sauce
¼ teaspoon celery seed
1 2-ounce can mushrooms
(stems, pieces)

¾ cup liquid (juice from
mushrooms and shrimp)
1 dozen shrimp, cooked and
chopped
1 tablespoon sherry
1½ pints oysters
Parmesan cheese
Paprika
Salt to taste

Make sauce of butter, flour, garlic, onion juice, Worcestershire sauce, celery seed, and liquid. Add mushrooms, shrimp and sherry. Slide oysters under broiler until edges just curl. Pour off liquid. Sprinkle liberally with Parmesan cheese; then cover with sauce. Sprinkle with paprika. Slide back under broiler for 5 to 8 minutes, until bubbly. (This sauce may also be used for Trout Marguery.) Serves 4 to 6.

MRS. LAURENCE SIEGEL

OYSTER CASSEROLE

3 dozen oysters, drained
⅔ cup chopped parsley
⅔ cup chopped green onions
1 cup cracker crumbs, rolled
fine

1 stick butter, melted
1 small lemon
½ teaspoon dry mustard
2 teaspoons Worcestershire
sauce

Place 3 dozen drained oysters in shallow pyrex dish. (A pyrex pie plate will do.) Sprinkle with parsley and green onions and sprinkle cracker crumbs on top. Melt 1 stick of butter, add juice of one lemon, mustard and Worcestershire sauce and pour over the crumbs. This may be served in ramekins. Bake in 450° oven until oysters curl and crumbs are brown, about 10 to 15 minutes. Serves 4 to 6.

The late JULIA C. WOODSIDE

CREOLE DEVILED OYSTERS

3 dozen large or 4 dozen small oysters, put through meat grinder
1 cup celery
1 cup onions, chopped very fine
1 cup bell pepper, chopped very fine
½ cup parsley, chopped very fine
1 tablespoon shortening
2 eggs, well beaten
2 cups cracker crumbs
Oyster juice
2 tablespoons Worcestershire sauce
2 tablespoons catsup
1 tablespoon salt—optional
1 teaspoon red pepper—optional
2 tablespoons lemon juice
1 clove garlic
½ stick butter—more, if desired

Put oysters through meat grinder, saving juice. Sauté chopped onion, celery, bell pepper, and parsley in shortening until tender. Mix oysters, eggs and sautéed ingredients. Soak crackers in oyster juice; squeeze liquid out of crackers, then measure and add to oyster-seasoning mixture. Put into sauce pan and cook 20 minutes over slow heat, stirring constantly. Remove from heat, add Worcestershire, catsup, salt, pepper, lemon juice and garlic (put through a garlic press). If oysters seem too moist, add ½ to 1 cup cracker crumbs. Put mixture into oyster shells, or ramekins, cover with cracker crumbs, dot with butter and brown in hot oven. Garnish with fresh sprig parsley. Serves 6.

MRS. CHARLES PROSSER

OYSTERS EN CROUSTADES

¼ pound butter or margarine
1 medium onion, chopped fine
½ bunch shallots, chopped fine
½ cup flour
4 dozen oysters
½ bunch parsley, chopped fine
1 tablespoon finely chopped celery
2 bay leaves
½ teaspoon thyme
1 teaspoon salt
Dash red pepper
Parsley and pimento for garnish

Sauté onion in butter until light brown. Add shallots and flour, stirring until well blended. Add oysters and seasonings and oyster water that has been strained to remove any possible chips of shell. Simmer over low heat for 10 or 15 minutes. Serve in toasted bread boxes and garnish with parsley and a bit of pimento. Serves 4.

TOASTED BREAD BOXES

Trim off crusts of day old unsliced bread and cut into slices 1½ to 2 inches thick. Hollow out the centers so that the shell part is about ¼ inch thick. Brush inside and outside of boxes with melted butter. Place on a baking sheet and toast in a 450° oven until lightly brown. An ordinary size loaf of bread will yield about 5 boxes.

MRS. JOHN V. PHILIPPS

OYSTERS POULETTE

3 dozen oysters and juice	2 tablespoons butter
1 stick butter	2 egg yolks
4 tablespoons minced green onions	1 small can button mushrooms
4 tablespoons minced parsley	2 tablespoons sherry
2 tablespoons flour	4 slices ham
½ cup milk	4 Holland Rusks

Drain oysters and save oyster juice. Dry oysters well by spreading on a cloth. Salt and pepper them and brown in a skillet of hot butter until they curl, pouring off excess liquid, and adding more butter until browned. Sauté green onion and parsley in butter, and add to cooked oysters. Heat oyster juice and add to oysters. Make a white sauce of milk, butter, and flour. Remove from heat and beat in egg yolks and mushrooms. Stir this sauce into cooked oysters, add sherry and heat thoroughly. Serve on a piece of hot broiled ham laid on a buttered and heated Holland Rusk. Serves 4.   THE EDITORS.

OYSTERS JOHNNY REB

1 quart select oysters, drained	¼ teaspoon pepper
	1 teaspoon lemon juice
2 tablespoons minced parsley	1¼ cups bread crumbs
2 tablespoons minced shallots and tops	¾ stick butter
	¾ cup milk
¼ teaspoon salt	Red pepper to taste

Butter 1 - quart shallow casserole (a pyrex loaf pan is a good size), put a layer of oysters in bottom. Sprinkle with parsley, shallots, salt, pepper, lemon juice, bread crumbs and dot with butter. Then make another layer of oysters and repeat. Cover top with bread crumbs and dot with ample butter. Just before baking pour milk over all. Be sure to mix well with oysters. Bake in 325° oven for 30 minutes. Serves 8.

MRS. WILLIAM E. ROBINSON, JR.

OYSTER PIE

3 tablespoons bacon drippings	3 tablespoons flour
2 medium sized onions, chopped	9 dozen oysters, drained
	1 tablespoon Worcestershire
1 cup chopped celery	Dash hot sauce
1 cup chopped bell pepper	Salt to taste
1 cup chopped parsley	

Sauté onions, celery, bell pepper and parsley in drippings, until all ingredients are well cooked, stirring constantly; this takes 30 minutes. Make a very dark roux by browning flour in drippings, stirring constantly. When onions, celery, etc., have finished cooking add to roux. Mix thoroughly; add oysters. Simmer 5 minutes. The oysters generally make enough juice after cooking, but if it seems too dry, add a little oyster liquor. Season with Worcestershire, hot sauce, and salt to taste. Pour into deep dish casserole, lined with your favorite unbaked pie crust. Place a top crust over mixture and make several knife slices in top. Bake in 300° oven until crust is golden brown.

MR. GROVER ALFORD

OYSTERS ROCKEFELLER I

For 4 dozen oysters:

1 bunch green spinach
2 bunches green onions
1 stalk green celery
1 bunch parsley
1 pound butter, melted
1½ cups bread crumbs

3 tablespoons Worcestershire sauce
1 tablespoon anchovy paste
Salt to taste
Hot sauce to taste
2 ounces absinthe
¾ cup bread crumbs

¾ cup grated Parmesan cheese

Grind spinach, onion, celery and parsley, very fine. Mix in 1 pound butter, melted, and 1½ cup bread crumbs. Season with Worcestershire sauce, anchovy paste, salt and hot sauce to taste. Put oysters in shells, which are on rock salt, and cover each with some sauce. Cover with cheese and bread crumbs. Bake in 450° oven until brown. Serve hot. Serves 4. Sauce may be frozen, but do not add absinthe until sauce is thawed and ready to spread on oysters.

MRS. JEAN FREY FRITCHIE

OYSTERS ROCKEFELLER II

Take out the oysters, wash them and dry them. Put them back in the shells after cleaning shells well. Set on a pan of hot ice-cream salt and run them under the broiler. Broil at a low temperature for about 5 minutes. Then cover with the Rockefeller Sauce and return to broiler, still using low temperature, and broil until sauce begins to brown (about 5 minutes). If shells are not available, grease a pan on which to place oysters and proceed as above but without the ice-cream salt. Remove oysters very carefully to very hot plates, decorate with parsley and serve at once.

Sauce for Oysters Rockefeller:

¼ cup fresh parsley, packed
4 shallots
1 cup spinach, packed
1 tablespoon anise seed
1 cup water
¼ to ½ teaspoon hot sauce

½ cup butter, oleo, or bacon drippings
½ teaspoon salt
½ teaspoon thyme
1 tablespoon anchovy paste
½ cup bread crumbs

Grind the three vegetables in the meat grinder. Simmer anise seed in 1 cup of water for about 10 minutes. Strain and discard seeds. Bring anise water to a vigorous boil, add ground vegetables, cover and reduce heat to "simmer" as soon as mixture steams well. Cook 10 minutes. Stir in shortening, seasonings, and toasted bread crumbs. This can be made up ahead and kept in the refrigerator for over a week. Thin with a little oyster liquor if necessary. It is enough for about 2½ to 3 dozen medium-sized oysters.

MRS. FRANCES L. FUCHS
Beaumont, Texas

OYSTERS ROCKEFELLER III

4 dozen oysters and shells
1 bunch green onions
1 stalk celery
1 bunch parsley
½ teaspoon anise seed
2 packages frozen spinach, cooked

1½ pounds melted butter
½ cup bread crumbs (toasted)
2 ounces Worcestershire sauce
1 ounce absinthe
Salt and pepper to taste

Cayenne to taste

Grind all greens in a blender, using melted butter as liquid. Then add bread crumbs, Worcestershire, absinthe, salt, pepper and cayenne. Place oysters in half shells, and in pans filled with rock salt. Run in oven without sauce. When edges curl, remove, and pour water from each shell. Then cover each oyster with Rockefeller sauce and put back under broiler and brown slightly. Serves 4.

MRS. LEROY WARD III

SHRIMP

TO BOIL SHRIMP: Wash shrimp and drop into boiling water to cover that is well seasoned with onion, salt, black pepper, red pepper, celery, garlic, and sliced lemon. Large shrimp should boil 10 to 15 minutes.

TO CLEAN SHRIMP: Pull off the heads, peel shell off the body and pinch off tail. The black line may be removed with a small sharp knife for esthetic reasons, but not for hygienic ones.

SHRIMP AMANDINE

1 pound raw shrimp, shelled
¼ cup olive oil
¼ cup lemon juice
3 tablespoons oleo or butter
1 clove garlic, cut in half

½ cup chopped blanched almonds
2 dashes hot sauce
2 tablespoons dry vermouth
Rice (¾ cup cooked rice per serving)

Marinate shrimp in olive oil and lemon juice about 2 hours. Remove shrimp, reserve sauce. Sauté shrimp in butter and garlic until pink. Remove garlic; place shrimp on warm platter; add almonds and reserved marinade to butter in skillet. Add hot sauce and vermouth. Let simmer 2 to 3 minutes. Pour over hot platter of shrimp. Serve over rice mounds. Serves 4.

MRS. DON H. WEBB

SHRIMP À LA CRÉOLE

4 pounds large lake shrimp
¼ cup salad oil
3 tablespoons flour
1 bunch shallots or 1 large onion

1 can tomato paste
4 green bell peppers
2 teaspoons salt, or to taste
2 teaspoons black pepper

Clean shrimp and boil 5 minutes, saving stock. Using an iron skillet, make a roux by heating oil and mixing in flour, stirring constantly until well browned. Add onion and brown slightly. Add shrimp, salt and pepper. Stir until shrimp are coated with roux and none of the roux and onion sticks to skillet. Add tomato paste and green peppers. Stir 15 minutes over moderate heat. Pour in 1 cup of hot shrimp stock and cook 15 minutes over moderate heat. Cook 1 hour slowly, and add more salt and pepper if desired. Serve over rice if desired. Serves 10 to 12.

MRS. CLAY RICHMOND

SHRIMP AU VIN

5 pounds shrimp
½ stick butter
2 teaspoons flour
1 cup heavy cream
½ cup light cream

1 stick butter (add more if needed)
Salt to taste
Red and white pepper to taste
1 bunch green onions, minced

1 cup dry white wine

Wash, peel, devein, and chop raw shrimp coarsely. Set aside. Make cream sauce as follows: melt butter, add flour gradually, blending well. Add cream and seasoning to taste. Cook about 20 minutes stirring constantly in double boiler until rather thick. Keep warm in double boiler. Sauté shrimp in butter until pink. Add green onions and then mix in cream sauce. Simmer all for 15 minutes. Add 1 cup of white wine and let the mixture steep. To serve, grease individual ramekins lightly with butter. Make a ruff of creamed potatoes around the edge of each dish. Spoon in the center some shrimp mixture. Sprinkle the creamed potaotes lightly with grated yellow cheese and run under broiler until the cheese is melted and the potatoes brown a little. Serves 8.

MISS KATHERINE BRES

SHRIMP BALLS

Shrimp Balls:

1 pound lake shrimp
1 cup bread crumbs
2 eggs
1 large onion, chopped
4 cloves garlic, crushed

1 tablespoon Worcestershire sauce
Chopped parsley, chopped green onions
Salt and pepper to taste

Gravy:

½ cup flour
¾ cup oil
1 small onion, chopped
1 bell pepper, chopped
1 quart water

1 can tomato paste
3 bay leaves
2 good size pinches sweet basil
Salt and pepper to taste

Grind shrimp, onions and garlic in food chopper. Place in mixing bowl; add remaining ingredients. Mix well with hands. Shape into small balls; then roll in flour and fry until brown. Add balls to gravy. *Gravy:* Make a roux with flour and oil. Sauté onions and bell pepper in roux; add water and remaining ingredients. Cook 2 hours on low heat. Serves 4.

MRS. NAVEN O. COUVILLON

BARBECUED STUFFED SHRIMP

2 tablespoons butter
2 tablespoons chopped onions
2 tablespoons chopped celery
2 tablespoons chopped green
  pepper
2 tablespoons flour
½ cup milk

¼ cup bread crumbs
1 cup cooked crab meat
1½ teaspoons Worcestershire
  sauce
½ teaspoon chopped parsley
¼ teaspoon salt
¼ teaspoon pepper

3 dozen large shrimp

Melt butter in skillet; sauté onion, celery, and green pepper, using medium heat. Stir in flour and milk, stirring constantly until thick. Add bread crumbs, crab meat, Worcestershire sauce, chopped parsley, salt and pepper. Mix well. Remove shell and vein from shrimp, leaving tails on. Slit back of shrimp. Put two shrimp together with crab stuffing. Hold together with toothpicks. Chill in refrigerator until ready to cook. Place shrimp in broiler pan, 5 inches from broiler unit. Baste occasionally with sauce (below) until shrimp are done, about 5 minutes on each side. Serves 6.

Barbecue Sauce

1 tablespoon fat
2 tablespoons chopped onion
2 tablespoons vinegar
2 tablespoons brown sugar

1 cup catsup
⅓ cup lemon juice
½ teaspoon salt
Dash hot sauce

3 tablespoons Worcestershire sauce

Sauté onion in fat, add other ingredients and simmer 5 minutes on low heat.

DEVILED SHRIMP

1 pound shrimp, raw and
  chopped coarsely
1 stick butter
3 tablespoons minced onions
½ teaspoon dry mustard

Dash red pepper
6 tablespoons flour
1 cup milk
1 tablespoon sherry
1 cup bread crumbs

Salt and pepper to taste

Clean raw shrimp and chop coarsely. Sauté onions until clear in melted butter. Add mustard, seasoning, shrimp, and flour, stirring constantly. Add milk and cook until mixture boils, stirring constantly. Remove from heat and add sherry. Pour into greased casserole and cover with bread crumbs. Bake 30 minutes at 350°. Serves 6 for cocktails or 4 as main dish.

MRS. JOSEPH K. HOPKINS III

SHRIMP FONDUE

1 pound shrimp (medium
  size)
5 slices white or cracked
  wheat bread
1 stick butter

2 cups grated American
  cheese
3 eggs, beaten slightly
2 cups milk
1 teaspoon salt

1 teaspoon pepper

Clean and devein shrimp. Remove crusts from bread. Spread bread generously with butter and cut into $\frac{1}{2}''$ cubes. Arrange alternate layers of bread, shrimp, and cheese in 8-inch casserole. Combine slightly beaten eggs, milk, salt and pepper and pour over contents in casserole. Set casserole in hot water. Bake at 350° for one hour. Serves 6 to 8.

MRS. HERMA FARNSWORTH

SHRIMP AND MUSHROOM CASSEROLE

1 large can mushrooms
  (sliced) <u>or</u>
2 cans stems and pieces
1 pound raw shrimp
8 deviled eggs

$\frac{1}{4}$ cup butter
$\frac{1}{4}$ cup flour
2 cups milk
1$\frac{1}{2}$ cups grated American
  cheese

Cover bottom of 2-quart casserole with mushrooms. Top with deviled eggs and uncooked shrimp. Make white sauce of butter, flour and milk. Stir in 1 cup cheese and cook over low heat until cheese melts. Pour over mushrooms and shrimp. Cover with $\frac{1}{2}$ cup grated cheese. Bake at 350° for 30 minutes.

MRS. HERMA FARNSWORTH

SHRIMP PIE

4 tablespoons butter
4 tablespoons flour
2 cups milk
2 tablespoons butter
$\frac{1}{2}$ pound fresh or canned
  mushrooms

1 pound cooked shrimp
1 tablespoon sherry
$\frac{1}{2}$ teaspoon mace
Dash black pepper
$\frac{1}{2}$ teaspoon salt
2 cups corn flakes

Make a cream sauce with butter, flour and milk. Sauté mushrooms in a bit of butter if using fresh ones. Add shrimp, mushrooms, and sherry to sauce and other seasonings. Put in casserole and top with crushed cornflakes dotted with butter. Heat 20 minutes in 375° oven. This may be used in individual ramekins if desired. Serves 6.

MRS. P. M. SMITH, JR.

SHRIMP FLORIDIAN EN PAPILLOTE

2 pounds shrimp
½ pound of blue cheese,
  Roquefort or Gorgonzola
8-ounce package cream
  cheese

1 tablespoon chopped chives
1 tablespoon chopped parsley
1 clove garlic, finely chopped
¾ cup dry white wine

Mash cheese and cream cheese and add parsley, chives, garlic and wine to make sauce. Pour over raw, cleaned and shelled shrimp. Bake in a covered baking dish at 400° for 30 minutes. Serves 4.

MRS. O. R. MENTON

PARTY SHRIMP

½ pound processed cheese
⅓ cup milk
1½ teaspoons chopped onions
½ cup chopped green pepper
8 toast points

¼ cup margarine
2 cups cooked shrimp
2 tablespoons chopped
  pimento

Melt cheese in top of double boiler, add milk gradually, stirring until smooth. Sauté onion and green pepper in margarine. Add shrimp and pimento. Cook until hot. For each serving cover 2 toast triangles with shrimp mixture and top with sauce. Serves 4.

MRS. PERCY E. ROBERTS

BAKED RED SNAPPER WITH SAVORY TOMATO SAUCE

3 pound red snapper
½ cup flour
Salt and pepper to taste
6 tablespoons butter
½ cup chopped onion
2 cups chopped celery
¼ cup chopped green pepper
3 cups canned tomatoes
1 tablespoon Worcestershire sauce

1 tablespoon catsup
1 teaspoon chili powder
½ lemon, finely sliced
2 bay leaves
1 clove of garlic, minced
1 teaspoon salt
Dash of red pepper
Lemon slices—parsley

Dredge fish inside and out with flour, salt and pepper. Place it in a baking dish. Melt the butter in a saucepan. Sauté onion, celery, green pepper until celery is very tender. Press the tomatoes, Worcestershire, catsup, chili powder, lemon slices, bay leaves, garlic, salt and red pepper through a potato ricer; add to sautéed ingredients. Pour the sauce around the fish. Bake in a moderate oven, 350°, for about 45 minutes. Baste frequently with the sauce. Garnish with lemon slices and parsley. Serves 4 to 6.

MRS. EDWARD BROUSSEAU

BAKED RED SNAPPER OR BASS

1 large red snapper (5-8
  pounds)
4 tablespoons butter
¼ cup chopped green pepper
¼ cup chopped onion
¼ cup chopped chives
    ¼ cup chopped parsley

1 teaspoon dried tarragon
Salt and pepper to taste
½ cup red wine
4 slices bacon
2 cups canned tomatoes or 1
  No. 2 can

Melt the butter and sauté the green pepper and onion gently. When they are tender add chives, parsley, tarragon, salt and pepper, wine and tomatoes. Place fish in a greased baking dish and top with strips of bacon. Pour liquid mixture over the fish and bake at 350° for 40 minutes. Baste with the sauce and a little additional red wine. Serves 8 to 10.

MRS. O. R. MENTON

BERNICE'S RED SNAPPER

1 4-pound red snapper
½ cup olive oil
½ cup flour
¼ cup chopped onions
4 cloves garlic, minced

½ cup chopped celery
2 1-pound cans tomatoes
1 bay leaf
Pinch thyme and oregano
Salt and pepper to taste

Make dark brown roux of oil and flour. Add onions, garlic, celery and cook until soft. Then add tomatoes, bay leaves, thyme and oregano and salt and pepper. Cook slowly 1 hour. Clean red snapper and place in oblong pan. Pour sauce over fish and bake in 350° oven, until fish is easily pierced with fork, about 30 minutes. Baste fish with sauce throughout cooking time. This recipe makes about a quart of sauce. Serves 6 or 8.

MRS. LOUIS CURET

COLD RED SNAPPER

1 3-pound red snapper
1 large onion, chopped
1 stalk celery, chopped
1 tablespoon salt
1 tablespoon red pepper
1 teaspoon black pepper
  1 teaspoon Worcestershire sauce

1½ cups home-made mayon-
  naise
1 teaspoon salt
½ teaspoon red pepper
1 teaspoon onion juice
Capers (optional)

Wrap the red snapper in cheese cloth and drop in boiling water seasoned with cut up onion, celery, red pepper, black pepper and salt. When very tender, almost falling off bone, remove from water and cool. Remove cheese cloth and debone, trying to leave in a whole piece if possible. Refrigerate several hours and serve cold on a platter topped with mayonnaise seasoned with Worcestershire, salt, red pepper, onion juice and capers. Serves 4 to 6.

MRS. JACK REITZELL

REDFISH SUPREME

1 4- to 5-pound red fish
1 teaspoon salt
1 teaspoon black pepper
1 cup water
½ cup salad oil
1¼ sticks butter
8 tablespoons flour
2 tablespoons chopped green onions
2 Birdseye red peppers, chopped, or ½ teaspoon crushed dried red peppers

1 cup chopped celery
½ cup chopped parsley
1 pound shrimp, cooked
2 dozen oysters, drained dry
1 medium can mushrooms, sauteed
½ stick butter
½ cup grated American cheese
½ cup bread crumbs
Salt to taste
Pepper to taste

Dress red fish, rub inside and out with salt and pepper and oil. Place on rack in roaster and add water. (Do not let fish touch water.) Cover and cook at 400° about 40 minutes. Save drippings. To make sauce, melt butter in large saucepan, add flour, stir constantly until golden brown. Add finely chopped onion, celery, parsley and red peppers. Cook about 5 minutes. Add drippings from roaster, water from mushrooms and enough plain water to make a thick smooth sauce. Sauté mushrooms in butter in separate pan. Place fish in a large flat baking dish about 3 or 4 inches deep. Cover with sauce. Add sautéed mushrooms, oysters and shrimp. Sprinkle grated cheese over and then sprinkle bread crumbs on top. Bake at 400° until well browned and bubbly, about 15 minutes. Serves 8.

MRS. L. LORIO

TUNA FISH PIE

½ cup chopped green pepper
1 small onion, chopped
3 tablespoons butter
6 tablespoons flour

½ teaspoon salt
3 cups milk
1 large can tuna fish
1 tablespoon lemon juice

Sauté pepper and onion in butter until soft; add flour; blend. Add milk and salt. Boil 2 minutes, being careful not to burn. Add tuna and lemon juice. Put in baking dish. Add cheese rolls on top of mixture and bake in oven 450° for 30 minutes.

Cheese Rolls:

2 cups flour
3 teaspoons baking powder
½ teaspoon salt

3 tablespoons shortening
½ cup milk
¾ cup grated cheese
2 pimentos, chopped

Roll dough out. Add cheese and pimento. Roll as jelly roll. Cut the roll, making pinwheels. Serves 6.

MRS. FRED BLANCHE, JR.

TUNA CASSEROLE

1 large can tuna
1 can undiluted mushroom soup
1 cup diced celery
1 small diced onion
Bread crumbs

Parsley and pimento for color
1 can mushrooms, drained
1 dozen salted crackers, crumbled
Pepper to taste

Combine all ingredients in a 1½ quart casserole, saving bread crumbs for top. Bake at 325° for 20 to 25 minutes. This can be made a day in advance. Serves 4 to 6.

MRS. CLYDE MADDEN

TUNA MOLD

2 envelopes gelatin dissolved in ½ cup water
1 cup mayonnaise
2 cups tuna (oil drained)
2 eggs—hard cooked and chopped

½ cup stuffed olives, chopped
3 pieces pimento
½ bell pepper
2 whole stuffed olives

Dissolve gelatin and water in a double boiler. Cool. Add mayonnaise, tuna, eggs and olives. Grease a fish mold and pack in mixture. Refrigerate several hours and unmold. Use a strip of pimento for mouth, several pimento strips for tail, a ridge of sliced green pepper down back and olives for eyes. Serves 6.

MRS. L. M. DAVIS

BAKED FLOUNDER WITH CRAB STUFFING

3 or 4 large flounders
(¾ to 1 pound)

Salt to taste
1 stick butter

Stuffing

1 cup crab meat
2 tablespoons bacon drippings
1 medium onion, chopped fine
1 shallot, chopped
2 cloves garlic, minced
2 tablespoons celery, chopped
2 tablespoons bell pepper, chopped

1 teaspoon salt
½ teaspoon pepper
⅛ teaspoon thyme
1 tablespoon parsley, chopped
1 egg
¾ cup bread crumbs

Have the butcher slit a big "pocket" in each fish. Place generous amount of stuffing (made by sautéing vegetables in drippings, then mixing with remaining ingredients) into each slit. Melt butter in pan or pans to lay fish, not overlapping. Place fish dark side down; then flip. This butters stuffed side, too. Bake 375° or 400°, covered, for 30 minutes. Uncover last 5 or 10 minutes.

MRS. LAURENCE SIEGEL

TRUITES AUX AMANDES
(TROUT WITH ALMONDS)

4 medium sized trout,
1-1½ pounds
¾ cup flour (or less)
⅔ cup butter

½ cup heavy cream
⅔ cup toasted, slivered
  almonds
Salt and pepper to taste

1 thinly sliced lemon

Clean, wash and scale trout. Dry thoroughly and roll lightly in flour. Melt the butter in a frying pan. When it is hot, but not brown, put in trout. Cook over low heat 5 to 7 minutes; turn carefully, and cook on other side for the same length of time. When golden brown, salt and pepper them and lay them carefully on a heated serving platter. Add cream to the butter remaining in pan; mix rapidly; add almonds and stir carefully so that the almonds will not be broken and heat again just to the boiling point. Do not boil sauce. Spoon sauce over trout; add thin rounds of lemon and serve immediately. Serves 4.

MRS. FRANK RIEGER, JR.

POTATO AND SALMON SCALLOP

Sliced cold potatoes (cooked
  leftovers)
1 small sized can salmon
Salt and pepper to taste
Grated onion

1 can of condensed cream of
  celery soup
¼ cup milk
Crushed potato chips (to
  cover top)

Arrange potatoes and salmon alternately in a buttered casserole. Season well with salt, pepper, and grated onion. Mix soup and milk and pour over potatoes and salmon. Cover with potato chips, dotted with butter. Bake in moderate oven, 350°, for 30 minutes

MRS. HELEN CRERAR

SEAFOOD TETRAZZINI

1 package (8 ounce)
  spaghetti
2 cups tomato juice
1 pound raw shrimp
1½ pounds scallops
2 teaspoons salt

1 teaspoon caraway seeds
2 tablespoons vinegar
2 tablespoons butter
2 tablespoons flour
2 cups milk
¼ cup sherry

Cook spaghetti until tender. Drain. Pour tomato juice over it and cook slowly 30 minutes. Stir frequently. Peel shrimp and cover cleaned shrimp and scallops with boiling water seasoned with salt, caraway seeds and vinegar. Cook 20 minutes. Make a cream sauce melting butter and stirring in flour until smooth and bubbly. Add milk and stir. Add drained seafood to sauce, season with sherry and stir in spaghetti-tomato mixture. Transfer to a large baking dish (2 quart), dot with a little butter and broil 4 inches from flame, until surface is brown. Serve hot. Serves 6 to 8.

MRS. S. G. HENRY, JR.

BAKED SEAFOOD CASSEROLE

I.

2 6-ounce cans crab meat or 1 large can fresh crab meat
2 cans shrimp or 1 pound fresh, cooked shrimp

½ green pepper, chopped fine
½ cup chopped onion
½ can pimento, chopped
1 cup chopped celery

1 small can mushrooms

II.

1 cup salad dressing—mayonnaise may be used, but makes it very rich
½ teaspoon salt

1 cup top milk
⅛ teaspoon pepper
1 tablespoon Worcestershire
½ to 1 cup raw rice, cooked

Mix all ingredients in each of the two groups, then blend together. Place in 2-quart buttered casserole. Sprinkle with bread crumbs and bake 30 minutes at 375°, though it does not seem to affect it to stay in oven longer. Amounts of pepper, onion, pimento, and mushrooms may be increased if desired. Makes 8 large servings.

MRS. J. W. KISTLER

SCALLOP AND FISH NEWBURG

½ cup bread cubes
½ cup butter
3 tablespoons flour
1 cup water
½ cup evaporated milk
1 bouillon cube
½ teaspoon salt

⅛ teaspoon pepper
1 tablespoon grated onion
2 tablespoons sliced stuffed olives
1 package frozen fish fillets (cut in pieces)
1 package frozen scallops

Dash paprika

Brown bread cubes in ¼ cup butter. Set aside. Make a white sauce of ¼ cup butter, flour, milk and water. Season with bouillon cube, salt, pepper and onion. Arrange fish pieces and scallops in sea shells. Pour white sauce over. Decorate each serving with olives and bread cubes. Bake at 350° for 40 minutes. Serves 4.

MRS. J. M. CADWALLADER

SAUCE FOR FISH

1 can mushroom soup
1½ teaspoons Worcestershire sauce
1 tablespoon lemon juice
¼ teaspoon mustard
Dash black pepper

3-4 drops of hot sauce
2 tablespoons milk
2 shallots, chopped
1 teaspoon chopped parsley
2 tablespoons white wine
6 or 8 shrimp

Mix all ingredients and pour over a pound of fresh or frozen fish. Bake at 375° about ½ hour. Serves 2 or 3.

MRS. C. BRYAN LUIKART, JR.

SAUCE MEUNIÈRE

½ cup butter
1 tablespoon chopped parsley
1 tablespoon chopped green
  onions

2 tablespoons lemon juice
½ teaspoon salt
½ teaspoon pepper
Dash of hot sauce

Dash of Worcestershire sauce

Mix ingredients in order over low heat. Simmer briefly and serve over fish.

MRS. NEAL GORDON

REMOULADE SAUCE

4 tablespoons lemon juice
4 tablespoons vinegar
4 tablespoons prepared
  mustard
4 tablespoons prepared
  horseradish
2 teaspoons salt

½ teaspoon black pepper
2 teaspoons paprika
Dash cayenne
2 tablespoons catsup
  (optional)
1 cup salad oil
½ cup celery, chopped fine

½ cup green onions, minced

Combine lemon juice, vinegar (tarragon, if you have it) and seasonings. Gradually add oil. Stir with fork or rotary beater to blend well. Add celery and onion. Makes 2 cups.

MRS. LENTON SARTAIN

REMOULADE SAUCE

(A Shrimp Dip to Serve 100 People)

1½ cups vinegar
3 6-ounce jars Mister Mustard
1 can paprika
1 jar horseradish

Salt and pepper to taste
1 quart olive oil
4 bunches green onions
  finely minced

1 big bunch parsley, finely minced

Combine vinegar, mustard, paprika, salt, pepper and horseradish. Mix well. Add olive oil and beat vigorously. Lastly, add the shallots and parsley. This makes enough sauce to serve 100 people as a cocktail party shrimp dip.

MRS. JOHN BARTON
MRS. RALPH BODMAN

POULTRY

BAKED CHICKEN AND MUSHROOMS

2-pound chicken, quartered
2 tablespoons oil (salad or
   olive)
½ teaspoon salt
½ teaspoon pepper

Juice of 1 large or 2 small
   cloves garlic
Juice of ½ lemon
1 can mushrooms (stems and
   pieces) and juice

1 cup sherry wine

Quarter chicken. Mix together with oil, salt, pepper, garlic, and lemon juice. Let this stand for 5 or 10 minutes to let the flavor go through the mixture; then rub well into the chicken.

Place the chicken in a baking pan. Put into 450° oven for 10 minutes, then lower temperature to 350° for 15 minutes. If chicken begins to dry out, add one-half cup wine and one-half of the mushrooms. Fifteen minutes later add the remaining one-half cup wine and the mushrooms and their liquid. Let cook for 15 to 25 minutes longer or until well done. Serves 4.

Miss Marie Barrett

BASTING SAUCE FOR BROILED CHICKEN

2 cloves garlic, crushed
¾ cup olive oil
Juice of 2 lemons

1 tablespoon Worcestershire
   sauce
1 tablespoon salt

½ teaspoon ground pepper

Combine all ingredients in saucepan; use to baste chicken. This sauce may be kept in the refrigerator for several days.

Mrs. E. R. Strahan
Mrs. Clarence Ives

BREAST OF CHICKEN FLAMBÉ

12 large halves chicken
   breasts (or 6 whole Cornish
   hens)

1 stick butter
Salt, pepper, paprika to taste
1 ounce brandy

Season chicken breasts with salt, pepper, and paprika and brush with butter. Cook for 30 minutes or until tender under the broiler. (This may be cooked for about 45 minutes in a 300° oven.) Remove to a chafing dish and pour cherry sauce over chicken just before serving. To "flambé," pour an ounce of brandy over the sauce and ignite by holding a match under a spoon filled with more brandy. Serves 12.

Cherry Sauce:

1 No. 2½ can black Bing
   cherries
¼ cup burgundy wine

2 tablespoons sugar
¼ teaspoon salt
2 teaspoons cornstarch

Drain juice from cherries; combine juice with wine, sugar, and salt. Bring mixture to a boil and thicken with cornstarch. Add the drained cherries.

Mrs. R. Gordon Kean, Jr.

CHICKEN AND ASPARAGUS CASSEROLE

1 package frozen asparagus spears (or 1 No. 2 can)
Cooked turkey or chicken slices
2 tablespoons butter

3 tablespoons flour
½ cup white wine
½ cup of chicken stock or gravy
4 tablespoons Parmesan cheese

Cook asparagus according to directions on package. Drain and place in shallow baking dish. Arrange chicken slices on asparagus. Cover with sauce made by melting butter and stirring in flour. Add wine and chicken stock slowly. Add 2 tablespoons cheese and cook until thick, stirring constantly.

Sprinkle 2 tablespoons cheese over top and bake in 350° oven for 20 minutes (or until heated through). Serves 2 or 3.

MRS. FRANK JORDAN

CHICKEN BAKED WITH OYSTERS

1 3-pound chicken, cut in pieces
½ stick butter (not margarine)
Salt and pepper to taste
1 pint oysters, drained

1 cup consommé
1 teaspoon herb seasoning
1 teaspoon monosodium glutamate
⅔ cup cream

Brown seasoned chicken pieces in butter in the pan or skillet you plan to cook this dish in. Pour consommé over chicken and sprinkle with monosodium glutamate and herb seasoning. Cover and bake in 375° oven for 40 minutes. The dish may be set aside to "wait" now. Before serving add cream, warmed slightly, and oysters. Bake in 350° oven just long enough to curl oysters, about 10 or 15 minutes.

MRS. CHARLES DUCHEIN, JR.

BRUNSWICK STEW

1 large hen
1 No. 2 can tomatoes
1 tablespoon olive oil
1½ tablespoons flour
3 tablespoons shortening
2 white onions, chopped
2 cloves garlic, chopped
Heart of celery, chopped
4 hard cooked eggs, cut in half

1 pint broth
1 No. 2 can creamed corn
½ bunch green onions, chopped
½ bunch parsley, chopped
1 tablespoon chopped bell pepper
Salt and pepper to taste

Boil the chicken until very tender in enough seasoned water to make 1 pint broth. Save the broth and cut the chicken into small pieces. Cook the canned tomatoes in the olive oil until they thicken. Make a roux with the flour, shortening, onions, garlic, and celery. Add to the roux the broth, tomatoes, chicken, corn, green onions, parsley, bell pepper, mushrooms, and salt and pepper to taste. Cook for one hour, adding more broth if needed. When cooked, add the hard cooked eggs. Serves 6.

MRS. AUGUSTINE RENAUD FOSTER

ARROZ CON POLLO
(Rice with Chicken)

1 large fryer	1 bay leaf
1 cup salad oil	2 tablespoons salt
1 medium onion, chopped	Pinch of saffron
2 cloves garlic, chopped	½ medium-sized bell pepper,
6-ounce can tomatoes (drain-	sliced
ed, but save juice)	1¾ cup long grain rice
1½ quarts water	6-ounce can peas

1 small pimento, sliced

Cut chicken into quarters and fry in salad oil. When chicken is well browned, add onion, garlic, and drained tomatoes. Use the liquid from the tomatoes to make up the 1½ quarts water. Add the water, bay leaf, salt, saffron, and green pepper. Stir thoroughly and let cook slowly for 20 minutes.

Place chicken in a covered baking pan, add liquid and rice, and cook in 350° oven for about 20 minutes or until rice is tender. Heat peas and serve over rice. Garnish with pimento. Serves 4.

MRS. W. S. CADE
Sulphur, Louisiana

CHICKEN CACCIATORE

1 large hen (4 to 5 pounds)	1 can Italian pack peeled
3 tablespoons olive oil	tomatoes
1 large onion, chopped	1 bell pepper, chopped
3 cloves garlic, minced	1 teaspoon salt
1 rib celery, chopped	¼ teaspoon pepper
1 can tomato sauce	½ teaspoon oregano

½ cup red wine (optional)

Cut chicken into serving pieces, rinse and dry. Heat oil in heavy skillet and sauté chicken until brown. Add onion and garlic and brown lightly. Add celery, tomato sauce, tomatoes, and seasoning. Simmer slowly for 45 minutes to 1 hour. Add wine 5 minutes before serving. Serve over noodles or spaghetti. Serves 4 to 6.

MRS. J. N. CAZAYOUX

CHICKEN ÉTOUFFÉE

2 large fryers	1 medium bell pepper,
Salt, red and black pepper	chopped
4 tablespoons salad oil	2 ribs celery, chopped
2 large onions, chopped	

Cut chicken into serving pieces and season generously. Cover the bottom of a heavy skillet with 2 tablespoons of salad oil and heat to frying temperature. Put in chicken pieces and move them around enough to keep them from sticking. Brown on both sides.

Sauté the onion, bell pepper, and celery in the remaining oil. Add this to the chicken. Cover and cook in a 325° oven for about 1½ hours (may be left in longer).

Before serving, remove chicken to plate, spoon off the grease in the pan, and serve the remaining gravy over rice. Serves 8.

MRS. F. S. CRAIG, JR.

CHICKEN BAKED WITH RICE (JAMBALAYA)

1 3-pound fryer
1 cup flour
1 tablespoon salt
¼ cup olive oil
⅔ cup uncooked rice
1 clove garlic, minced
1 medium onion, chopped
2 tablespoons olive oil

1 large can (No. 2½)
  tomatoes
2 teaspoons chili powder
  (optional)
1 teaspoon salt
Red and black pepper to
  taste

Cut chicken into frying pieces. Coat chicken by placing in paper bag with flour and salt. Brown lightly in oil and place in a three-quart casserole with tight fitting cover.

Brown rice, garlic, and onion in pan in which chicken was browned, using the additional oil. Add tomatoes, additional salt, and other seasonings. Pour over chicken. Cover and bake in 350° oven for 1 hour and 15 minutes. Serves 4 to 6.

This can also be simmered, covered, on top of range for 1 hour. Stir occasionally and add water if too dry.

EVELYN WILSFORD

CHICKEN CHOW MEIN

1 large hen
4 tablespoons butter or fat
4 tablespoons flour
4 cups chicken broth
6 thinly sliced onions
Pepper, to taste
½ cup soy sauce (or to taste)

Variety of Chinese vegetables
  (2 cups vegetables to each
  4 cups diced chicken)
1 large can mushrooms
2 cans water chestnuts, diced
Toasted almonds
Green olives

Boil hen until tender. Save stock. Dice the chicken and measure by cupfuls. Brown the flour in the butter and stir in the broth to make a brown gravy. Add onion. Season to taste with the pepper and soy sauce.

Drain Chinese vegetables and mix with the chicken. Gradually stir in the onion gravy until the mixture has the consistency of hash. Reserve any extra gravy to serve in the gravy bowl. Serve chow mein hot over rice. Garnish with toasted slivered almonds and green olives. Serves 10.

Glazed apples go well with this dish.

MRS. J. C. ROBERT
Lexington, Virginia

CHICKEN JAMBALAYA

1 3-pound fryer
Salt and black and red
  pepper, to taste
Flour—enough to coat
  chicken
3 tablespoons fat
3 large onions, chopped

5 ribs celery, chopped
2 cloves garlic, chopped
¼ bell pepper, chopped
2 cups rice, washed
1 can beer
2½ cups water
2 teaspoons salt

Cut chicken into serving pieces. Season well with salt, black pepper, and red pepper. Coat well with flour. Melt fat in an iron skillet or heavy aluminum pot. Fry chicken until brown, then remove from skillet.

To the fat add the onions, celery, garlic, and bell pepper and cook until wilted. Put the chicken back in the skillet and cover. Cook slowly until the chicken is tender (about 30 minutes).

Add rice to chicken. Stir thoroughly for 2 or 3 minutes. Pour beer over the mixture and stir thoroughly. Add salt and cook slowly (about 30 minutes) until rice is cooked. Serves 6.

MRS. JOHN FRIDGE

CHICKEN ITALIAN

1 3-pound hen
2 tablespoons oil or bacon drippings
4 ribs celery, diced
2 white onions, chopped
3 bunches green onions, chopped
1 bell pepper, chopped fine
2 small cloves garlic, minced
Few sprigs parsley, chopped
2 small cans ripe olives, drained and cut in small pieces (or small can of chopped ripe olives)

2 large cans of mushrooms, cut in small pieces, not drained
Salt and pepper to taste
Juice of ½ lemon
1 tablespoon chili powder (optional)
1 12-ounce package egg noodles, cooked in chicken stock
1 can tomato paste
1 pound sharp cheese, grated

Boil hen in enough seasoned water to make one quart of stock. Let hen remain in stock until cool. Remove when cool and bone. Save stock to use in cooking noodles.

Sauté celery, onions, green pepper, and garlic in hot oil until clear and limp. Add parsley, olives, mushrooms, and seasonings. Combine with cooked noodles, chicken, tomato paste, and grated cheese. Cook until thoroughly hot on low heat for about 45 minutes. This can be prepared the day before serving and reheated. Serves 6.

MRS. JAMES LAROCHE

CHICKEN DIVAN

1 3-pound fryer, split
1 bunch broccoli (or 2 packages frozen)
2 tablespoons butter
3 tablespoons flour

2 cups broth
Salt and pepper to taste
3 tablespoons sherry wine
¼ pound grated Parmesan cheese

Boil chicken in seasoned water until tender. Save broth. Bone the chicken in large pieces, then slice.

Cook broccoli until just tender, drain, and place in casserole dish.

Melt butter in top of a double boiler and blend in the flour. Measure the chicken broth. If there is not enough to make 2 cups, add milk to make up the difference. Add the broth to the butter and flour, stirring until thickened. Add salt, pepper, and sherry.

Cover the broccoli in the casserole dish with a layer of chicken, then add the sauce. Sprinkle with grated cheese. Bake in 400° oven for about 12 minutes. Serves 4.

MRS. STUART JOHNSON

JELLIED CHICKEN

1 large fat hen	1 pint stock
1 large bell pepper	1 package gelatin
1 rib celery	¼ cup cold water
3 hard cooked eggs	¼ cup lemon juice

Salt and pepper, to taste

Boil hen in seasoned water until tender. Save stock. Cut the chicken, bell pepper, celery, and eggs into small pieces.

Bring the stock to boil and add the gelatin that has been softened in the cold water and lemon juice. Cool and pour over the chicken and other ingredients. Season to taste with salt and pepper. Pour into individual molds and refrigerate until firm. Serve on lettuce leaf with a dressing. Serves 6 to 8.

MRS. LENTON SARTAIN

CHICKEN MAYONNAISE

1 5- to 6-pound hen	Fresh ground peppercorns,
Salt and pepper	to taste (or black pepper)
1 rib of celery	Salt, to taste
2 sprigs parsley	2 teaspoons sugar
1 egg yolk, slightly beaten	6 egg yolks, hard cooked
4 teaspoons cider vinegar	Approximately 1 pint olive oil
2 teaspoons fresh ground	Hearts of lettuce
mustard seed (or 3	Garnishes: tomato wedges,
teaspoons dry or 4	avocado rings, hard cooked
teaspoons prepared	eggs, ripe olives
mustard)	

Boil hen slowly in water seasoned with salt, pepper, celery, and parsley. Use sufficient water so that hen is half covered; turn hen during cooking. Boil until meat is tender enough to be stripped from bone and stock reduces to 1 pint. Allow chicken to partly cool in the stock. Skim fat off stock and reserve in refrigerator. Strip (do not cut) white and dark meat from the bone and chill in refrigerator.

To make the mayonnaise, add to the slightly beaten raw egg yolk the vinegar, mustard, salt, pepper, and sugar. Then mash the hard cooked eggs with a fork, and add one at a time, alternately, with the oil, until all the oil is used.

This mayonnaise is spooned over the chilled meat placed across the hearts of lettuce. A spoonful of the jelled stock is placed at the side of the chicken. Garnish with tomato wedges, avocado rings, quartered hard cooked eggs, and ripe olives, this makes a delightfully cool luncheon. Serves 6.

This is an old French recipe from the Simon family in St. Martinville. The fresh ground mustard seed and peppercorns are in the original recipe. The mayonnaise is delightful—an interesting blend of sweet and sour with the tang of mustard and a perfect consistency.

MRS. GEORGE M. SIMON, SR.

CHICKEN LOAF

1 3- to 4-pound hen	1½ cups bread crumbs
1½ cups chicken broth	1½ cups milk
1 cup cooked rice	1 pimento, chopped

4 well beaten eggs

Boil the hen until tender in enough lightly salted water to make 1½ cups broth. Bone the hen and cut the meat into bite size pieces. Save the broth to use later. If there is not enough broth to make 1½ cups, add a litle hot water.

Mix all the ingredients well in the order given. Put in a 9" x 13" loaf pan. Bake in a 350° oven for 45 minutes. Allow to cool in the pan before turning out. This dish may be prepared the day before using. Serve with sauce. Serves 10.

Sauce for Chicken Loaf:

½ cup butter	¼ cup chopped pimento
2 tablespoons flour	1 small can mushrooms
½ to 1 cup medium cream	(sauteed in butter)

¼ cup chopped parsley

Make white sauce of butter, flour, and cream. Add mushrooms, pimento and parsley. Serve warm over chicken loaf.

Mrs. Hugh A. Neal

CHICKEN PIE

1 3-pound hen	¼ cup flour
4 cups broth	2 sliced hard cooked eggs
½ cup canned milk	1 cup drained petit pois peas

1 can biscuits

Cut hen up and boil in salted water (1 teaspoon salt). When chicken is tender, remove from broth and bone. Cut meat into bite-sized pieces.

To the 4 cups of broth add milk and flour mixed with water to form a thick paste. Let simmer until thickened. Then add eggs, peas, and chicken meat. Pour mixture into a casserole and cool. When cooled, place biscuits on top and bake in 400° oven until the biscuits are golden brown (about 15 minutes). Serves 8 to 10.

Mrs. Charles Holloway

CHICKEN ROUNDELAY

4 breasts from 2-pound fryers	1 teaspoon nutmeg
½ cup butter or oleo	2 eggs, beaten
½ cup flour	4 5-inch baked pastry rounds
2 cups canned milk	Garnishing: 1 teaspoon
2 cups chicken broth	chopped parsley, 2 chopped
2 bouillon cubes	hard cooked egg yolks,
1 teaspoon poultry seasoning	strips of pimento

Place chicken breasts in salted water to simmer. When tender, cool, then remove bones and skin.

For the sauce blend butter with flour in double boiler. Stir until smooth and gradually add milk, broth and bouillon cubes. Stir constantly to keep smooth and add beaten eggs. Cook until thick and creamy.

Bake 4 five-inch pastry rounds. When serving, place one chicken breast on each round of pastry, pour on sauce, and garnish with chopped parsley, chopped egg yolk, and strips of pimento. Serves 4.

MRS. WILLIAM R. McGEHEE

CHICKEN SPAGHETTI I

2 large hens	Salt and pepper to taste
½ pound butter	2 tablespoons chili powder
2 large onions, chopped	3 packages spaghetti
4 cloves garlic, chopped	Chicken stock
4 pounds round steak, ground	2 pounds American cheese,
3 No. 1 cans tomatoes	grated

Boil hen in enough seasoned water to cover. Save stock. Bone chicken and cut into bite sized pieces.

Put butter in a large skillet, add onions and garlic and simmer. Add ground steak, fry slightly, add tomatoes, and cook until like hash. Add salt, pepper and chili powder.

Using a large baking dish, put a layer of cooked spaghetti, a layer of sauce, a layer of chicken and a layer of cheese. Repeat this three times, ending with the cheese on top. Bake in 200° oven (or electric roaster) for 2 hours. Serves 14 to 16.

MRS. BECK HOFFMAN
St. Gabriel, Louisiana

CHICKEN SPAGHETTI II

1 large hen	1 can tomato sauce
2 large onions, chopped	1 can tomato soup
3 cloves garlic, chopped	½ can tomato paste
4 ribs celery, chopped	Salt and pepper to taste
1 bell pepper, chopped	1 bay leaf
1 bunch green onions,	Dash of hot sauce
chopped	2 tablespoons Worcestershire
½ bunch parsley, chopped	sauce
2 tablespoons bacon drippings	2 cups broth

Boil hen in seasoned water (enough to cover). Save broth. Bone chicken and cut into large pieces.

Sauté onions, garlic, celery, bell pepper, and green onions in hot bacon drippings, adding the parsley as this cooks. Be sure to use a large, heavy pot. Add to this the tomato sauce, soup, paste, and seasonings. Thin the mixture with the broth and add the boned chicken. Cover and simmer for about 1 hour or until the sauce has thickened. Serve over spaghetti. Serves 6.

MRS. E. O. SPILLER

CHICKEN SAUTERNE

2 broilers, halved
1 cup sauterne wine
3 tablespoons chopped green onions
3 tablespoons chopped parsley
¼ cup melted butter
Salt, pepper, and paprika, to taste
Small can of whole mushrooms

Marinate chicken halves in wine for several hours in refrigerator. Pour wine from chicken. To wine add onions, parsley, and butter. Salt and pepper chicken, sprinkle with paprika, and place skin side down in a shallow baking dish. Pour wine mixture over and bake in a 450° oven for 25 minutes, basting often. Turn skin side up, add mushrooms, and continue baking for 20-25 minutes, or until tender and brown. Serves 4.

MRS. J. A. NOLAND

CHICKEN-SPAGHETTI CASSEROLE

1 large hen
1 stick butter or oleo
3 medium onions, minced
2 bell peppers, minced
1 cup celery, chopped
1 clove garlic, crushed
2 cups canned tomatoes
1 16-ounce package spaghetti (very thin)
¼ pound mild cheese, grated

Boil hen in enough water to make 2 quarts of stock.

Sauté onions, peppers, celery, and garlic in butter. Add 1 quart stock and tomatoes and simmer together.

Bone chicken and cut into rather large pieces. Mix with sauce and put in casserole. Add spaghetti which has been cooked in chicken stock (drain before adding), mixing well with chicken and sauce. Bake 40 minutes in 350° oven, sprinkle with grated cheese, and bake 20 minutes more. Serves 8-10.

MRS. ROBERT SCHEFFY

CHICKEN-SPANISH RICE CASSEROLE

1 large hen
3 cups water
1 teaspoon salt
¼ pound sausage
1¼ cup raw rice
3 tablespoons shortening or bacon drippings
½ cup sliced onions
1 clove garlic, minced
½ cup tomato sauce
1 teaspoon salt
2 cups hot chicken broth
2 cans green peas
Pimento

Simmer chicken in water and salt and seasonings. Remove meat from bones in large pieces. Place in large greased casserole.

Quarter sausage and fry in skillet. Scatter over chicken.

In shortening, fry raw rice until golden brown, stirring constantly. Drain rice and sprinkle over chicken and sausage. Add onions, garlic, tomato sauce, and salt to hot broth. Pour over chicken and rice. Cover. Bake 1¼ hours in 325° oven. Heap hot drained peas around edge. Garnish with pimento. Serves 6-8.

MRS. C. W. ROBERTS

CHICKEN IN WINE

8 chicken breasts
¼ cup butter
2 tablespoons brandy
1 small can mushrooms
18 small pearl onions (or
  bottoms of 1 bunch green
  onions)

1 bouillon cube, dissolved in
  ¼ cup water
2 tablespoons flour
1 teaspoon tomato paste
1 cup chicken stock
¾ cup red wine
Salt and pepper to taste

Brown the chicken breasts well in hot butter. Pour the brandy over the chicken and ignite. Let the burning finish; then remove the chicken from the pan and brown the mushrooms and onions in the butter. Stir in the dissolved bouillon cube and remove the pan from the heat. Stir in the flour. Add the tomato paste, stock and wine. Return to heat and stir while heating to boiling point. Add salt and pepper to taste. Add chicken breasts. Cover and simmer for 30 minutes or until chicken is tender. Very good served with brown rice or rice dressing. Serves 8.

MRS. BERT TURNER

CHICKEN TERIYAKI

1 large fryer
Pepper and garlic salt to taste
⅔ cup cooking or salad oil

⅔ cup soy sauce
⅔ cup bourbon whiskey

Cut chicken in serving pieces and season to taste with pepper and garlic salt. Marinate for several hours in equal portions of soy sauce, whiskey, and cooking oil.

Place chicken pieces in shallow baking pan. Bake in 325° oven for about 45 minutes, or until chicken is well done. Turn the pieces frequently, basting with the marinating sauce. The remainder of the sauce may be used as gravy. Serves 4.

MRS. JAMES W. LORIO

DE LUXE CHICKEN A LA KING

3 tablespoons butter
1 bell pepper, shredded
½ cup celery, chopped
1 small can mushrooms
1 small onion, grated
3 tablespoons flour
2 cups milk (or 1 cup milk
  and 1 cup cream)

2 cups cold diced chicken
2 egg yolks, beaten into
  cream
Few drops lemon juice
Salt, pepper, paprika to taste
1 small can green peas

Melt butter in pan and add bell pepper, celery, and mushrooms. Cook about 5 minutes. Add grated onion, flour mixed with part of the milk, then the remaining milk. Stir until thickened and add the chicken and the cream with the egg yolks beaten in. Cook a few minutes longer, stirring constantly. Add a few drops of lemon juice and the seasonings. Stir in the green peas. Serve in patty shells or on toast. Serves 8.

MRS. LENTON SARTAIN

CHICKEN TETRAZZINI

1 tablespoon flour	1½ cups cooked chicken (turkey or veal), cut in pieces
1 tablespoon butter	
1 cup milk	¾ cup cooked spaghetti
¼ teaspoon salt	½ cup chopped mushrooms
¼ teaspoon pepper	2 tablespoons butter
¼ teaspoon paprika	¼ lb. grated Parmesan or
¼ teaspoon dry mustard	Cheddar cheese (or ¼ lb.
Few drops onion juice	processed cheese)
1 teaspoon lemon juice	¾ cup buttered crumbs

Make a medium white sauce of the flour, butter, milk, and salt. Add the pepper, paprika, mustard, and onion and lemon juices to the white sauce and heat to the boiling point. Add chicken, spaghetti, and the mushrooms which have been sautéed in the butter. Fill greased individual casseroles or one large casserole with the mixture and top with cheese and buttered bread crumbs. Bake in 425° oven for about 15 minutes or until the crumbs are very brown and ingredients are warmed through and bubbly. Serves 8.

MRS. LENTON SARTAIN

GARLIC CHICKEN

1 medium broiler	2 sprigs parsley
Salt and pepper, to taste	2 large cloves garlic
½ stick butter	1 stick oleo or butter
Juice of 1 lemon	

Generously salt and pepper fowl inside and out. In cavity of chicken put butter, parsley, and one clove garlic, and seal the opening with foil.

In a saucepan melt 1 stick of oleo or butter, 1 crushed garlic clove, and the juice of 1 lemon. Place chicken in a Dutch oven and bake in 300° oven. Baste constantly with sauce and turn frequently until the chicken is golden brown and tender. Remove parsley and garlic from cavity before serving. Serves 4.

MRS. CHARLES DUCHEIN, JR.

GARLIC FRIED CHICKEN

1 egg, well beaten	1 2½-pound fryer
1 pinch baking powder	Salt and pepper, to taste
2 teaspoons garlic puree	Seasoned flour
2 tablespoons olive oil	¼ cup shortening

Mix together the egg, baking powder, garlic purée, and olive oil. Cut the chicken into serving pieces. Salt and pepper it and put it into the egg mixture, allowing it to soak several hours (even overnight). Use a china bowl. Rework the liquid into the chicken before removing from the bowl. Roll the chicken in flour that has been seasoned with salt and pepper. Heat shortening on low heat until very hot and fry chicken on low heat until done and brown (about 30 minutes). Serves 4.

MRS. LENTON SARTAIN

CHICKEN WITH SPINACH NOODLES

1 4-pound hen	½ pound processed cheese
1 stick margarine	6-ounce jar stuffed olives
1 cup bell pepper, chopped	6-ounce can sliced mushrooms
1 cup celery, chopped	1 package spinach noodles
1 cup onion, chopped	4 cups chicken stock

1 can mushroom soup

Boil hen in seasoned water (lightly salted so that stock will not be too salty). Be sure to use enough water to make 4 cups of stock. Save stock. Bone chicken and cut in large pieces.

Sauté in margarine the bell pepper, celery, onion. Stir in the cheese. Add olives and mushrooms, then stir in the chicken.

Boil noodles in three cups of stock. Boil until all the stock is absorbed. Add 1 can of mushroom soup to the noodles.

Mix all the ingredients together in a pan and serve hot. One cup of stock can be used to moisten the mixture if needed. If the dish is prepared ahead of time, it can be reheated in a casserole by placing it in a 300° oven for about 45 minutes. Serves 6 to 8.

MRS. FLORENCE PETERS

CHICKEN LIVERS WITH MUSHROOMS

1 pound chicken livers	Pepper to taste
1 teaspoon salt	1 4½-ounce can mushrooms
¼ cup flour	(stems and pieces)
¼ cup butter or oleo	1 can chicken soup
1 small onion, chopped	1 soup can milk

Few sprigs parsley, finely chopped

Place livers on waxed paper. Sprinkle with salt and half the flour to coat. Heat butter in large skillet, add livers, onions and mushrooms, and sauté 5 or 6 minutes, turning occasionally. Remove livers from skillet. Blend remaining flour into fat in skillet until smooth, then gradually add soup, milk, and pepper. Cook gently 4 or 5 minutes, stirring to keep smooth. When thickened, stir livers into the sauce. Serve on cheese waffles or toast and sprinkle with parsley. Serves 6.

MRS. THOMAS B. PUGH, II

COUNTRY CAPTAIN

1 hen	1 teaspoon salt
2 medium onions, chopped	1 teaspoon sugar
1 clove garlic, chopped	⅛ teaspoon red pepper
1 bell pepper, chopped	½ cup soaked currants
3 tablespoons olive oil	1 small can blanched almonds
2 No. 303 cans tomatoes	2 cups brown or wild rice
2 teaspoons curry powder	Ground peanuts (optional)
1 teaspoon powdered thyme	Shredded coconut (optional)

Chutney (optional)

Cook hen as usual in salted water over low heat until tender. Cool and bone chicken, cutting meat into bite size pieces. Save the chicken stock. Sauté onions, garlic, and bell pepper in olive oil. Add tomatoes and cook

5 minutes. Add curry powder, thyme, salt, sugar, and red pepper. Cook 10 minutes. Add chicken and bake uncovered in 350° oven for 45 minutes. Add currants which have been soaked in ½ cup chicken stock. Add blanched almonds. Cook rice during baking period and serve meat mixture over the rice. You may serve as a curry using chopped peanuts, shredded coconut, and pieces of chutney. This may be reheated if made ahead of time. It also freezes well. Serves 6 to 8.

MRS. RONALD COCO

INDIA CHICKEN CURRY

1 5-pound hen
½ cup onion, finely chopped
½ cup celery, finely chopped
¼ cup chicken or other fat
⅓ cup flour
2 cups chicken stock
1 cup strained tomato juice
½ teaspoon Worcestershire
  sauce
1 teaspoon curry powder
Salt and pepper to taste

Condiments:
  Apple chutney (see Index)
  Slivered almonds or peanuts
  Finely chopped crisp bacon
  Shredded coconut
  Finely chopped hard cooked
    eggs
  Canned fried onion rings

Boil hen in seasoned water until meat leaves bone. Cool and dice chicken as for salad. Save stock.

Lightly brown onions and celery in fat. Add flour and stock, stirring until thick. Add tomato juice and other ingredients. Add diced chicken. Serve over rice with the condiments in small bowls so that they may be added to individual servings. Be sure to use the apple chutney.

Cooked shrimp or lamb may be substituted for the chicken. Serves 6 to 8.

MRS. J. H. BENTON

PARTY CHICKEN DISH

1 large hen
1½ pints stock
2 medium onions, chopped
  Salt and pepper to taste

1 large bell pepper, chopped
2 packages egg noodles
½ pound processed cheese

Boil the chicken in enough seasoned water to make 1½ pints stock (or cook in pressure cooker for 25 minutes). When cool, skim off the fat and save. Bone the chicken and cut into pieces. It is best to do this the day before you prepare the dish.

Sauté the onion, bell pepper in the chicken fat. Cook the noodles in salted boiling water for 5 minutes. Cut the cheese into small pieces. Combine all the ingredients. Place in covered pan and steam over water for 2 hours. (To steam, place covered pan in larger pan containing boiling water and let the water simmer.) Season to taste. Serves 10.

MRS. J. M. HUDDLESTON
Shreveport, La.

VINEYARD CHICKEN

1 3-pound chicken, quartered	¼ cup melted butter
1 cup dry white wine	¼ cup finely chopped green
1 tablespoon lemon juice	onions
¼ teaspoon black pepper	3 teaspoons salt
½ teaspoon paprika	¼ cup minced parsley

Place chicken, skin side down, in large casserole. Blend all other ingredients together and pour over the chicken. Cover with foil and bake 1 hour in 325° oven. Remove the foil. Turn chicken skin side up; increase temperature to 375° and bake 30 minutes, basting two or three times. increase temperature to 425° for the last 30 minutes of baking time. Baste frequently (total cooking time is 2 hours). Serves 4.

MRS. RODNEY COCO

TURKEY ROCHAMBEAU

6 slices toast	6 thin slices cooked turkey
6 thin slices cooked ham	(white meat)

Sauce Poulette

On each slice of toast place one slice of ham and one slice of turkey. Cover with sauce poulette. Serves 6.

Sauce Poulette:

2 tablespoons butter	2 egg yolks
1 tablespoon flour	Juice of 1 lemon
2 cups chicken broth	1 teaspoon parsley, finely
½ teaspoon salt	chopped
1 teaspoon pepper	1 4½-oz. can mushrooms,
2 sprigs parsley	drained

Heat one tablespoon of the butter; add flour and cook for 1 minute. Stir in the chicken broth and add salt, pepper, and parsley sprigs. Bring the mixture to a boil, then lower the heat and simmer for 30 minutes. Discard the parsley. Remove the sauce from the heat and blend in the egg yolks. Add lemon juice, chopped parsley, the remaining one tablespoon of butter, and the drained mushrooms.

Serve over ham and turkey slices on toast. Serves 6.

MRS. DAVID VAN GELDER

DRESSINGS

CORNBREAD DRESSING

Cornbread (use recipe calling for 2 cups dry ingredients), cooked and cooled
2 cups cooked rice
1 tablespoon chili powder
Salt to taste

2 bunches green onions, chopped
4 ribs celery, chopped
1 bunch parsley, chopped
3 sticks butter or oleo

Crumble cornbread fine and combine with rice. Add chili powder and salt to taste.

Sauté onions and celery in a stick of butter or oleo, adding parsley as it cooks a little.

Mix all the ingredients together, then return to the skillet and brown slightly in the remaining butter or oleo, stirring dressing as it cooks. If the dressing becomes too dry as it browns, add a small amount of water. This dressing can be used separately or used as a stuffing for fowl. Serves 8 to 10.

MRS. C. VERNON PORTER

LOUISIANA CORNBREAD DRESSING

5 cups corn bread
6 slices whole wheat bread (or French bread), slightly toasted
2 cups finely cut celery
1½ cups shallots with tops, cut fine
½ cup finely cut onion

½ cup minced parsley
¼ cup butter or margazine
4 teaspoons salt
¼ teaspoon cayenne
½ teaspoon black pepper
1 teaspoon celery seed
1 teaspoon sage (optional)
Giblets

Simmer gizzard, heart and neck in a quart of water until tender. Add liver and cook a few minutes more until done. Cut all meat fine for dressing. Sauté celery, shallots and onion in the butter until done but not brown; add seasonings, more or less than amounts suggested to suit individual taste.

Soak the toasted bread in cold water, squeeze dry and mix well with the crumbled corn bread. Combine with the sautéed seasonings, parsley, minced giblets and sufficient liquor from the giblets to make a moist dressing. Stuff turkey; allow about one cup of stuffing for each pound of turkey.

Golden Corn Bread: (Doubled this recipe will give slightly over 5 cups)

1 cup yellow corn meal
¾ cup flour
5 teaspoons baking powder
2 tablespoons melted shortening

¾ teaspoon salt
1 slightly beaten egg
1 cup milk

Sift dry ingredients into bowl and add the slightly beaten egg, milk and melted shortening. Beat thoroughly. Pour into greased shallow pan. Bake in 425° oven for 25 minutes.

MISS EVELYN WILSFORD

RICE AND OYSTER DRESSING

½ cup butter
10-12 chopped green onions
1 cup chopped celery
2 small, chopped bell peppers
1 quart oysters

Cooked giblets, chopped
3 cups cooked rice
½ cup chopped parsley
Salt
Red and black pepper

Melt butter and add onions, celery, and pepper. Cook until soft. Add oysters and giblets. Pour over rice and add parsley. Mix well. Salt and pepper to taste. If dressing is too dry, add some of the liquid in which giblets were cooked. Stuff turkey.

RICE DRESSING

1½ cups raw rice
1½ teaspoon salt
3 cups water
3 softened chicken bouillon
cubes
2 medium bell peppers, diced
Salt and pepper to taste

3 tablespoons chopped green onion
½ cup minced onion
½ cup diced celery
4 teaspoons chopped parsley
½ cup salad oil

Place rice and salt in cold water. Cover and bring to a boil. When boiling, add 3 softened bouillon cubes (chicken or beef, depending on the meat you are using). Reduce heat and cook until tender.

Sauté the pepper, green onions, onion, celery, and parsley in ½ cup oil. Add these ingredients to the cooked rice and mix thoroughly. Salt and pepper to taste. Serves 4.

MRS. CHARLES HOLLOWAY

TURKEY DRESSING

1 bunch green onions (tops included), chopped
3 cloves garlic, minced
1 cup celery, chopped
2 tablespoons bacon drippings
1 pound chicken livers, chopped
1 pound hot pork sausage

Cornbread (using recipe calling for 4 cups cornmeal), cooked and cooled
Broth
Salt, pepper, monosodium glutamate to taste
¾ cup chopped parsley
Pecans (optional)

Sauté onions, garlic, and celery in bacon drippings until tender. Add livers and sausage and cook until tender and done. Add crumbled cornbread. Soften the mixture with enough broth to make mixture moist. Season to taste. Add chopped parsley before baking. Chopped pecans may be added if desired. Bake in casserole in 350° oven for 1 hour or use to stuff turkey. Serves 10.

MRS. JOHN BARTON

GAME

GAME

The joy of Louisiana's "chasseurs" (or hunters) invariably becomes the pride of the gourmet, for the venison, wild duck, rabbit, squirrel, and quail—to mention but a few—lend themselves to many a gala dish.

GAME AIDS

TO PREPARE SQUIRREL OR QUAIL FOR COOKING

Skin squirrel or pick birds and wash in cold water. Then soak in a solution of salty water 15 to 25 minutes. (If the game has been shot up pretty badly, put about 1 tablespoon vinegar to a quart of water when soaking.) Wash again well and dry well. Wrap carefully in foil and freeze before using. Do not keep game too long in the freezer.

GAME BIRDS

Game Birds include grouse, quail, partridge, pheasant, wild duck and goose, pigeon and woodcock. All are prepared for cooking the same way as domestic poultry. If the bird has a decided odor, it can be soaked in salt water for an hour before cooking. The method of cooking will vary with the size and age of the bird. Small birds may be split and broiled. Larger but still tender birds are usually roasted. If there is any question as to the tenderness of the bird, it should either be steamed for a short time before roasting or should be cooked until brown in a rack in an open pan and then have water added and cooked covered until tender when pierced with a fork. Allow 1 whole small bird, half a larger bird, or about 1 pound per person.

Broiled Game Birds (Grouse, Partridge, Pheasant, Quail). Split the tender young birds; brush with melted butter; broil like chicken. Baste with melted butter or other fat each time the birds are turned. The time of cooking will vary with the size of the bird and whether the family prefers rare or well done meat. In general small birds will cook in 15 to 20 and larger birds in 30 minutes. Season to taste.

Roasted Small Game Birds (Grouse, Partridge, Quail, Woodcock, Small Wild Duck.) Prepare the birds according to the directions for Roast Chicken. They are not stuffed but the cavity may be sprinkled with salt. Place the birds in a pan; cover the breasts with thin slices of fat, salt pork or bacon. Roast uncovered in a hot oven 450° for 30 to 45 minutes. If the breast does not appear tender, add ½ cup water, cover and continue cooking in a moderate oven 350° for about 30 minutes.

Roasted Larger Game Birds (Larger Wild Ducks, Geese, or Pheasants.) Prepare the bird according to the general directions for roasting. Fill with any desired stuffing, making about 1 cup for a 3 pound bird. Cover the breast with thin slices of fat, salt pork or bacon (salt pork preferred.) Place breast side up on a rack in a shallow pan; cook in a moderate oven (350°) for about 30 minutes.

Braised Game Birds (Pheasants or Pigeons.) Cut older birds in pieces as for a larger broiler; coat with seasoned flour; brown in a small quantity of fat in a frying pan; transfer the pieces to a casserole; rinse the frying pan with 1 cup boiling water, dry wine or cream (½ water, ½ wine), pour over birds and bake in a slow oven 250° for 1 hour or until tender. Make a gravy by thickening the liquid; return to the casserole for serving.

PHEASANT

2 pheasants	Seasoning salt
1 can consommé	1 can beef gravy
Flour to dredge	½ bunch parsley, chopped
½ cup sherry	1 large can mushrooms
Salt and pepper to taste	4 large green onions, chopped

1 teaspoon monosodium glutamate

Halve or quarter each pheasant; clean with damp cloth and dry thoroughly. Season with salt, pepper, seasoning salt, and dredge with flour. Brown to golden brown on both sides under broiler or in Dutch oven on top of stove. Remove to roasting pan and add consommé, sherry, and gravy. Cook, covered, at 300° until tender (40 to 45 minutes). Baste frequently. When birds are cooked, remove from pan and add green onions, parsley and monosodium glutamate. Simmer until tender. Add mushrooms and more consommé if there is not enough juice for gravy. Sprinkle pheasant with chopped parsley to serve. Serves 4.

MRS. CHARLES DUCHEIN, JR.

COON À LA DELTA

1 coon	1 cup celery, chopped
Cayenne pepper to taste	1 medium bell pepper,
Black pepper to taste	chopped
Salt to taste	Flour for gravy
3 cloves garlic, chopped	Shortening for gravy and
1 large onion, chopped	browning coon

6 medium sweet potatoes

After coon has been dressed properly, soak for 1 hour in mild vinegar solution. Drain. Cut up or cook whole as desired. Salt and pepper coon and cover with water. Add cayenne pepper, chopped garlic, onion, celery, and bell pepper and parboil until partially tender. Remove from heat and drain. Brown coon in a small amount of shortening, then place in roasting pan. Make a thin brown gravy, seasoned as desired. Pour over coon in roasting pan and place peeled sweet potatoes around and bake in 350° oven until potatoes are done.

MRS. ORVILLE E. COMER
Tensas Parish

CORNISH HEN ALEXANDER

6 Cornish hens	½ cup white dry wine
1 stick butter or oleo	1 tablespoon chopped parsley
1 4-ounce can mushrooms	Salt and pepper to taste

Rub the birds with salt and pepper inside and out and place in refrigerator for several hours before cooking. Melt butter in baking pan. Turn each bird over in butter. Place bird on back with legs tied with string. Place a tight fitting top or cover tightly with aluminum foil and bake for 45 minutes at 325°. Remove top and brown for the last 15 minutes at 400° Remove birds to warm serving platter. Drain mushrooms and sauté in drippings; add wine. If more liquid is needed, add mushroom juice. Pour this over birds and then sprinkle lightly with chopped parsley.

MRS. ROBERT SLOWEY

BAKED CORNISH HEN

Cornish hen (or chicken or   Butter
  pheasant)   1 small onion, cut in rings
Salt and pepper   1 bell pepper, cut in rings
Paprika   1 cup white wine, optional

Rub Cornish hen (chicken or pheasant) with butter and a generous amount of salt and pepper. (It is better if this is done right before cooking.) Coat the hen well with paprika and attach alternating rings of onion and bell pepper to the breast with toothpicks. Place in uncovered baking pan with 1 cup white wine (optional) and cook in oven at 325° until tender. (Large Cornish hens, 1 hour baking time; small, 45 minutes.) One hen serves 1 or 2.

Mrs. F. S. Craig, Jr.

DOVES

14-16 doves   ½ cup chopped onion
Salt and pepper   (preferably green onions)
Flour   1½ cups water
½ cup salad oil   1 cup sherry
          ¼ cup chopped parsley

Salt, pepper, and flour doves. Brown in oil in heavy roaster in 400° oven. Add chopped onions and water. Cover. Reduce heat to 350°; cook until tender. Add sherry; baste during cooking. Add chopped parsley to gravy before serving. Serves 6-8.

Mrs. John Barton

DOVE AND OYSTER PIE

16 doves   1 quart water, or 3 inches
2 cups chopped celery   above doves
1 cup chopped onions   4 dozen oysters
3 slices bacon, chopped   4 tablespoons flour
Salt and pepper to taste   ¼ cup water

Have doves picked and drawn; do not split open. Wash in cold water, dry. Keep in refrigerator several days. Place doves in heavy pot. Add celery, onion, bacon, salt and pepper; cover with water. Let come to a boil; reduce to low heat, stir; cover with heavy top and let simmer until doves are tender, about 30 minutes. Remove from heat. With open spoon or tongs dip out each bird on to a flat pan, let cool enough to handle. Drain oysters, then stuff as many oysters as possible into each dove. Mix flour with ¼ cup water to make paste; then add enough liquid from pot to blend well. Add this to the pot in which doves were cooked; put on low heat and stir constantly until thickened about consistency of cream. To this add the remaining oysters and remove from heat. Line casserole, bottom and sides, with flaky pastry, and bake for about 10 minutes in preheated oven at 350° just to set pastry. Remove from oven and let cool. Put in layer of doves, layer of liquid with oysters. Repeat until casserole is within ½-inch of top. Cover with pastry rolled thin. Prick top of pastry to let out steam and bake at about 350° until pastry is golden brown top and bottom. Serve hot. Serves 8.

Mrs. Jane Evans
Tensas Parish

WILD DUCK

2 ducks, wild or domestic	1 cup sherry
2 onions	1 tablespoon flour
1 rib celery	¼ cup water
¼ cup salad oil	4 tablespoons chopped parsley
1 cup water	Salt and pepper to taste

Salt and pepper ducks well inside and out. In the cavity of the ducks place ½ onion and ½ rib of celery. Brown ducks in open, heavy roasting pan at 400° in the oil. Wilt the chopped second onion in the fat around the ducks. Add a cup of water and a cup of sherry. Reduce heat to 350° cover and cook until done. Baste and add more liquid if needed. Toward the last make a paste of flour and water. Add this to drippings. Add chopped parsley. If desired, add more sherry. Serves 6.

MRS. JOHN BARTON

BRAISED DUCK

1 duck	½ cup dry red wine or sherry
½ onion	1 can mushrooms
1 apple, quartered	1 cup grapes (white seedless
Salt and pepper (coarse	or tokay, cut in half and
ground)	seeded)
Butter	

Rub duck with seasoning and stuff with onion and apple. Brown well in butter in a deep kettle on top of stove. About 30 minutes before finished cooking, add mushrooms with the juice from the can, and grapes. Add red wine, salt and pepper and cover tightly. Reduce heat to very low and cook until tender. If additional liquid is needed, add more red wine. Ducks may be turned once during cooking. Use gravy to serve over wild rice. One duck will serve 2 to 3 persons.

This is the recipe which my cook, Hattie, learned when she grew up on Bayou Lafourche.

MRS. GORDON KEAN

FRICASSEED DUCK BREAST

4 breasts of duck	3 cups water
4 tablespoons bacon drippings	1 can mushroom sauce
or shortening	1 teaspoon garlic purée
4 tablespoons flour	Salt and pepper
¾ cup chopped onions	Seasoned salt

Salt and pepper breast of ducks; flour and brown. Remove ducks. Make a roux by browning the flour in the bacon drippings. Add and sauté onions. Add water, mushroom sauce, garlic, seasoned salt, salt and pepper to taste. Cover. Simmer for 2 hours. Optional: ½ cup sherry may be added. Serves 4.

MRS. KILEY SANFORD

QUAIL

8 Quail   Butter

Sauce:

1 stick butter   3 lemons
2 tablespoons Worcestershire sauce (or any barbecue sauce)

Brown quail in butter. Place breast up in heavy Dutch oven. Baste with sauce and cook in covered oven until tender, about 30 minutes. Remove cover and brown about 10 minutes. Place quail on serving dish and pour sauce over them. Serves 6 to 8.

Mrs. J. W. Adcock
Monroe, La.

BAKED QUAIL

Quail, usually 2 per person   Worcestershire sauce
Salt and pepper   Any favorite stuffing
Bacon strips   1 cup bouillon

Split whole quail down back only. Salt and pepper birds and stuff with favorite cornbread, giblet, or rice dressing. Frozen prepared dressings may be used. Wrap a strip of bacon around each bird and sprinkle with Worcestershire sauce. Bake in 350° oven and baste frequently with bouillon. Cook 1 hour and 45 minutes to 2 hours.

Mrs. Louis Christian

CHICKEN FRIED QUAIL

Quail   Eggs, optional
Salt and pepper

Use only tender birds which have been kept in refrigerator several days. You may dip birds in beaten eggs (optional). Season birds with salt and pepper and roll in flour. Drop in deep hot fat and fry until crisp and brown on both sides, 10 to 15 minutes. Drain well. May be served with cream gravy. Allow 1 quail per serving.

Mrs. I. P. Collier

These may be smothered in a thickened gravy with a few drops of Worcestershire sauce in cavity of each bird. Cover tightly and simmer 1 hour. Water may be added if the birds become too dry.

Mrs. Louis Christian

BAKED QUAIL

1 dozen quail	4 tablespoons truffle peelings
1 cup mushrooms	1 tablespoon flour
1 cup fresh bread crumbs	1 tablespoon oil
1 teaspoon salt	2½ cups chicken broth
¼ teaspoon cayenne pepper	¼ teaspoon minced onions
½ teaspoon minced parsley	

Salt and pepper quail inside and out. Combine mushrooms, bread crumbs, salt, cayenne, pepper and truffles; sauté in butter. Stuff quail with this mixture. Make roux by browning flour in oil. Add stock, onions and parsley to browned flour, then pour over quail which have been put into baking pan. Bake ¾ hour at 325°, basting frequently.

MRS. OVIDE B. LACOUR

RABBIT HASEN PFEFFER

1 rabbit

Marinade consisting of:

2 large onions, sliced	¼ teaspoon allspice
3 stalks celery, cut	1 bay leaf
6 sprigs parsley, chopped	¼ teaspoon red pepper
1 clove garlic	1½ teaspoons salt
¼ teaspoon cloves	Vinegar to cover rabbit
¼ cup oil	1 tablespoon sugar
1 No. 2 can tomatoes	1 cup vinegar
1 cup water	

Wash rabbit and cut into pieces; put into large bowl that can be covered. Pour the above marinade over rabbit and cover. Place in refrigerator overnight. When ready to cook, drain rabbit and fry brown all over in oil. Remove rabbit from skillet and fry the drained vegetables well. To this add the tomatoes and sugar. Cook about 15 minutes to cook down tomatoes. Add vinegar and water. Bring to a boil and add rabbit. Cook slowly for 1½ hours.

MRS. J. R. BLACK

SQUIRREL COUNTRY STYLE

2 squirrels	Flour to dredge
Salt to taste	3 tablespoons fat
Pepper to taste	2 cups water

Cut squirrel into serving pieces and shake in a paper bag containing seasoned flour to dredge well. Fry in skillet until golden brown. Remove squirrel from skillet and pour off all grease except 2 teaspoons. Add water and bring to a boil. Return squirrel to skillet; turn to low heat, cover, and cook for about 1 hour, until meat almost leaves bone. Turn squirrel occasionally and baste often. Serve with grits, hot biscuits, and honey. Serves 3 or 4. *Good!*

MRS. H. L. FIELD

SQUIRREL PIE

6 squirrels
2 cups chopped celery
2 cups chopped onions
1 cup coarsely chopped
  salt meat

1 quart water
Red and black pepper to taste
Salt to taste
2 hard cooked eggs

Cut squirrels in pieces; put into heavy pot and add celery, onions, salt meat and seasoning, cover with water 3 inches above squirrel. Let come to a boil; turn to low heat and simmer about an hour or until squirrels are tender.

2 tablespoons shortening
2 tablespoons flour

1 cup hot water
1 cup liquid from squirrel pot

In a separate skillet brown the flour in the shortening. Add water and liquid from squirrel pot. Stir well and remove from heat.

2 tablespoons flour
½ cup liquid from squirrel pot

¼ cup water to make smooth
  paste

Remove squirrel from pot, add the flour mixture and the browned flour mixture to liquid in the pot; mix well and cook about 2 minutes until it has started to slightly thicken. Line a casserole with pastry. Bake 10 minutes in preheated oven at 350° to set pastry. Remove and let cool slightly; then put in layer of squirrel, layer of 4 to 6 slices of hard cooked egg and a cup of liquid. Repeat until casserole is within ½ inch of the top. Try to use as much as possible of all liquid to avoid a dry pie. Cover with pastry top. Slit top of pastry to release steam and bake at 350° until top and bottom crusts are brown. Serves 6.

Mrs. Jane C. Evans
Tensas Parish

SQUIRREL BRUNSWICK STEW

2 squirrels
Salt and pepper
2 medium onions, sliced
1 cup lima beans
1 cup corn

1 ½-inch square piece salt
pork
2 medium white potatoes,
diced
1 large can tomatoes

3 or 4 small balls of butter rolled in flour

Cut two squirrels into serving pieces and salt and pepper them (pieces of chicken can be added to stretch the recipe). Place the squirrel in a deep well cooker (or deep iron pot), and cover with water. Bring the water to a boil and add onions, lima beans, and corn. Again let the mixture come to a boil and this time add salt pork (or bacon). Cover and cook for a total of 2 hours. During the second hour add potatoes, tomatoes, salt and pepper to taste. During the last 30 minutes drop in 3 or 4 small balls of butter rolled in flour. This will thicken the stew. Serves 4-6.

Mrs. Louis Christian

ROAST SADDLE OF VENISON

Marinade

1⅓ cups water	2 bay leaves
2⅔ cups dry red wine	1 teaspoon thyme
2 teaspoons mustard seeds	2 onions, sliced
½ teaspoon pepper	

Seasoning

2 cloves garlic, cut in slivers   1 teaspoon salt

Trim all fat off the venison. Soak meat in marinade for 24 hours, turning occasionally. Insert slivers of garlic in meat; salt it, and place in a 350° oven. Roast uncovered until tender, about 2 to 4 hours (time varies with age of animal), basting frequently with remaining marinade and then with meat drippings. Remove meat and add sauce ingredients to drippings in roasting pan; cook until the mixture thickens. Spoon sauce over servings of meat. Figure on ½ to ¾ pound venison per person.

This sauce has been suggested to me as a happy addition to the pan drippings before serving:

½ cup sour cream   1 glass currant jelly

1 tablespoon brandy

MRS. JOHN BARTON

VENISON ROAST

10-20 pound venison roast	1 tablespoon salt
1 quart vinegar	3 cloves garlic, chopped
1 quart water	3 bay leaves
1 tablespoon red pepper	1 teaspoon cloves
1 teaspoon black pepper	1 teaspoon allspice

Use a rump or loin roast which has been washed and rubbed clean. Mix the above ingredients and pour over roast which has been put into a bowl that can be covered. Place in refrigerator for at least 12 hours before cooking. Be sure to turn several times. When ready to prepare for cooking take out of refrigerator. Do not wash, just wipe off with cloth or paper towel. Use a sharp thin blade knife and punch holes deep into roast (about 10 for a 10-pound roast, 20 for a 20-pound roast) and insert into each hole one piece each of the following:

Salt meat, cut into 2-inch strips (thin)	Celery, cut into 2-inch thin strips
Onion, cut into thin strips	Garlic, cloves, cut into fourths

Use meat thermometer to determine when done. *This meat is also wonderful to serve cold, sliced thinly for a late cold supper.*

MRS. JANE C. EVANS
Tensas Parish

VENISON STEAKS

2 venison steaks
Garlic salt, to taste
1 lemon, juiced
½ stick oleo or butter

Salt and pepper to taste
1 tablespoon Worcestershire
    sauce
1 tablespoon tomato catsup

½ cup water

Sprinkle garlic salt over venison steaks. With edge of saucer, gently cut into the meat, turning several times. Sprinkle lemon juice over the meat and allow to set at least 3 hours. When ready to broil, heat an iron skillet until almost smoking. Add ½ stick oleo or butter which immediately browns. Quickly put in steak; brown on one side, turn and brown on other. (Serve on the more rare side.) Salt and pepper. Place steaks on warm platter, add to skillet drippings, Worcestershire sauce, catsup, and water. Bring to boil; then pour over steaks and serve at once.

MRS. B. W. BERRY
Tensas Parish

BROILED VENISON

Use only tender venison for broiling, preferably the tenderloin, bone out. Trim and slice about ¾ inch thick. Warm a heavy platter and put in as much melted butter or oleo as you will need, small amount of lemon juice, and Worcestershire sauce, salt, and pepper. Have heavy skillet very hot, put about ½ teaspoon oil, just enough to keep meat from sticking; put in sliced venison. Turn to medium heat and turn meat in 2 minutes; turn to high heat for 2 minutes. Turn meat and reduce heat again to medium. Repeat. Remove meat and drop into platter with butter sauce. Put ½ cup water in skillet, stir and pour over meat. Serve with yellow grits which have been cooked at least 1½ hours with milk.

Butter sauce variations:
1. The platter may be rubbed with clove of garlic.
2. Add chopped green onions to melted butter and seasoning.

MRS. JANE C. EVANS
Tensas Parish

GROUND VENISON MEAT PATTIES

Meat Patties

1 pound ground venison
1 teaspoon garlic salt
1 teaspoon seasoning salt
5 crackers, crumbled

1 egg
1 teaspoon salt
Pepper to taste
1 medium onion, diced

Mix all ingredients well and form into patties. Brown in shortening and remove from heat to make gravy. In the same shortening used to brown patties make the gravy. Salt and pepper to taste. Add small can drained mushrooms, and put the patties into the gravy. Simmer for a few minutes until the gravy thickens and seasonings cook through the gravy. Serves 4.

Gravy

2 tablespoons shortening
2 tablespoons flour
1 small can mushrooms

1 cup water
Salt and pepper to taste

MRS. CHARLES HOLLOWAY

BUTTERED RICE

To Be Served With Game

2 tablespoons butter
2 medium onions, diced
2 cups rice

2 cups hot consommé
2 teaspoons salt
1 tablespoon chopped parsley

Melt butter in covered pot and sauté onions. Add rice; stir until grains are well coated with butter. Add the consommé and salt. Stir and cover. Simmer over low heat for about 30 minutes, until grains are tender and liquid absorbed. Toss rice lightly with fork to release steam and put over warm burner without lid until each grain is separated. Toss rice with butter and chopped parsley before serving. Serves 8 to 10.

MRS. CHARLES DUCHEIN, JR.

STUFFING

(Duck, Goose or Turkey)

1½ quarts cornbread
3 or 4 slices whole wheat
  bread
3 cups chopped celery
3 cups chopped onions
3 cups chopped parsley

1 pint mushrooms with juice
2 cups chopped pecans
6 hard cooked eggs
Salt, black and red pepper,
  to taste
¾ cups long grain rice

Mix cornbread and whole wheat bread; add celery, onion and parsley. Dampen well with stock from boiled neck and gizzards in seasoned water. Mix dressing thoroughly and fry in small amount of salad oil until celery and onions look wilted. To this add eggs, mushrooms with juice and pecans. Season well with salt and pepper. In another skillet fry, in small amount of oil, the rice (do not wash rice, just pick over it) until golden brown. Add just enough stock to cover rice and let cook about 10 minutes, stirring constantly. Then add rice to first mixture; mix well. Stuff bird or bake separately.

MRS. JANE C. EVANS
Tensas Parish

RICE DRESSING FOR DUCK

Giblets of duck, cooked   2 ribs celery, chopped
   and chopped   ½ green pepper, chopped
1 tablespoon bacon drippings   2 cloves garlic, minced
   or shortening   ½ teaspoon red pepper
1 tablespoon flour   1 teaspoon salt
2 white onions chopped   1½ cups hot water
              3 cups cooked rice

Combine bacon drippings with flour in a skillet and brown slowly to make a roux. Stir in giblets, onions, celery, pepper, garlic, and seasonings. Add hot water and cook over low heat for 1 hour. Add cooked rice. Serves 8.

                                        Mrs. I. P. Collier

BARBECUE

BARBECUE

BARBECUED CHUCK ROAST

3½ pound heavy beef chuck blade roast, 2½ inches thick
Cover with: ¼ inch prepared mustard (about 1 large jar)
Also cover with rock salt on both sides.

Cook over coals as you would a steak, approximately 25 minutes on each side.

MRS. DAVID CAMPBELL

GRILL-BOUND SHISHKABOBS

6 1-inch lamb steaks cut in
  1-inch cubes
1 pound salami, cut in 1-inch
  cubes
3 cloves garlic, minced
⅓ cup salad oil

3 tablespoons soy sauce
3 tablespoons vinegar
1½ teaspoons sugar
¼ teaspoon pepper
¼ teaspoon Worcestershire
  sauce

2 large onions, sliced

Arrange lamb and salami cubes alternately on 6 skewers. Place in shallow pan. Combine all ingredients except onion; pour over skewered meat. Top with onions. Cover; let stand in refrigerator several hours or overnight. Broil kabobs over hot coals for 20-30 minutes, turning frequently. Cook onions in remaining sauce until golden; serve with kabobs. Serves 6.

THE EDITORS

BEEFKABOBS

Marinate 1½-inch cubes of sirloin tip in sauce overnight. Save sauce for basting.

Sauce:

1 cup red dry wine
½ cup soy sauce
1 cup orange juice
1 tablespoon thyme
1 tablespoon rosemary

¼ teaspoon Worcestershire
  sauce
1 cup finely chopped onions
1 tablespoon black pepper
6 cloves garlic, finely chopped

Place on skewers in this order:

Small new potatoes (raw)
Large button mushrooms

Cubes sirloin
Small whole tomatoes

Broil slowly and brush with sauce often. Brush with butter immediately before serving. Serve with tossed green salad and garlic bread.

MRS. JEAN FREY FRITCHIE

FOIL BAKED CHICKEN SUPREME

6 chicken breasts
1½ teaspoons salt
Dash pepper
2 tablespoons minced green
  onion

4 tablespoons minced parsley
2 cloves garlic, minced
1 teaspoon tarragon vinegar
2 cans condensed cream of
  mushroom soup

¼ teaspoon thyme

Sprinkle chicken with salt and pepper. Combine remaining ingredients; spread on surface and in cavity of chicken breasts. Place each piece of chicken on square of aluminum foil; bring edges together and seal with drug store wrap, folding corners under; place on cookie sheet. Cook over coals until tender, turning package once.

THE EDITORS

OVEN BARBECUED CHICKEN

1 frying chicken, cut up
6 tablespoons butter or
  shortening
Salt and pepper
1 small onion, finely chopped
1 clove garlic, chopped

2 tablespoons Worcestershire
  sauce
2 tablespoons A-1 sauce
4 teaspoons vinegar
4 tablespoons catsup
Few drops hot sauce

2 tablespoons sugar, if desired

Separate pieces of chicken. Melt butter in skillet, add chicken and sauté about 20 minutes, turning to brown both sides. Place in baking dish, sprinkle with salt and pepper and pour fat from skillet over chicken. Place onion and garlic in cheesecloth bag and place in corner of baking dish. Cover chicken with sauce made by mixing remaining ingredients. Bake in moderate oven (350°) for 30 minutes, basting frequently. Serves 4.

MRS. DERMARCUS SMITH III

BARBECUED DUCK

1 cup salad oil
½ cup vinegar
¼ cup soy sauce
6 buds garlic, crushed

1 sprig rosemary
1 tablespoon celery seeds
1 teaspoon salt
¼ teaspoon pepper

Combine all sauce ingredients; simmer 10 minutes.- Cut ducks into halves and barbecue, turning several times and swabbing sauce on generously, until tender.

MRS. JOHN BARTON

BARBECUED LEG OF LAMB

1 six-pound leg of lamb, boned and flattened

Marinade:

2 tablespoons vinegar   1 clove garlic, crushed
½ cup olive oil   1 teaspoon salt
                ½ teaspoon pepper

Combine sauce ingredients and marinate the lamb in this mixture for 2 hours. Broil over charcoal embers for 1½ to 2 hours, turning frequently and brushing every 5 minutes with this hot barbecue sauce:

2½ cups chili sauce   1 bay leaf
1 teaspoon chili pepper   2 teaspoons hot sauce
¾ cup olive oil   1 teaspoon dry mustard
½ cup lemon juice   ½ cup water
1 tablespoon brown sugar   2 cups finely chopped onion
2 tablespoons tarragon   2 cloves garlic, minced
  vinegar   1 teaspoon salt

Combine ingredients in sauce pan. Bring to a boil; reduce heat and simmer for 15 minutes. Best served with lamb, chicken, spare ribs. Serves 4 to 6.

THE EDITORS

SMOKED TURKEY

Rub turkey (10 to 15 pounds) with curing salt (can be bought from stores in 5-pound packages—5 pounds will do about 6 to 8 turkeys). Refrigerate for 5 days in plastic bag. Then wash inside and out thoroughly (be sure to clean out all the salt). The turkey must be smoked in a covered barbecue pit using dampened hickory sawdust. The sawdust may be added to the fire from time to time to keep the smoke going. Remember, you are not barbecuing; you are *smoking* the turkey. Smoke for 36 hours, turning every now and then. Baste every hour during the daytime with Coca-Cola, vinegar, and white wine (1 part each).

MRS. HEIDEL BROWN

BARBECUED HAM STEAKS

6 1-inch thick ham steaks   ½ cup dry mustard
½ cup melted butter   ½ cup brown sugar
4 cups sherry wine   4 teaspoons paprika
4 teaspoons powdered cloves 8 cloves garlic, finely chopped

Combine sauce ingredients and marinate ham steaks in mixture for 2 hours turning once. Broil 20 minutes, turning frequently and basting with marinade. Serves 6.

THE EDITORS

ROUND STEAK MARINADE

½ cup chopped onion
½ cup lemon juice
¼ cup salad oil
½ teaspoon salt
½ teaspoon celery salt

½ teaspoon pepper
½ teaspoon thyme
½ teaspoon oregano
½ teaspoon rosemary
2 cloves garlic, minced

2½ pounds round steak

Combine all ingredients except steak. Marinate steak 4 to 5 hours, turning several times. Cook on grill over hot coals to doneness you like. Baste with marinade during broiling. Serves 4.

THE EDITORS

BARBECUED PORK CHOPS

6 1-inch pork chops
Salt and pepper
1 8-ounce can (1 cup) seasoned tomato sauce
½ cup catsup

1 teaspoon Worcestershire
  sauce
1 teaspoon liquid smoke
½ teaspoon onion salt
Dash hot sauce

Brown chops in heavy skillet; season with salt and pepper. Combine remaining ingredients; pour over chops. Simmer until meat is tender, about 1 hour, turning occasionally. Serves 6.

THE EDITORS

BARBECUED RIBS

1 tablespoon celery seed
1 tablespoon chili powder
½ cup brown sugar
1 tablespoon salt

1 teaspoon paprika
2½ pounds loin back ribs
1 8-ounce can tomato sauce
  (1 cup)

¼ cup vinegar

Combine celery seed, chili powder, sugar, salt, paprika. Rub ⅓ of mixture on ribs. To remaining mixture, add tomato sauce and vinegar. Heat and use to baste ribs. Cook over hot coals until tender, basting occasionally with the sauce. Makes 4 servings.

THE EDITORS

BARBECUED SHRIMP

3 sticks butter or oleo, melted
2 cloves garlic, minced
Hot sauce, to taste
Paprika
Salt and pepper

1 lime or lemon, sliced
Dash of oregano
1 tablespoon chili sauce
1 cup white wine
1 pound shrimp

To prepare shrimp: Take heads off and with a very sharp knife, slice them down the back and remove black line. Leave shell and tail on. Marinate shrimp for 1 hour or more in the sauce made from the above ingredients. Broil shrimp over charcoal fire turning and basting often. If preferred, bake in a 300° oven, basting shrimp often with sauce. Baking time about 30 minutes. Do not overcook.

MRS. O. R. MENTON

SHRIMP ON SKEWERS

2 pounds medium shrimp
⅓ cup salad oil
⅓ cup lemon juice (fresh or frozen)
3 or 4 garlic cloves

½ teaspoon paprika
1½ teaspoons salt
6 bell peppers, quartered
2 large onions, quartered
4 tomatoes, quartered

6 lemon wedges

Peel and devein shrimp. Combine oil, lemon juice, and seasonings; pour over shrimp and refrigerate overnight. Place shrimp on skewers, reserving leftover sauce. Alternate with onion and green pepper. Use 3 or 4 shrimp, piece of pepper, piece of onion, etc. Broil them 3 inches from heat about 13 minutes, or until done, basting with sauce frequently. During last 2 or 3 minutes add tomatoes to end of skewers. Serve with lemon wedge. Serves 6.

MRS. HEIDEL BROWN

SHRIMP KABOB

3 pounds shrimp, peeled and cleaned
1 pound bacon, half slices
1 No. 2 can pineapple chunks

Marinade:
1 cup soy sauce
½ cup lemon juice

Combine sauce ingredients; marinate shrimp in mixture for ½ hour. On skewer, alternate shrimp, pineapple, bacon (½ slice folded). Broil until bacon is crisp. Serves 6 to 8.

THE EDITORS

BARBECUED PORK ON BUNS

1½ cups water
¼ cup vinegar
¼ cup sugar
4 teaspoons mustard
2 teaspoons salt
¼ teaspoon red pepper
2 slices lemon
2 chopped medium onions
¼ cup butter

4 cups thinly sliced left-over pork roast
1 cup catsup
3 tablespoons Worcestershire sauce
½ cup chopped celery (optional)
½ cup ripe olives, chopped (optional)

In Dutch oven combine first nine ingredients. Simmer uncovered 20 minutes. Add meat, catsup and Worcestershire sauce. Simmer slowly 45 minutes. If desired, add celery and olives before serving. Serve on buns or French bread.

MRS. J. N. SINGLETARY

BARBECUED BEANS

1 pound bacon (cut in thirds)	1 package brown sugar
1 large or 2 medium onions (chopped semi-fine)	(2¼ cups packed)
5 No. 1 cans pork and beans	¼ cup prepared mustard
1 bottle catsup	¼ cup Worcestershire sauce
	2 teaspoons liquid smoke

Fry bacon in a 4- to 6-quart capacity pot until crisp. Add onion and sauté until clear. Add beans and stir. Then add remaining ingredients. Stir well and lower heat to simmer. Let simmer uncovered until cooked down to consistency desired (about 2 hours or more). Serves 20.

MRS. JACKIE RUSS
Shreveport, Louisiana

BARBECUED LIMA BEANS

1 pound large fresh or frozen lima beans   Piece of smoked ham or salt pork

1 clove garlic

Sauce:

1 large onion, chopped	2 tablespoons Worcestershire sauce
1 clove garlic	Salt to taste
½ cup bacon drippings	1 can tomato soup
1½ tablespoons prepared mustard	¼ cup vinegar

1 tablespoon chili powder

Boil lima beans according to directions on package, adding ham or salt pork and 1 clove garlic. To prepare sauce, fry onion and garlic in bacon drippings. When onions are clear add remaining ingredients. When beans are tender, drain and save juice. Add 2 cups bean juice to sauce. In greased casserole alternate layers of beans and sauce. Strip top with bacon, and bake 40 minutes in 300° oven. Cut off oven and let beans remain in oven until ready to serve. (Note: ¾ pound of dried lima beans may also be used satisfactorily; however, longer cooking time must be allowed—two hours or more—until beans are tender. Then proceed with sauce and rest of directions.)

MRS. JACK DE CORDOVA
San Antonio, Texas

GRILLED CINNAMON APPLES

Place cored apple in center of 24-inch length of aluminum foil folded in half. Fill hole with a tablespoon each of cinnamon candies and raisins. Dot with butter. Bring foil up loosely over apple and twist ends together to seal. Cook over glowing coals 30 minutes, or until done. Serve with cream if desired.

THE EDITORS

FRUIT KABOB

1 No. 2½ can peach halves	2 apples, cut in wedges
3 bananas, thickly sliced	1 fresh pineapple, cubed

3 grapefruit, sectioned

Marinade and basting sauce:

1 cup grapefruit juice	½ cup honey
2 tablespoons Cointreau	½ teaspoon chopped mint

Combine sauce and ingredients and marinate the fruit for ½ hour. Alternate fruit on skewer and broil 5 to 8 minutes, basting with marinade.

THE EDITORS

BARBECUE SAUCE (FOR 20 PEOPLE)

1 quart salad oil	Chicken giblets
5 pounds onions, chopped	2 pounds ground meat
1 whole pod of garlic, chopped	3 tablespoons Worcestershire sauce
2 pounds bell peppers, chopped	1 jar prepared yellow mustard
1 stalk celery, chopped	1 bunch parsley, chopped
1 pound margarine	Salt and red pepper, to taste

3 lemons, sliced

In cooking oil, cook onions, garlic, pepper and celery. In margarine cook giblets and ground meat. Remove the oil from the cooked onion, garlic, pepper and celery; use this oil to baste chicken. Add cooked vegetables to cooked meat. Then add Worcestershire sauce, lemons, mustard and parsley. Season to taste. Serve with chicken on buns or small French breads.

MRS. RAY B. THEAUX
Lafayette, La.
MRS. EUGENE GRAUGNARD
St. James, La.

SAUCE JANE

(Sauce for Steaks or Hamburgers)

4 tablespoons butter	Salt and pepper to taste
6 green onions, finely chopped	Pinch of dried sage
½ pound fresh mushrooms, sliced (or 1 can stems and pieces)	¼ teaspoon paprika
	½ cup red or white dry wine (or water)
	1 cup sour cream

Sauté onions and mushrooms in butter until golden and tender. Add salt and pepper, sage and paprika. Add wine (or water) and stir to mix; heat through. Just before serving, add sour cream. Heat, but do not boil. This serves 4 to 6 as sauce, spooned over grilled hamburgers or small steaks.

MRS. DAVID VAN GELDER

BARBECUE BASTING SAUCE
(FOR BEEF OR PORK ROAST)

½ cup salad oil
½ cup lemon juice
½ cup red wine vinegar

¼ cup soy sauce
½ teaspoon monosodium
   glutamate

Dash of Worcestershire sauce
Salt and pepper to taste

Mix all ingredients and keep covered in refrigerator until needed. This is enough for 5 to 10 lb. roast.

MRS. W. H. WRIGHT, JR.

SAUCE FOR BARBECUED STEAK

1 cup salad oil
¼ cup vinegar
½ bottle A-1 Sauce (medium size)
¼ bottle Worcestershire sauce

1 teaspoon sugar
2-4 tablespoons grated onion
Salt and cayenne pepper
1 clove garlic, grated (optional)

This sauce is used only to *cook* the steaks.

MRS. GEORGE M. SIMON, SR.

JIFFY HAMBURGER SAUCE

½ cup salad oil
¾ cup onion, chopped
½ bell pepper, chopped fine
½ cup celery, chopped fine
¾ cup tomato catsup
¾ cup water
⅓ cup lemon juice

Sliced peel of ½ lemon
3 tablespoons brown sugar
3 tablespoons Worcestershire sauce
2 tablespoons prepared mustard
Salt and pepper, to taste

Cook onion, bell pepper, and celery in hot oil until soft. Add remaining ingredients. Simmer at least 15 minutes, preferably ½ hour. Yield: enough sauce to baste and serve with two chickens. Also good with hamburgers, hot dogs, and other favorites.

MRS. EARL P. DUGAS

BARBECUE SAUCE FOR CHICKEN

½ cup salad oil
1 cup water
2 tablespoons chopped onion
1 clove garlic, crushed
1½ teaspoons sugar
1 teaspoon salt
1 teaspoon chili powder
1 teaspoon paprika
1 teaspoon pepper

½ teaspoon dry mustard
Dash cayenne
1 teaspoon Worcestershire sauce
1 teaspoon hot sauce
¼ cup lemon juice
½ bottle tomato catsup
¼ bottle steak sauce
½ green pepper, chopped

1 tablespoon vinegar

Combine all ingredients and simmer one hour. As chicken broils or smokes, brush frequently with sauce.

MRS. W. E. ROBINSON

CHICKEN BARBECUE SAUCE

1 stick butter
½ bottle Steak Sauce,
  medium size
¼ bottle Worcestershire
  sauce

1 or 2 tablespoons onion juice
Juice and rind of 1 lemon
1 clove garlic, grated
  (optional)
1 teaspoon sugar

Mix all ingredients and cook slowly about 15 minutes. Use sauce to baste chicken; the remainder of the sauce may be served with the barbecued chicken. If the sauce is allowed to cool down slightly, it congeals and adheres to the chicken more readily. Enough sauce for 2 whole chickens. *This is the best barbecue sauce and really has a "twang" all of its own.*

MRS. GEORGE M. SIMON, SR.

BARBECUE SAUCE

2 large cloves of garlic
Juice of one lemon
1 teaspoon smoke sauce
1 teaspoon sugar
1 14-ounce bottle catsup

3 ounces hickory smoked
  mustard
1 16-ounce bottle Worcestershire sauce
4 ounces vegetable or olive
  oil

Pulverize garlic and add all ingredients in order listed. The oil must be well blended. This mixture keeps indefinitely in the refrigerator and gives an "outdoor" barbecue flavor to meats cooked in the oven.

MRS. HANSEN SCOBEE

BARBECUE SAUCE FOR "LEFT-OVER" MEAT

1 cup bacon drippings
2 cups catsup
4 cups water
1 teaspoon salt

1 teaspoon pepper
4 teaspoons chili powder
1 teaspoon celery seed
¼ teaspoon curry powder

1 teaspoon liquid smoke

Melt bacon drippings; add catsup and water; add all ingredients except smoke. Bring to a quick boil; then add smoke. Pour over leftover meat such as ham, roast, etc. and heat. Serve on bun; top with grated cabbage. This sauce may be stored in refrigerator for future use.

MRS. W. R. SMITH

DESSERTS

Á LA MODE

Brownies   Vanilla ice cream

Whipped cream

Cut up several brownies in bite size pieces. Put in parfait glasses—layer of brownies—layer of ice cream. Repeat and top with whipped cream.

Do you remember the good old days of curb service when this came to 7¢ at the nearest drug store? So good and gooey.

MISS ELLEN ROY JOLLY

ALMOND MACAROON SOUFFLÉ

1 dozen almond macaroons   3 eggs, separated
1 cup milk   Pinch salt
½ pint whipping cream, whipped

Scald 1 dozen almond macaroons in hot milk. Pour gradually into yolks of eggs which were beaten with pinch of salt and cook over hot water until thickened slightly. Fold the stiffly beaten egg whites into the mixture and pour into greased baking dish 7" x 3" deep. Place dish in pan of hot water and bake 30 minutes at 350°. Serve hot with whipped cream. Yield 8.

MRS. J. W. C. WRIGHT

APPLE CRANBERRY CRISP

4 medium sized cooking   1 cup uncooked quick rolled
   apples (about 1⅓ pounds)   oats
1 1-pound can whole cran-   ½ cup flour
   berry sauce   1 cup dark brown sugar
1 teaspoon cinnamon   (firmly packed)
½ cup butter

Peel apples and slice thin. Arrange in square baking dish about 10" x 6". Sprinkle with cinnamon. Spoon cranberry sauce over this. Stir rolled oats (oatmeal), flour, and brown sugar together. Cut in butter until evenly mixed and crumbly. Sprinkle this over cranberry layer. Bake in moderate oven—350°—until apples are cooked through and top is lightly browned. About 40 minutes. Good served plain or with whipped cream or vanilla ice cream. Serve hot. Serves 8.

MRS. DAN MOORE, JR.

OZARK PUDDING

1 egg	⅛ teaspoon salt
¾ cup sugar	½ cup nuts, broken
2 tablespoons flour	1 apple, diced and peeled
1½ teaspoons baking powder	1 teaspoon vanilla
½ pint whipping cream, whipped	

Beat eggs and sugar until smooth. Add flour, baking powder and salt. Add nuts, apple, and vanilla. Bake in buttered 8″ pie pan 35 minutes at 350°. Serve with whipped cream, whipped cream with cointreau as flavoring, ice cream, or hard sauce. *This is one of Mrs. Harry Truman's favorites.* Yield 6-8.

MRS. DUDLEY W. COATES, JR.

BANANAS FOSTER

2 tablespoons butter	Pinch cinnamon
4 tablespoons brown sugar	1 tablespoon banana liqueur
2 bananas	1 ounce rum or brandy
Ice Cream	

Mix butter and brown sugar in saucepan. Cook over medium heat until it is caramelized. Cut bananas in quarters. Add and cook until tender. Add cinnamon and liqueur; stir. Add rum or brandy to top of mixture. DO NOT STIR. Light. Spoon over vanilla ice cream while flaming. Yield 6.

MRS. DEAN GEHEBER

TROPICAL STYLE BAKED BANANAS

4 tablespoons butter	½ cup sugar
6 firm medium sized bananas	1 lemon

Place 3 tablespoons butter in heavy skillet. Add bananas 2 or 3 at a time and brown. Lift gently wth spatula and place side by side in shallow baking dish. Sprinkle with sugar and squeeze lemon juice over all. Dot with remaining butter and bake in 325° to 350° oven until bananas are tender and syrup thickens. About 30 minutes. Yield 6.

MRS. W. FLOYD WILLIAMSON, JR.

GRAPEJUICE DESSERT

16 marshmallows	½ cup grapejuice
½ pint whipping cream, whipped	

Melt marshmallows in grapejuice. Cool. Add whipped cream and mix. Put in individuals dishes and place in refrigerator. Serve with additional whipped cream. Yield—8.

MRS. DUDLEY W. COATES, JR.

BEST EVER CHEESE CAKE

15 graham crackers
¼ cup butter or oleo
4 eggs, separated
3 eight-ounce packages soft cream cheese

1 cup sugar
1 teaspoon vanilla
1 pint sour cream

Set oven at 350°. Grease bottom and sides of 9″ x 3″ aluminum spring form pan generously. Roll graham crackers fine. Melt butter or oleo and combine with 12 of rolled crackers. Cover bottom of pan with this mixture. Beat egg whites stiff and set aside. In large mixing bowl of mixer combine cream cheese, egg yolks, ¾ cup of sugar, and vanilla. Beat until smooth. Fold in stiff egg whites. Place mixture in pan on top of cracker crumbs and bake for 40 or 50 minutes or until slightly brown. Remove from oven and pour slowly over top the sour cream mixed with remaining ¼ cup of sugar. Sprinkle crumbs of 3 crackers on top and return to oven at 475° for 5 minutes. Remove from oven and cool. When cold, glaze and place in refrigerator for at least 12 hours before serving.

Mrs. Jake Dampf

GLAZE—CHERRY

1 #2½ can of Bing cherries
1 cup juice from cherries

½ cup sugar
2 tablespoons cornstarch

Drain cherries and cover top of cake with them. Heat liquid drained from cherries to the boiling point. When boiling rapidly, add sugar mixed with cornstarch. Let mixture strike hard boil, stirring constantly. Boil for 1 minute and remove from stove. When cold, spoon over top of cherries. Return to refrigerator. (Cake best when allowed to remain out of refrigerator at least one hour before serving.)

Mrs. Jake Dampf

GLAZE FOR CHEESE CAKE—STRAWBERRY

3 boxes fresh strawberries (washed and hulled)
2¼ tablespoons cornstarch

1⅛ cups strawberry juice
⅔ cup sugar

Wash and hull berries and drain them. Do not sugar them. Save largest, firm berries from top of boxes. Take remaining berries and mash well. Then strain the juice, using 1⅛ cups juice (if not this much, add water to make 1⅛ cups). Put juice in saucepan. Boil. Add sugar mixed with cornstarch and when mixture again reaches boiling point, boil for 1 minute. Remove and cool. Add red coloring if desired. When cheesecake is cool arrange large berries on top. Spoon glaze over it. Return to refrigerator for 2 hours. Remove from refrigerator 30 or 40 minutes before serving.

Mrs. Jake Dampf

CHEESE CAKE

Very fattening! Very good! (Not Lindy's, but almost.)

3 large packages of soft cream cheese	¾ cup sugar
4 eggs	1 teaspoon vanilla
	1 pint sour cream

1 box zwieback

Cream the cream cheese and then add ¾ cup of sugar and eggs one at a time. Add vanilla. Pour into greased spring pan lined with zwieback crumbs at bottom. Bake in 350° oven for 30 minutes. Whip 1 pint sour cream with ¼ to ½ cup of sugar and pour over cake. Return to same oven for 10 minutes. Put in refrigerator and chill at least 2 hours before serving. Serves 8. *Delicious with hot coffee.*

MISS WINNIE THOMAS

DE LUXE CHEESECAKE

(Cookie Mixture)

1 cup sifted all purpose flour	¼ teaspoon vanilla
¼ cup sugar	½ cup soft butter
1 teaspoon grated lemon rind	1 egg yolk

(Cheese Filling)

5 8-ounce packages soft cream cheese	3 tablespoons flour
1¾ cups granulated sugar	¼ teaspoon salt
¼ teaspoon vanilla	½ teaspoon grated lemon rind
½ teaspoon grated orange rind	5 medium eggs and 2 yolks
	¼ cup heavy cream
	1 cup sour cream

Mix flour, sugar, and lemon rind. With pastry blender or 2 knives, cut in butter, vanilla and 1 egg yolk. Shape into ball; wrap in waxed paper. Refrigerate 1 hour. Heat oven to 400°. Roll out ⅓ of dough between floured pieces of waxed paper or pastry cloth into 9½" circle. Place on bottom of 9" x 3" spring form pan. Trim to fit. Bake at 400° or until golden brown. Grease side of pan. Fit over base and roll rest of dough into 15" x 4" rectangle. Cut in half and line side of pan, patching if necessary.

Increase oven to 500°. Mix cheese in mixer until fluffy. Combine sugar with vanilla, orange rind, flour, salt, and lemon rind. Slowly add to cheese, beating until smooth. Add eggs and 2 yolks, one at a time, beating after each addition. Stir in cream. Turn into lined pan. Bake at 500° 12 minutes or until dough is golden. Reduce oven to 200°. Bake 1 hour. Cool on rack. Remove side of pan. Refrigerate until cool. Cover with ¼" layer of sour cream to serve. Yield 12-14.

MRS. LOUIS MAYER

CHEESE CUPCAKES

2 cups graham-cracker crumbs
⅓ cup melted butter or margarine
½ cup granulated sugar
2 eggs (unbeaten)

1½ 8-ounce packages soft cream cheese
½ teaspoon vanilla
1 cup sour cream
Fresh or frozen strawberries or canned or frozen pineapple chunks

Morning or afternoon before: Line twelve 2½″ muffin tin cups with paper liners. In bowl, blend crumbs and melted butter. Press some of this crumb mixture to bottom and sides of each lined muffin tin cup; refrigerate for 1 hour. Meanwhile, with electric mixer at medium speed, beat sugar, eggs, cheese, and vanilla until smooth and creamy. Spoon this mixture into cups; fill each cup almost to top of crumb crust. Refrigerate till served.

Just before serving: Remove from pans. Spread sour cream on each cupcake, then top with fruit. Makes 12.

MRS. J. D. AYMOND, JR.

DATE PUDDING

2 eggs
1 cup granulated sugar
2 tablespoons flour
1 teaspoon baking powder
1 cup chopped nuts

1 cup chopped dates
1 teaspoon vanilla
½ pint whipping cream, whipped

Beat eggs and sugar together. Sift in flour and baking powder. Add nuts, dates and vanilla. Butter and flour 8″ cake pan. Pour pudding into pan. Bake at 350° for about 20 minutes. When it rises during baking and begins to brown (about 10 minutes), stir well and let it settle and continue cooking. Do not let pudding bake until dry. May be served with whipped cream. Yield 10-12.

THE LATE MRS. F. L. CLOSE
Shreveport, La.

LEMON CAKE TOP PUDDING

3 tablespoons butter
1 cup sugar
4 eggs, separated
3 tablespoons flour
⅓ cup fresh lemon juice

2 teaspoons grated lemon rind
¼ teaspoon salt
1 cup milk
⅓ cup toasted, slivered almonds (optional)

Cream butter; add sugar gradually. Cream together until light and fluffy. Add egg yolks; beat well. Add flour, lemon juice, rind, salt, and mix well. Stir in milk. Blend in ¼ cup almonds. Beat egg whites until stiff and fold into mixture. Pour into loaf baking dish 9″ x 5″. Set in pan of hot water and bake in slow oven 325° for 40 minutes. Turn oven to 350° and bake until brown (about 10 minutes). Sprinkle with remaining almonds and serve warm or chilled. This may be poured into individual pyrex cups. Yield—8.

MRS. CHARLES I. BLACK

PINEAPPLE-ALMOND DESSERT

1 #2 can pineapple tidbits
¼ pound (16) marshmallows,
   cut in eighths

¼ cup maraschino cherries,
   cut in fourths
1 cup heavy cream, whipped

½ cup slivered, toasted, blanched almonds

Drain pineapple, reserving syrup. Combine pineapple, marshmallows, cherries, and ¼ cup of the pineapple syrup. Let stand about an hour. Fold in whipped cream. Spoon into dishes and sprinkle with nuts. Chill. Yield 6-8.

MRS. R. W. SCHEFFY

HONOLULU PINEAPPLE CAKE

½ cup sugar
¼ cup water
4 eggs, separated
1 cup butter (½ pound)
2 cups confectioners' sugar
½ pint whipping cream,
   whipped

1 cup drained crushed pineapple
¼ teaspoon vanilla
2 tablespoons confectioners'
   sugar
2 dozen lady fingers or strips
   of sheet sponge cake

Melt sugar in water in double boiler. Heat slowly and add the beaten egg yolks gradually. Stir and cook until mixture thickens. Cool. Cream butter and sugar. Add pineapple and first cooled mixture. Beat egg whites until stiff. Add vanilla and 2 tablespoons powdered sugar. Fold this into mixture. Line bottom and sides of 8" x 12" large flat dish with lady fingers or sponge cake. Refrigerate for 12 hours. When serving, garnish with whipped cream and bits of candied fruit if desired. Yield: 10-12.

MRS. HARRY L. HAGAN

PINEAPPLE BAVARIAN CREAM

1 tablespoon gelatin
¼ cup cold water
1 small can chunk pineapple
Boiling water
½ cup sugar

Dash salt
2 tablespoons lemon juice
½ cup whipping cream,
   whipped

Soak gelatin in cold water. Drain syrup from pineapple. Measure and add enough boiling water to make 1½ cups. Heat this to boiling point and pour over gelatin. Add sugar, salt, and lemon juice, and stir until dissolved. Cool until mixture begins to stiffen. Then add whipped cream and pineapple chunks and mix thoroughly. Pour into molds and allow to congeal. Yield 6.

MRS. A. P. RABENHORST

PLUM PUDDING

1 cup finely chopped beef suet (¼ pound)
1 cup and 2 tablespoons brown sugar
½ cup milk
2 eggs, well beaten
1 cup currants or seedless raisins
1 pound chopped mixed fruits or 1 jar chopped mixed fruits

1 cup sliced blanched almonds or pecans
1¼ cup sifted all-purpose flour
1 teaspoon baking soda
1 teaspoon salt
½ teaspoon nutmeg
1 teaspoon cinnamon
¼ teaspoon mace
1 cup soft bread crumbs
½ cup brandy or whiskey

Combine suet, brown sugar, milk and eggs. Mix fruits and almonds with ¼ cup of flour. Sift remaining flour with soda, salt, and spices. Add fruits, crumbs, flour and spice mixture to suet mixture. Mix well. Turn into well greased 2 quart covered pudding mold. Steam 3 hours with water ½ depth of mold, replenishing water during steaming to keep proper depth. Turn out on hot platter. Heat brandy in pan. Pour over pudding. Light brandy and serve pudding flaming. Yield: 8.

Hard Sauce for Topping

6 tablespoons butter or oleo
1½ cups confectioners' sugar

1½ teaspoons vanilla
Sherry to taste

Cream butter well. Add sugar gradually. Add vanilla and sherry.

MRS. JOHN V. PHILLIPS

ENGLISH PLUM PUDDING

2 cups seeded raisins, cut
1 cup currants
⅔ cup mixed candied peel
2 teaspoons mixed ground spices
1 cup sugar
½ teaspoon salt

Grated rind of 2 lemons
1½ cups bread crumbs
1 cup sifted flour
2 cups beef suet, finely chopped
1 cup grapejuice
6 eggs

Combine fruits, peel, spices, sugar, salt and lemon rind. Blend separately crumbs, flour and suet. Add to fruits and moisten with grapejuice and well-beaten eggs. Turn into two well greased bowls or molds, filling not more than two-thirds full. Place in deep well on rack over 2 cups water. Bring to steam on high and turn to low to steam for six hours.

If puddings are to be kept for any length of time, remove greased paper and replace with fresh paper before storing away. At the time of serving, steam one hour and serve with hard sauce or a clear dessert sauce.

Foamy Sauce

2 eggs, separated
3 tablespoons wine

1 cup powdered sugar

Beat yolks very lightly. Add sugar and heat again. Add stiffly beaten egg whites and wine. Pour over plum pudding.

THE EDITORS

SHERRIED ANGEL LOAF

1 angel loaf cake	1 cup chopped pecans
½ cup sherry	1 quart vanilla ice cream
½ pint whipping cream, whipped	

Slice cake into 3 layers. Soften ice cream and add sherry and pecans. Spread between layers of cake. Frost entire loaf with whipped cream. Put in freezer. Serve sliced. Yield 6-8.

MRS. EVANS HOWELL

BISCUIT TORTONI

Whites of 3 eggs	1 tablespoon sherry
½ pint whipping cream, whipped	1 dozen almond macaroons, crumbled or rolled
½ cup confectioners' sugar	

Whip eggs. Whip cream and when nearly done, add confectioners' sugar gradually. Fold in egg whites, sherry and macaroons alternately, leaving some crumbs to sprinkle on top. Fill small fluted paper cups and sprinkle with crumbs. Cover with waxed paper and put in freezer until hard. A cherry tops this prettily. Yield: 8.

MRS. CHARLES DUCHEIN, JR.

COFFEE BISCUIT TORTONI

2 dozen medium size or 2½ dozen small almond macaroons	3 eggs beaten separately
¾ cup sugar	2 tablespoons sugar
¾ cup strong coffee	1 pint whipping cream, whipped

Toast and crush or grind macaroons. Line bottom and sides of two 8″ pie pans with most of them. Save some. Make a syrup of sugar and coffee. Pour slowly into beaten egg yolks. Let cool. Beat whites until stiff, adding sugar. Fold these into above mixture. Fold in whipped cream. Cover with more crumbs. Freeze and serve. Yield—12.

MRS. P. M. SMITH

COFFEE DELIGHT

20 marshmallows, chopped	½ pint whipping cream, whipped
1 cup hot strong coffee	½ cup chopped maraschino cherries
1 envelope gelatin	
¼ cup coffee	
1 cup chopped pecans	

Put marshmallows into double boiler. Add 1 cup coffee. Melt. Soften gelatin in ¼ cup coffee and add to above mixture. Cool until jelly-like consistency. Fold in whipped cream; then add other ingredients. Pour into 8″ x 8″ pan and chill several hours. Yield—6.

MRS. CHARLES BEADLES

CHRISTMAS DAY TREAT

1 quart milk
6 eggs, separated
6 tablespoons sugar
3 envelopes gelatin
⅓ cup water
Vanilla or sherry to taste

2 cups chopped pecans
1 medium package vanilla
   wafers
½ pint whipping cream,
   whipped

Heat milk slowly. Beat egg whites and yolks separately. Add 6 heaping tablespoons sugar to egg yolks. Stir yolks slowly into milk and cook
until custard has thickened. Soak gelatin in cold water and stir into milk
and eggs. Cool slightly then stir in whipped whites. Flavor. Into a large
oblong dish pour a cup of the pudding then a layer of pecans followed by
wafers. Continue until all ingredients are used. Place in refrigerator.
Serve with whipped cream. *Good for afternoon gatherings and late evening snacks, too.* Yield—12.

MRS. CHARLES DUCHEIN, JR.

FROZEN FRUIT CAKE
(A holiday specialty)

2 cups milk
½ cup sugar
¼ cup flour
¼ teaspoon salt
2 eggs, beaten
1 cup white raisins
1 cup broken pecans

2 cups crumbled almond
   macaroons
½ cup chopped candied
   cherries
1 cup whipping cream,
   whipped
1 teaspoon vanilla

Scald milk. Blend sugar, flour and salt. Add to milk. Stir until
smooth. Cook 10 minues. Pour over beaten eggs. Cook until thick stirring constantly. Cool. Add other ingredients, folding in whipped cream
last. Freeze. May top with additional whipped cream if desired. Place in
refrigerator ice trays and serve either sliced frozen or allow to soften
enough to serve in parfait or sherbert glasses. Yield—6.

MRS. CHARLES PROSSER

CHOCOLATE REFRIGERATOR YUMMY

5 small bars almond chocolate
8 marshmallows
¼ cup milk
½ pint whipping cream,
   whipped

Vanilla to taste
16 graham crackers, rolled
¼ cup butter or margarine
¼ cup sugar

Put candy bars, marshmallows and milk into double boiler. Melt.
Cool. (Not too cold.) Fold in whipped cream and a little vanilla. Mix
together by hand the crackers, margarine, and sugar. Put half of the crumb
mixture in the bottom of refrigerator tray and pat out. Add filling, then
remaining cracker mixture on top. Freeze. Yield—6-8.

MRS. KIMBROUGH OWEN

CHOCOLATE CRUNCH ICE CREAM PIE

1 six-ounce package semi-
   sweet chocolate bits
3 tablespoons butter
2 cups crisp rice cereal

½ gallon vanilla ice cream,
   slightly softened
Fresh or frozen sliced strawberries

In top of double boiler, melt chocolate and butter over hot water. Blend and add rice cereal. Press into unbuttered 9″ pie plate. Chill until firm. Spoon in vanilla ice cream until filled. Top with strawberries and freeze until firm. Let stand at room temperature 10-15 minutes before serving.

MRS. ALBERT McQUOWN

FAT MAN'S MISERY

14 chocolate wafers
1 stick butter
1 cup confectioners' sugar
1 egg
Few drops almond flavoring

½ pint whipping cream,
   whipped
½ tablespoon sugar
1 teaspoon vanilla
1 cup chopped pecans

Crush chocolate wafers. Line pie pan with these. Cream butter and sugar. Add eggs; cream again. Add almond flavoring. Spread this on crumbs. Whip cream with sugar; add vanilla and chopped pecans. Fold these until well blended. Spread this on first mixture. Cover with more crushed wafers. Let stand in refrigerator for 24 hours. Yield—6-8.

THE EDITORS

CHOCOLATE REFRIGERATOR CAKE

2 packages German chocolate
4½ tablespoons confectioners'
   sugar
6 eggs, separated
   ½ cup whipping cream, whipped

Pinch salt
1½ cups whipping cream,
   whipped
3 dozen lady fingers

Melt chocolate and sugar in double boiler. Set aside. Beat yolks. Beat whites until stiff. Add yolks, salt, 1½ cups of the whipped cream and beaten egg whites to above mixture. Pour ⅓ of this mixture into torte pan lined with lady fingers. Add more lady fingers, then remaining mixture. Top with remaining whipped cream. Chill well. Yield—12-15.

MRS. W. FLOYD WILLIAMSON, JR.

CHOCOLATE ROLL

5 eggs, separated
1 cup sugar
3 tablespoons cocoa
2 tablespoons flour, sifted
   three times

1 teaspoon vanilla
1 pinch salt
½ pint whipping cream,
   whipped

Beat yolks until creamy. Add sugar, then cocoa and flour. Add vanilla and salt. Fold in egg whites that have been beaten until stiff. Pour this on cookie sheet, lined with waxed paper which has been greased on both sides. Bake 20 minutes at 350° Turn out on damp towel. Cover with whipped cream, then roll. Store in refrigerator. Slice when firm. Yield—10.

MRS. EDWARD SUTTER

CHOCOLATE MOLDS WITH BUTTER CREAM FILLING AND PRALINE TOPPING

Chocolate Molds

1 package bitter-sweet chocolate

Melt chocolate and pour immediately in small paper cups that have been placed in muffin tins. Coat inside with chocolate. Place in refrigerator and chill thoroughly or freeze before removing papers. Let stand at room temperature 10 minutes before serving.

Butter Cream Filling

1½ cups sugar	**1 teaspoon cornstarch**
4 egg yolks	**Scant cup boiling milk**

1½ sticks butter, softened

Mix sugar, egg yolks and cornstarch, and dilute with milk. This will not be thick but stir over heat (do not boil) to thicken. Cool. Whip the mixture and the butter together. It will then change in texture and thicken. The flavor can be changed with either coffee or melted chocolate or vanilla. Can tint filling with vegetable coloring if desired.

Praline Topping

1 cup sugar   **½ cup pecans, roasted**

Caramelize sugar and add nuts. Pour immediately on greased platter while runny. When hard, powder it with a rolling pin. Sprinkle on top of filling. Serve on doily with fork. Yield—12-14. *Wonderful.*

MRS. DAVID CAMPBELL

CHOCOLATE REFRIGERATOR PIE

2 cups fine vanilla wafer crumbs	**2 eggs**
⅓ cup melted butter	**¼ cup sugar**
½ cup butter	**2 tablespoons cocoa**
1½ cups sifted confectioners' sugar	**1 cup heavy cream**
	1 cup chopped walnuts
	1 ripe banana, mashed

¼ cup maraschino cherries, chopped

Mix together crumbs and melted butter. Reserve 2 tablespoons for top. Press remainder in bottom of refrigerator tray. Cream together ½ cup butter and sugar. Add eggs one at a time, beating well after each. Spread over crumbs. Combine sugar, cocoa and cream. Whip. Fold in nuts and fruit. Pile on mixture in pan. Sprinkle reserved crumbs over all. Chill 24 hours. 9-12 servings.

MRS. ROY JORDAN

ANGEL PIE

3 egg whites, beaten
1 tablespoon almond flavoring
¼ teaspoon cream of tartar

1 cup sugar
½ teaspoon baking powder
12 saltines, crushed very fine

Make a meringue of egg whites, flavoring, sugar, cream of tartar, and baking powder which have been mixed together. Add saltines. Butter a pie tin lightly and put in the mixture—making the sides high. Bake in a 325° oven for 30 minutes. This keeps well in freezer.

Filling

4 egg yolks
½ cup sugar
3 tablespoons lemon juice

1 tablespoon lemon rind
⅛ teaspoon salt
1 cup heavy cream, whipped

To make the filling, beat the egg yolks lightly; stir in the sugar, lemon juice, rind, and salt. Cook over boiling water until thick. Cool. Fold in whipped cream. Pour into the shell and chill in the refrigerator.

Mrs. Walter Prichard
Mrs. Thomas Pugh, II
Mrs. Ernest Eanes

BROWNIE PIE

3 egg whites
Dash salt
¾ cup sugar
¾ cup fine chocolate wafer
   crumbs
½ cup chopped pecans

½ teaspoon vanilla
½ pint cream, whipped and
   sweetened
1 square unsweetened chocolate, shaved

Beat egg whites and salt until soft peaks form. Gradually add sugar, beating until stiff peaks form. Fold in crumbs, nuts and vanilla. Spread evenly in lightly buttered 9″ pie plate. Bake in slow oven, 325° for 35 minutes. Cool thoroughly. Spread top with sweetened whipped cream. Chill 3 to 4 hours. Trim with curls of shaved chocolate. Will serve 6.

Mrs. Calvin L. Simpson, II

WALNUT PIE OR RITZY DESSERT

16 Ritz crackers
1 cup chopped walnuts or
   pecans
3 egg whites

1 cup sugar
1 teaspoon vanilla
¼ pint whipping cream,
   whipped

Combine chopped nuts and crackers which have been finely crumbled (use rolling pin). Beat egg whites stiff; add sugar. Fold into nut mixture; add vanilla. Pour into 9″ pie pan and bake in slow oven (300°) for 45 minutes until golden brown. This cooks like a meringue. Cool and refrigerate. Top with ¼ pint whipped cream or ice cream before serving. This pie may be made a day before serving.

Mrs. J. B. Arbour

CHOCOLATE ANGEL PIE

2 egg whites
⅛ teaspoon salt
⅛ teaspoon cream tartar
½ cup sifted sugar
½ cup finely chopped pecans
½ teaspoon vanilla

1 package German sweet chocolate
3 tablespoons water
1 teaspoon vanilla
1 cup whipping cream, whipped

Beat egg whites with salt and cream of tartar until foamy. Add sugar slowly, beating until very stiff peaks are formed. Fold in nuts and ½ teaspoon of vanilla. Spread in a greased 8-inch pie pan and build up sides ½ inch above the pan. Cook in 300° oven for 50 to 55 minutes. Cool this meringue shell.

Now melt chocolate and water over low heat (or in double boiler), stirring constantly. Cool until thick. Add 1 teaspoon vanilla and then fold in the whipped cream. Pile the chocolate mixture in the meringue shell and chill for 2 hours. *It is delightful to eat.*

MRS. J. H. SIMPSON, JR.

GRAHAM CRACKER TORTE

3 egg whites
1 cup sugar
¾ cup graham cracker crumbs

½ cup chopped pecans
1 teaspoon baking powder
1 teaspoon vanilla

Beat egg whites until stiff. Add sugar gradually and continue beating. Fold in remaining ingredients gradually. Drop by tablespoons onto greased waxed paper on a greased cookie sheet; spread into 3-inch patties 1 inch thick. Bake 15 minutes in 350° oven. Pull off onto wet tea towel to loosen. To serve place scoop of vanilla ice cream on each torte and top with additional chopped pecans. Or torte may be baked in greased pie pan for 35 minutes and topped with ice cream or whipped cream. Yield—10.

MRS. J. H. BENTON
MRS. TOWSON ELLIS

FROZEN LEMON SHERBET PIE

½ cup sugar
3 eggs, separated
3 tablespoons lemon juice
Pinch of salt
1 tablespoon lemon rind

½ pint whipping cream, whipped
Vanilla wafers or graham crackers, crushed

Cook sugar, egg yolks, lemon juice, rind and salt in double boiler until thick, stirring frequently. Cool. Fold in whipped cream and stiffly beaten egg whites. Line 9″ pie plate or refrigerator tray with crushed vanilla wafers. Pour in filling. Top with more crushed vanilla wafers and freeze. Yield—8.

MRS. EDWARD WALL

LEMON CREAM SHERBET

1 pint milk
1 cup sugar
1 tablespoon grated lemon
  rind

½ pint cream, whipped
2 lemons (juice)
2 egg whites
2 tablespoons sugar

Add sugar to milk and allow to dissolve. When thoroughly dissolved, add grated rind and juice of lemon. Stir while adding lemon juice. Freeze in tray 45 minutes to 1 hour or until mushy. Beat egg whites adding 2 tablespoons sugar. Combine whipped cream and egg whites. Add frozen mixture and mix lightly. Return to freezer for 2 to 2½ hours. Serve garnished with mint. Will fill 2 regular ice trays. (After adding the lemon to the milk it might have a slightly curdled look. This will disappear in freezing.)   Yield—12-14.

MRS. GALE CREED

LEMON SHERBET—FOR CRANK TYPE FREEZER

3 cups sugar (if all lemon
  juice is used)
2¾ cups sugar (if part orange
  juice is used)

1⅓ cups lemon juice
  (or 1 cup lemon and ⅓
  cup orange)
2 quarts milk

Mix juice and sugar. Add milk gradually. Freeze in hand crank or electric freezer. Add the cream from the milk to the sherbet just before it freezes. Yield—14-16 servings or one gallon.

MRS. EUGENE CAZEDESSUS

MINCE MEAT ICE CREAM PIE

1 jar mince meat
1 quart vanilla ice cream
½ pint whipping cream, whipped

2 tablespoons rum
9″ baked pie shell

Mix mince meat, rum, and ice cream. (Don't let it melt any more than necessary.) Put into pie shell. Top with whipped cream. Keep in freezer. Yield—6-8.

MRS. WILLIAM T. BAYNARD

OOO LA LA (LIME FREEZE)

1 cup graham cracker
  crumbs
3 tablespoons melted butter
2 eggs, separated
1 can condensed milk
½ cup fresh or "real" lime
  juice

1 tablespoon grated lime rind
  or 1 can Florida limeade
¼ teaspoon vanilla
¼ cup sugar
3 or 4 drops green coloring

Combine crumbs and butter. Keep ¼ cup of mixture for top. Line refrigerator tray with this. Beat egg yolks; add all other ingredients except sugar. Beat egg whites and add sugar. Fold in. Put in tray and add remaining crumb mixture on top. Yield—6.

MRS. WRAY E. ROBINSON, JR.

PINEAPPLE MARSHMALLOW FROZEN DESSERT

40 marshmallows
2 cups milk
2 eggs
1 #2 can crushed pineapple, drained

1 small jar cherries, drained and chopped
½ pint whipping cream, whipped

Heat marshmallows and milk over low heat until marshmallows have melted, stirring constantly. Slowly add 2 well beaten eggs; continue stirring constantly about 3 minutes. Remove from heat and cool. Add pineapple, cherries and whipped cream to first mixture. Place in refrigerator tray and freeze. Stir several times while freezing. Yield—10.

MRS. FRANK RICKEY

PINEAPPLE SHERBET

1 #2 can crushed pineapple
¼ cup pineapple juice
¾ cup sugar
½ cup water

2 tablespoons lemon juice
1 cup whipping cream, whipped
2 egg whites, beaten

Drain juice from pineapple. Cook sugar, pineapple juice and water for 10 minutes. Add pineapple and lemon juice. Cool. Pour into tray and freeze to mush. Fold whipped cream and beaten egg whites into mush. Put in freezer tray and freeze until firm. Serves 8.

MRS. J. H. SIMPSON, JR.

FROZEN RUM CREAM

4 egg yolks
4 tablespoons sugar
3 egg whites, beaten stiff

1½ cups whipping cream, whipped
½ cup rum

Beat egg yolks and sugar until thick. Fold in egg whites and cream. Stir in rum. Freeze for 8 hours. Yield—10.

MRS. ROBERT E. LEE, JR.

STUFFED ORANGE WITH CREAM SHERBET

2 envelopes plain gelatin
½ cup cold water
1½ cups sugar
1½ cups hot water
1 cup lemon juice
1½ cups orange juice

2 cups heavy cream, whipped
2 eggs, separated
½ cup sugar
¼ teaspoon salt
Grated rind of 2 oranges
12 oranges

Soften gelatin in cold water. Add sugar and hot water and stir until dissolved. Add orange juice and lemon juice. Put in freezer tray until mushy. Beat cream until stiff. Beat yolks of eggs with sugar and salt until lemon colored. Then beat whites until stiff and add cream and remaining ingredients. Freeze until it holds its shape. Cut tops off of 12 oranges. Scrape out membrane, and stuff with sherbet; wrap each orange in foil and freeze. Serves 12.

MRS. NAVEN O. COUVILLON

SUNSHINE SHERBET

1½ cups sugar
3 cups water
Juice of 2 lemons
Juice of 2 oranges

1 can halved apricots (2 cups) cut into small pieces
1 small jar maraschino cherries, cut up

1 #2 can crushed pineapple

Boil sugar and water for 5 minutes. Cool. Mix thoroughly with all other ingredients. Pour into 3 ice trays and freeze, stirring a couple of times during freezing process. Yield—12-16.

Mrs. W. H. Ashby

STRAWBERRY BLANC MANGE

½ cup milk
½ cup sifted cake flour
3½ cups half and half milk (rich milk)
⅓ cup sugar

3 egg yolks
1 teaspoon vanilla
1 quart strawberries, washed, hulled and sliced
½ cup sugar

Mix ½ cup milk and flour in mixer until well blended. Scald 3½ cups milk; stir in ⅓ cup sugar. Add above flour-milk mixture and mix with mixer until well blended. Bring this to boil; lower heat and simmer gently for 6 or 7 minutes, stirring constantly from bottom of pan. Cool. When quite cold beat in egg yolks, one at a time, beating well after each addition. Return to low heat and cook gently, stirring constantly until mixture boils. Remove from fire and add vanilla. Turn into wet ring mold 8″ x 2½″ and chill thoroughly in refrigerator ½ hour before serving. Mix washed, hulled, and sliced strawberries with ½ cup sugar. Let stand. At serving time turn mold on plate and fill center with strawberries. Frozen strawberries, raspberries, peaches, or any fruit may be substituted for fresh strawberries. Yield—8-10.

Mrs. D. V. Cacioppo

CAKES

BANANA CUP CAKES

½ cup shortening
1½ cups sugar
2 beaten eggs
2 cups flour
½ teaspoon salt

1 teaspoon baking powder
¾ teaspoon soda
¼ cup milk (sour)
1 cup mashed bananas
1 teaspoon vanilla

Cream shortening and sugar. Add beaten eggs. Add sifted dry ingredients, alternating with milk, banana, and vanilla. Fill greased muffin tins half full. Bake in moderate oven 375° for 20 minutes. This may also be baked in two eight-inch pans at 350° for 25 minutes.

Mrs. William R. Smith

POUND CAKE

8 eggs, separated	3½ cups flour
6 tablespoons sugar	½ cup light cream
1 pound butter	1 tablespoon vanilla
2¾ cups sugar	

Separate eggs and beat whites stiff with 6 tablespoons sugar. Place in refrigerator. Cream butter and sugar, add egg yolks. Alternate flour and cream. Add vanilla. Fold in stiffly beaten egg whites. Bake in large tube pan in 325° oven for approximately 1½ hours.

MRS. ASHTON STEWART

GRANDMOTHER'S POUND CAKE

1 cup shortening or butter	Juice of one lemon
2 cups sugar	1 teaspoon vanilla
2¼ cups all purpose flour	Dash of salt
6 eggs	

Use mixer and cream together shortening and sugar. Sift and then measure flour. Add alternately flour and eggs, one at a time. Add lemon juice, vanilla, and salt. Bake 1 hour and 20 minutes in greased and floured angel cake pan at 312°. Let cool slightly in pan and then turn out on cake rack.

GRANDMOTHER OF MRS. CHARLES B. MOORE

BISHOP'S CAKE

½ pound (2 sticks) butter	1 tablespoon lemon juice
2 cups sugar	1 teaspoon vanilla
5 whole eggs	2 cups sifted cake flour

Cream butter and sugar in mixing bowl. Add eggs, lemon juice, and vanilla. Beat well. Add sifted flour. Bake in angel food cake pan that has been greased and floured for 1 hour and 15 minutes in 325° oven. Let cool before removing from pan. *This is an old fashioned pound cake. As a variation I sprinkle crushed blanched almonds over the top of the cake right before putting it in the oven to bake.*

MRS. JAMES H. HUGUET

HOT MILK CAKE

4 eggs	¼ teaspoon salt
2 cups sugar	1 cup milk
2 cups flour	1 stick butter
2 teaspoons baking powder	1 teaspoon vanilla

Set oven at 350°. Grease and flour 3 layer cake pans. Beat eggs until thick. Add sugar gradually. Then add slowly flour, baking powder, and salt that have been sifted together. Put milk in pan and butter. When it comes to a boiling point stir rapidly into egg mixture. Bake for 20 minutes. Ice with lemon or coconut icing.

MRS. R. E. LEE, JR.

CARAMEL CAKES

6 tablespoons caramel syrup	2½ cups flour, sifted
1 cup butter	¾ cup milk
1½ cups sugar	3 teaspoons baking powder
5 eggs, separated	1 teaspoon vanilla

Make caramel syrup: Melt ½ cup sugar in iron skillet, add ½ cup of hot water. Let simmer five or ten minutes. Cream butter and sugar well; add yolks, beat thoroughly. Add two cups of flour alternately with the milk, beat well, then add vanilla, caramel syrup, the remaining ½ cup of flour with baking powder and lastly, fold in beaten whites. I always add 5 tablespoons of the 1½ cups of sugar to the beaten whites. Bake in tube pan 45 minutes or in 3 greased 8-inch layer pans 25 to 30 minutes. Bake in 325° oven. Frost with a caramel icing.

MRS. J. E. LAWTON

CLABBER CAKE

2 sticks margarine	2 teaspoons soda (dissolved
2 cups sugar	in a little water)
2 eggs	2 cups buttermilk
¼ to ½ cup cocoa	1 pinch salt
3½ cups cake flour	1 teaspoon vanilla

Cream butter and sugar. Add eggs. Sift cocoa and cake flour. Add alternately flour and cocoa with milk, salt, soda, and vanilla. Bake in large flat pan 13" x 9" x 2" at 350° for 45 minutes. Ice with chocolate or butterscotch icing.

MRS. JOHN E. COXE

FUDGE CAKE

1¾ sticks butter	1 teaspoon vanilla
4 ounces bitter chocolate	1 cup all purpose flour
4 eggs	2 cups pecans
2 cups sugar	

Grease and line two 8" layer cake pans. Set oven at 350°. Melt chocolate and butter over steam. When cool, add sugar, vanilla, and eggs beaten together. (Do not use mixer.) Do not reheat after combining these. Dredge pecans in flour and add last. Put a pan of water in oven while baking. Bake about 30 to 40 minutes. Let cake get cold before removing from pan.

ICING FOR FUDGE CAKE

1 to 2 boxes of powdered sugar	Evaporated milk
2 tablespoons cocoa	1 teaspoon vanilla
¼ cup butter	1 cup pecans

Mix 1 box of sugar and cocoa. Cream in butter. Add milk and vanilla, a little at a time until really thick. If more sugar is needed to achieve this, add it. Spread on cake and add pecans. Put in refrigerator for 24 hours before cutting.

MR. HUGH MEANS

GERMAN CHOCOLATE CAKE

2 cups sugar
1 cup shortening
4 egg yolks
¼ pound German sweet
   chocolate
½ cup boiling water

2½ cups all purpose flour
1 cup buttermilk
1 teaspoon soda
1 teaspoon vanilla
Pinch of salt
4 stiffly beaten egg whites

Cream together sugar and shortening. Add egg yolks one at a time. Melt chocolate in boiling water and add to mixture. Add flour alternately with buttermilk, with soda dissolved in ¼ cup of the buttermilk. Add vanilla and salt. Fold in stiffly beaten egg whites. Pour into three 9-inch cake pans. Bake 30 minutes at 350°. Ice with special icing for this cake or fudge icing.

FILLING AND ICING FOR
GERMAN CHOCOLATE CAKE

1 cup sugar
1 cup evaporated milk
1 stick butter or margarine
3 beaten egg yolks

1 cup flaked coconut
½ to 1 cup chopped pecans
1 teaspoon vanilla

Cook together in double boiler, stirring constantly, sugar, milk, butter and egg yolks. Cook until thick. Add coconut, pecans and vanilla. Spread.

Mrs. Richard Gregg

DEVIL'S FOOD CAKE

4 tablespoons butter
2 cups sugar
2 eggs
4 squares of chocolate

2 cups flour
3 teaspoons baking powder
1½ cups milk

Cream butter. Into the butter cream 1½ cups of sugar. Add egg yolks and cream well. Melt chocolate in a double boiler. Add to sugar mixture. Sift flour and measure. Sift again with the baking powder. Add milk and flour alternately. Fold in beaten egg whites, to which the remaining ½ cup of sugar has been added one tablespoon at a time. Pour batter into greased 9 x 9 x 2 inch pan which has been lined on the bottom with wax paper. Bake 40 minutes in a moderate oven 350°.

CHOCOLATE DELUXE ICING

4 cups sifted confectioners'
   sugar
⅔ teaspoon salt

2 eggs
⅔ cup soft shortening
4 squares chocolate, melted

Beat ingredients with electric mixer until fluffy. Spread on cooled cake. This is really enough for a two layer cake.

Mrs. Thomas P. Roberts

COCONUT CAKE

½ pound butter	4 teaspoons baking powder
2 cups sugar	1 cup sweet milk
4 eggs	Pinch of salt
2⅔ cups cake flour	1 teaspoon vanilla

Grease and line 3 eight-inch cake pans. Set oven for 375°. Cream butter and sugar well. Add egg yolks. Sift flour, baking powder, and salt together and add alternately with the milk. Add vanilla. Beat egg whites until stiff and fold into mixture. Bake at 375° 20 to 25 minutes.

THE EDITORS

COCONUT FILLING

1 egg yolk	1 tablespoon cornstarch
1 cup milk or part coconut milk	1 teaspoon vanilla
	1 grated coconut
1 cup sugar	

Mix together all ingredients except coconut and cook in double boiler over low heat until thickened. Cool partly, then add coconut before icing cake.

THE EDITORS

GINGERBREAD

½ cup sugar	1 teaspoon soda
½ cup butter	1 teaspoon ginger
2 eggs	1 teaspoon allspice
½ cup molasses	½ cup buttermilk
1½ cups cake flour	1 teaspoon cinnamon

Cream butter and sugar, add eggs and beat well. Add molasses. Sift flour, soda, and spices together; fold in flour mixture alternately with buttermilk. Bake in square pan 25 to 30 minutes at 350°

MRS. COURTLAND HULINGS

TOPPING FOR GINGERBREAD

½ cup brown sugar	¼ cup soft butter
2 teaspoons cinnamon	½ to 1 cup chopped nut
¼ cup flour	meats

Combine all ingredients with hands or fork until crumbly. Spread over gingerbread for last ten minutes of cooking.

MRS. BEN DOWNING

JELLY ROLL

3 eggs	1 cup flour
1 cup sugar	1 teaspoon baking powder
3 tablespoons cold water	⅓ teaspoon salt

Beat eggs and sugar until thick. Add water, then flour, baking powder and salt, sifted together. Line cookie sheet with waxed paper and rub with oil, then flour. Pour in batter. Bake in quick oven 425°, 12 to 15 minutes. Turn on cloth on which you have sifted powdered sugar. Trim edges and spread with jelly or lemon sauce and roll in cloth.

LEMON SAUCE FOR JELLY ROLL

Grated rind and juice of 1 lemon	**2 tablespoons butter**
1 cup sugar	**Salt**
3 tablespoons flour	**1 egg**
	1 cup hot water

Cook ingredients until thick. Cool. This is enough for two jelly rolls. Will keep in refrigerator.

MRS. WALTER PRICHARD

MARBLE MOLASSES CAKE

½ cup butter	⅔ cup milk
1 cup sugar	1 teaspoon cinnamon
2 eggs, beaten	½ teaspoon cloves
2 cups sifted cake flour	¼ teaspoon ginger
2 teaspoons baking powder	3 tablespoons molasses
¼ teaspoon salt	

Set oven at 350° and grease loaf pan. Cream butter, add sugar gradually and beat until light and fluffy. Add beaten eggs and continue to cream. Next add flour, which has been sifted together with baking powder and salt, alternately with milk. Beat after each addition. Then remove ⅔ of batter from bowl. Add spices and molasses to the remaining batter and beat well. Drop by tablespoons into greased loaf pan, alternating light and dark mixture. Bake in moderate oven 350° for one hour. *Serve plain or frost with your favorite icing. Nice to serve with coffee or tea and is good without frosting.*

MRS. RALPH DUFF

JAM CAKE

½ cup butter	1 teaspoon soda
1 cup sugar	½ teaspoon cinnamon
3 eggs	½ teaspoon nutmeg
1 cup jam	½ cup buttermilk
2 cups flour	1 teaspoon vanilla

Cream butter. Add sugar and cream well. Add beaten eggs one at a time. Add jam. Sift dry ingredients together and add alternately with milk. Add vanilla. Bake at 350° 20-30 minutes in two large or three small layer cake pans that have been greased and floured.

FILLING

2 tablespoons flour	½ cup butter
1 cup sugar	1 egg
1 cup cream	1 teaspoon vanilla

Mix flour and sugar. Add other ingredients and cook over hot water until thick.

MRS. C. C. MORELAND

PINEAPPLE MERINGUE CAKE

½ cup shortening
½ cup sugar
4 egg yolks
1 cup cake flour, sifted

2 teaspoons baking powder
⅛ teaspoon salt
1 teaspoon vanilla
5 tablespoons milk

Cream shortening and sugar together; add egg yolks and mix thoroughly. Add the cake flour, which has been sifted with the baking powder and salt, alternately with the vanilla and milk. Pour into two 8-inch round layer cake pans, which have been greased and floured, and add:

MERINGUE TOPPING

4 egg whites
1 cup sugar

1 teaspoon vanilla
¾ cup chopped nut meats

Beat egg whites stiff, then add a light sifting of sugar, continue beating and adding until all sugar has been used. Add vanilla and spread meringue on each cake. Sprinkle with nut meats. Bake at 350° 20 to 30 minutes. Allow to cool, then remove from pans and spread with pineapple filling.

PINEAPPLE FILLING

1 cup heavy cream, whipped
1 cup drained crushed
pineapple

1½ teaspoons powdered
sugar
¼ teaspoon vanilla

Combine all ingredients. Place one layer meringue side down on cake plate and spread filling on cake. Place second layer on top of filling with meringue side up. Serve.

NOTE: This cake can be made without the pineapple in the filling.

THE EDITORS

PINEAPPLE TURNOVER

1 stick of butter
1½ cups white sugar
2 eggs, separated
2 cups flour
2 teaspoons baking powder

1 cup milk
1 teaspoon vanilla
1½ cups brown sugar
5 slices of pineapple
5 cherries

To make batter, cream ½ stick of butter with white sugar. Mix in well the egg yolks. Sift together flour and baking powder, and add alternately with milk. Add vanilla. Beat egg whites and fold into batter. Set aside. In cast iron skillet, place ½ stick of butter in small dabs, and add brown sugar, pouring evenly over butter. Place 1 slice of pineapple in center of pan and other slices around, centering each with a cherry. Pour batter over this and bake in a slow oven, 300° for 1 hour or until done. Test by inserting straw in center of cake and when straw comes out clean, it is done.

MRS. BEN THOMPSON

PRALINE CAKE

1½ cups sifted cake flour   ¾ cup sugar
1½ teaspoons baking powder   1 teaspoon vanilla
¼ teaspoon salt   1 egg
¼ cup shortening   ⅔ cup milk

Sift together cake flour, baking powder and salt. Cream shortening, sugar, and vanilla. Beat in egg thoroughly. Add flour mixture alternately with milk, beating just until smooth after each addition. Pour into well greased heat resistant glass round cake dish. Bake in slow 325° oven about 40 minutes. Cool slightly in dish.

ICING

½ cup brown sugar   2 tablespoons water
4 teaspoons flour   4 tablespoons butter
                ¾ cup chopped pecans

Mix together brown sugar, flour, water, melted butter and pecans. Carefully spread on top of slightly cooled cake. Return to slow oven 325° and bake 10 minutes.

MRS. CHARLES I. BLACK

RAISIN APPLE CAKE

First Part:

3 tart cooking apples   ½ cup seedless raisins
⅓ cup sugar   1 tablespoon butter

Slice apples. Put in buttered baking dish, add raisins, sugar and bits of butter.

Second Part:

1 egg   ½ cup milk
½ cup sugar   2 tablespoons melted butter
1 cup flour   ½ teaspoon vanilla
1 teaspoon baking powder

Beat egg until very light, add sugar. Sift flour and baking powder and add alternately with milk. Beat until smooth. Add melted butter and vanilla. Pour over fruit mixture and bake in moderate oven 350° about 35 minutes.

MRS. JAKE DAMPF

STRAWBERRY CAKE

1 box white cake mix   1 cup salad oil
3 tablespoons flour (heaping)   4 eggs
1 package strawberry gelatin   ½ cup water
            ½ package frozen strawberries

Mix cake mix, flour, and gelatin. Add oil. Beat in eggs. Add water and strawberries. Mix well. Bake in greased tube pan 35 to 40 minutes in 350° oven. Frost with the following icing.

ICING

½ stick butter   ½ package strawberries
About 2 cups powdered sugar

Melt butter with ½ package strawberries. Mash in. Mix in the powdered sugar until spreading consistency.

MRS. GERALD BYARS

PERFECT SPONGE CAKE

(By Electric Mixer)

1¼ cups sifted cake flour   1½ cups sugar
¼ teaspoon baking powder   ⅓ cup cold orange juice
6 eggs   ¼ teaspoon salt
¾ teaspoon cream of tartar   1 teaspoon vanilla

Set oven at 325°. Use a 12″ tube-cake pan. Sift flour with baking powder. Separate eggs, putting whites in large bowl of your electric mixer, yolks in next size bowl. Beat whites at high speed until frothy, then sprinkle in the cream of tartar and continue beating until whites stand in peaks but still cling to the side of the bowl (takes about 3 minutes). Add ½ cup sugar very gradually, still beating at high speed, until you have a smooth, satiny meringue. Set aside. Beat the yolks at high speed for 2 minutes. Pour in the orange juice, beating for 1 more minute, still at high speed. Add remaining sugar very gradually to yolks; add salt and vanilla and continue beating until mixture looks light and smooth. Remove from mixer and fold flour into egg yolks until batter is smooth. Do not beat. Pour this batter into the meringue and fold batter very gently again until all patches of egg white disappear. Pour into ungreased tube pan and bake 1¼ hours. Cool, upside down on a rack, for one hour, then pull cake carefully away from pan with your hands. When cool cover with powdered sugar or Pineapple Glaze.

PINEAPPLE GLAZE FOR PERFECT SPONGE CAKE

2 tablespoons butter   3 tablespoons crushed pineapple, drained
Rind of ½ small lemon
1 egg yolk   2 tablespoons pineapple juice
    1¼ cups confectioners' sugar

Melt butter; grate rind from lemon. Beat egg yolk for 1 minute at high speed on electric mixer. At low speed pour in melted butter, crushed pineapple, pineapple juice, lemon rind, and confectioners' sugar. Beat 2 minutes. Spoon this thin glaze over top of Sponge Cake allowing some of it to trickle over the cake sides.

Excellent!

MRS. RALPH DUFF

TREASURE CAKE

1 cup butter	Dash of salt
1 cup white sugar	2 cups cake flour
2 whole eggs	1 teaspoon baking powder
2 teaspoons vanilla	1 teaspoon soda

1 cup sour cream

Cream butter, sugar, vanilla, eggs, and salt. Sift together flour, baking powder, and soda. Add half flour mixture and half of the sour cream to butter mixture. Beat 1 minute. Then add rest of both and beat one minute. Grease and flour 9″ x 12″ x 2″ pan and spread ½ of cake batter in pan. Mix icing mixture and sprinkle ½ on batter. Then carefully pour and spread remaining cake batter on top of this. Then sprinkle remaining icing mixture on top. Bake in 350° oven for 35 to 38 minutes.

ICING

½ cup brown sugar	1 cup chopped pecans or
¼ cup white sugar	walnuts
1 teaspoon cinnamon	

MRS. G. W. COURTERS' GRANDMOTHER

DATE FRUIT CAKE

8 eggs	1 teaspoon almond extract
2 cups white sugar	8 cups nuts
3 cups flour	1 pound candied cherries
2 teaspoons baking powder	1 pound candied pineapple,
2 teaspoons salt	cut up
3 teaspoons vanilla	2 pounds pitted dates

Set oven at 250° and grease and flour loaf or tube pans. Beat eggs together. Add sugar slowly, then 2 cups flour, baking powder and salt, which have been sifted together. Add flavoring. Use other cup flour to flour fruit and nuts. Then add to cake mixture. Pack in lined, greased, floured tins. Bake 2½ hours at 250° with pan of hot water in oven under cake. Leave fruits and nuts in original pieces except for pineapple.

MRS. L. C. KUTTRUFF

DATE AND NUT CAKE

1 cup flour	1 pound nuts, chopped
2 teaspoons baking powder	4 eggs, separated
1 teaspoon salt	1 cup sugar
1 pound dates, chopped	1 teaspoon brandy

1 teaspoon vanilla

Sift flour, baking powder, and salt and mix with dates and nuts. Beat egg yolks and sugar. Add vanilla and brandy. Fold in stiffly beaten egg whites and bake in two loaf pans which are greased and lined with brown or waxed paper. Grease and flour paper. Bake in moderate oven 350° for 2 hours. It is best to put a pan of water in the oven.

MRS. A. M. CULPEPPER

VARIATION:

Use same recipe as above and add ½ pound candied cherries and ½ pound crystalized pineapple. Cut in small pieces and add with dates and nuts. Bake in two loaf pans which are greased and lined with brown or waxed paper. Bake in slow oven 275° - 300° for 2 hours.

Mrs. H. Payne Breazeale

ORANGE DATE NUT CAKE

¾ cup butter	½ teaspoon soda
1½ cups sugar	1 cup buttermilk
3 eggs	1 6½ ounce package dates
3 cups flour	1 cup chopped nuts (pecans)

Rind of 1 orange, grated

Sauce:

Rind of another orange, grated	½ cup orange juice
	1 cup sugar

Cream the butter and sugar. Add eggs. Add 2 cups of the sifted flour and soda alternately with the buttermilk. Cut dates into small pieces and flour with the other cup of sifted flour. Stir in by hand the dates, nuts, and grated rind. Grease and flour a tube pan or angel food cake pan. Bake in 350° oven for approximately 1 hour. While cake is baking, grate the rind of another orange and add to orange juice and sugar (granulated or powdered). When cake is done invert pan and place cake top side down on cake plate. Pour half of mixture gradually over bottom of cake as soon as it is removed from oven. The cake will absorb the orange juice mixture. Turn cake with top side up and pour remaining mixture on the top and sides.

This cake is better when served cold. Do not try to slice while still warm. This cake will stay fresh for one to two weeks if kept in a cake box.

Mrs. Don R. McAdams
Mrs. C. E. Phillips

CHRISTMAS NUT CAKE

2 cups sifted sugar	1 teaspoon nutmeg
¾ pound soft butter	Pinch of salt
6 eggs	1 pound candied pineapple
4 cups flour	1 pound candied cherries
2 teaspoons baking powder	4 cups chopped pecans

1 cup whiskey

Set oven at 300°. Cream sugar and butter. Add eggs one at a time. Sift dry ingredients together. Divide flour and flour fruit and nuts well. Add whiskey to sugar and butter mixture. Then add flour and well floured nuts and fruits. Bake one hour and 20 minutes in a pan that has been lined with wax paper. Use two small loaf pans or one large tube pan.

Mrs. W. R. Smith

WHITE NUT CAKE

2⅔ cups sifted cake flour
3 teaspoons baking powder
1 teaspoon salt
⅔ cup shortening
1¼ cups sugar
1 cup milk

1 teaspoon vanilla
5 egg whites
½ cup sugar
1 cup chopped nuts (pecans or walnuts)

Sift flour once, measure, add baking powder, salt and sift 3 times. Cream shortening, and add 1¼ cups sugar gradually, and cream until light and fluffy. Add flour alternately with milk, beating each time until smooth. Add vanilla and blend. Beat egg whites until foamy and add ½ cup sugar gradually, and beat only until mixture holds soft peaks. Beat thoroughly into batter. Add chopped nuts and mix well. Bake in two 9″ layer pans, lined and greased at 375° for approximately 30 minutes. Cover with divinity icing and decorate with nut halves.

DIVINITY ICING

1½ cups sugar
6 tablespoons water
1 teaspoon vanilla

⅛ teaspoon cream of tartar
2 egg whites, stiffly beaten

Combine sugar, water, cream of tartar. Cook without stirring to 238°F. Pour ⅓ of syrup in fine stream over stiffly beaten egg whites, stirring constantly. Cook remainder of syrup to 248°. Pour half of remaining syrup in fine stream into mixture beating constantly. Cook remaining syrup to 268°. Pour into icing, beat thoroughly, add flavoring and spread at once.

Mrs. L. C. Kuttruff

LAYER FRUIT CAKE

1 cup nuts
1 cup raisins
1½ cups coconut
2 cups sugar
1 cup butter or margarine
1 teaspoon allspice

3 eggs
1 cup buttermilk
1 teaspoon soda
1 cup blackberry jam
3 cups flour

Run nuts (preferably pecans), raisins, and coconut through food chopper. Cream sugar and butter well. Add eggs and milk in which soda has been dissolved. Add jam, spice, and flour. Mix thoroughly. Add nuts, raisins and coconut. Bake in layer cake pans at 350° for 30 - 35 minutes. Put together with the following filling.

FILLING

2 cups sugar
1½ cups milk

1 cup butter or margarine

Boil until thick, about 7 minutes. Put between layers and over cake. This cake may be baked 30 days before serving.

Mrs. D. M. Benton, Sr.
Denham Springs, La.

ICINGS AND FILLINGS

CARAMEL CAKE FROSTING

1 cup brown sugar	2 tablespoons butter
½ cup granulated sugar	½ teaspoon vanilla
½ cup milk	⅛ teaspoon salt

Mix all ingredients together and cook over medium heat until drops of icing will form soft ball when dropped into cup of cool water (238°). Remove from heat and beat with electric beater until icing reaches spreading consistency (about 15 minutes). For a large cake, double recipe.

MRS. H. H. HOLLOWAY, JR.

CARAMEL ICING

3 cups sugar	1 cup milk
1 stick butter	½ teaspoon vanilla

Combine 2½ cups sugar, the butter, and milk in a 3 or 4 quart pot and begin cooking. Brown ½ cup sugar in skillet and add to the syrup already cooking. Cook to 238° (soft ball stage). Remove from heat; cool; add vanilla, and heat to consistency for spreading. If icing becomes too stiff, a little cream may be added to thin. *Good!*

MRS. FRANK MIDDLETON, JR.

FUDGE ICING

2 cups granulated sugar	1 box confectioners' sugar,
2 heaping tablespoons cocoa	sifted
1 stick butter	1 teaspoon vanilla
Enough undiluted evaporated	Chopped nuts, optional
milk to mix well	

Mix all ingredients but confectioners' sugar and bring to a boil. (Stir to prevent sticking.) Remove from heat and add powdered sugar. Add about ⅓ at a time and use an electric mixer for beating. Add vanilla and continue beating until the mixture is of spreading consistency. Add chopped nuts if desired. Variations: If you want caramel icing, use brown sugar instead of white and omit cocoa. For vanilla cream icing, use white sugar and omit cocoa. Shredded coconut may be added if desired.

MRS. A. J. BRYAN

LEMON JELLY FILLING

1 cup sugar	1 teaspoon flour
¾ stick butter	3 egg yolks
Juice of 2 lemons	

Beat sugar, butter, flour and eggs. Add lemon juice. Cook in double boiler to consistency of jelly. Place between layers of cake. Ice cake with white icing.

MRS. CLARENCE IVES

LEMON BUTTER

3 eggs   2 lemons, grated rind and
1 cup sugar   juice
                    1 tablespoon butter

Beat eggs and sugar together until thick and very light. Add lemon juice, rind and butter. Cook in top of double boiler over hot water, stirring constantly until mixture is consistency of mayonnaise (about 10 minutes).

                                    MRS. CLARENCE IVES

LEMON SAUCE FOR GINGERBREAD

½ cup sugar   1 egg yolk, beaten
4 teaspoons cornstarch   1 teaspoon grated lemon rind
1 cup hot water   3 to 4 tablespoons lemon juice
                    1 tablespoon butter

Mix sugar and cornstarch in a saucepan. Gradually add the hot water and blend until smooth. Cook on high heat, stirring until thick; reduce heat and cook 5 to 7 minutes until clear. Remove from heat. Blend in quickly the beaten egg yolk, to which a little of the hot mixture has been added. Cook 2 minutes. Add the lemon rind, lemon juice and butter.

                                    THE EDITORS

SAUCE FOR ANGEL FOOD CAKE

¾ cup sugar with 1 table-   Juice of one orange
    spoon cornstarch added   2 tablespoons of flour in a
2 eggs, beaten   little water
Juice of one lemon   1 cup whipped cream

Cook all ingredients except whipped cream in a double boiler. Cool the mixture and fold in the whipped cream.

                                    MRS. GLENN S. DARSEY

FLUFFY SEVEN MINUTE ICING

2 egg whites, unbeaten   Dash of salt
1½ cups light corn syrup   1 teaspoon vanilla

Combine egg whites, corn syrup, and salt in top of double boiler, beating with rotary egg beater until thoroughly mixed. Place over rapidly boiling water. Beat constantly with rotary beater for 7 minutes or until it stands in peaks. Remove from boiling water. Add vanilla and beat until thick enough to spread. One half tablespoon of vinegar or lemon juice may be added slowly to make not so sweet.

                                    MRS. A. A. WREN

PEACH SAUCE

1 tablespoon tapioca
¼ cup sugar
Dash of salt

1 box frozen peaches, thawed
  and drained
¾ cup peach syrup
1 tablespoon lemon juice

Place all ingredients except the lemon juice in a saucepan and cook over medium heat until mixture comes to a boil. Remove from heat and add lemon juice.

Use on angel food, butter or sponge cake, gingerbread, plain pudding, or ice cream.

THE EDITORS

WHITE ICING

2½ cups sugar
5 tablespoons white corn
  syrup

½ cup water
2 egg whites, beaten stiff
Vanilla to taste

Cook sugar, water and corn syrup to 242° or hard ball stage. Pour over beaten whites very slowly, beating constantly. Add vanilla. Beat until cool and mixture stands in peaks. Ice cake.

MRS. CLARENCE IVES

ORANGE FILLING FOR CAKE

2 eggs, whole
1 cup sugar
1 heaping tablespoon flour

Juice of 4 oranges
Juice of 1 lemon
¼ stick butter

1 grated orange rind

Beat eggs. Add sugar and flour. Then add juices and butter. Cook until thick. Add rind and let cool.

MRS. U. S. HARGROVE

TOPPING FOR YELLOW OR CHOCOLATE CAKE

1 cup light brown sugar
3 teaspoons cream
1 stick of margarine or butter

1½ cups coconut
Vanilla
Nuts

Mix all together and melt in saucepan. Pour on cake and run under broiler.

MRS. W. R. EIDSON

COOKIES

BROWNIES

2 squares bitter chocolate
1 stick butter
½ cup brown sugar
¾ cup white sugar
1 tablespoon white corn
  syrup

2 eggs
2 cups chopped pecans
½ cup flour
1 tablespoon vanilla

Set oven at 350° and grease an 8-inch square pan. Melt in top of double boiler first five ingredients. Cool; then add eggs one at a time. Beat well after each addition. Add chopped pecans. Mix well. Then add flour and vanilla. Bake 30 to 40 minutes or until cake springs back when touched. Cool and cut in squares.

MRS. JOSEPH S. SIMMONS

BROWNIES

2 sticks butter
2 cups sugar
4 eggs

1½ cups flour
6 tablespoons cocoa
2 tablespoons vanilla

2 cups chopped pecans

Set oven at 350° and grease a 9″ x 13″ pan. Blend butter and sugar. Add eggs one at a time and blend. Sift flour and cocoa and add to above mixture. Add vanilla and pecans. Pour into greased pan and bake about 30 minutes. This is the light, cake type brownie.

MRS. NELSON BOURGEOIS

MAPLE CHEWS

1 box brown sugar
1 cup all purpose flour,
  unsifted
1 teaspoon baking powder

4 eggs, unbeaten
Pinch of salt
1 teaspoon maple flavoring
1 cup chopped pecans

Grease and flour a 9x13x2 inch pan and preheat oven to 375°. Mix brown sugar, flour, and baking powder in a bowl. Add unbeaten eggs, salt, and maple flavoring. Mix well; add pecans. Pour into pan and bake for 20 minutes or until the middle is set, but not hard. Do not overcook. Cool 10 to 15 minutes in pan. Cut in squares and remove. Sprinkle with powdered sugar. Cookies keep well in covered tin and remain chewy.

MRS. GEORGE W. REYNAUD

Variation:
Vanilla may be used instead of maple flavoring, the squares cut larger and served with whipped cream or ice cream for an excellent dessert.

MRS. LAURENCE SIEGEL

EASY CHOCOLATE BROWNIES

4 squares unsweetened
  chocolate (4 ounces)
⅔ cup salad oil
2 cups sugar
4 eggs

1½ cups flour
1 teaspoon double acting
  baking powder
1 teaspoon salt
1 cup chopped pecans

Set oven at 350° and grease large, oblong pan. Melt over hot water the chocolate and salad oil. Beat in sugar and eggs. Sift together and stir in the dry ingredients. Add nuts. Spread in pan; bake 35 to 40 minutes. A slight imprint will be left when top is touched lightly with finger. Cool slightly and cut into squares.

MRS. WRAY E. ROBINSON, JR.

CARAMEL SQUARES

1 stick butter
1 cup brown sugar
1 egg
1 cup sifted flour

1 teaspoon baking powder
1 teaspoon vanilla
Pinch of salt
1⅓ cups nuts

Set oven at 350° and grease 9″ x 9″ pan. Put butter and sugar in saucepan and stir over heat until very smooth. Cool. Add unbeaten egg. Sift in flour, baking powder and salt; add vanilla. Mix well until smooth. Bake 30 to 40 minutes. Cook before cutting in squares. Makes about 36 small cookie squares.

MRS. J. BURTON LEBLANC
MRS. PAUL B. WALKER
MRS. A. P. RABENHORST

CHOCOLATE BARS

1 cup shortening
½ cup brown sugar
½ cup white sugar
3 egg yolks
1 tablespoon cold water

1 tablespoon vanilla
2 cups flour
¼ teaspoon salt
¼ teaspoon soda
1 cup chocolate chips

Cream shortening and add sugars. Beat and add egg yolks; beat well. Add remaining ingredients. Line a large shallow ungreased pan with this mixture. Sprinkle with chocolate chips.

Meringue

3 egg whites
1 cup chopped nuts
1 cup brown sugar, packed

Beat egg whites stiff, and add brown sugar gradually. Spread this meringue over the butter. Sprinkle with chopped nuts. Bake in 350° oven for 25 minutes.

MRS. CHARLES E. BEADLES

CHEWEY NOELS

2 tablespoons butter or margarine
2 eggs
1 cup brown sugar, packed

5 tablespoons flour
1/8 teaspoon soda
1 cup chopped nuts
1 teaspoon vanilla
Confectioners' sugar

Set oven at 350°. Melt butter or margarine in a 9-inch square pan over low heat. Then take off stove.

Beat eggs slightly. Combine sugar, flour, soda and nuts, and stir into beaten eggs. Add vanilla. Pour this mixture over the butter or margarine. Do not stir. Bake 20 minutes. Turn out of pan onto rack; cut into oblongs and dust bottom side with confectioners' sugar. If you want to be fancy, you can write "Noel" across the top using any type of white frosting. Makes 18.

MRS. HUGH MIDDLETON

CHOCOLATE DROPS

2 squares baking chocolate
1 can condensed milk (14 ounce size)
1 teaspoon lemon juice
1/2 teaspoon vanilla

2 cups shredded sweetened coconut
1/2 cup or more chopped pecans

Melt chocolate over hot water. Remove from heat and add condensed milk. Stir and add lemon juice and vanilla. Add shredded coconut and pecans. Drop from a spoon on a very well oiled cookie sheet. Bake at 325° for 10 minutes.

MRS. GEORGE W. REYNAUD

COCONUT CRUNCH

3/4 cup butter or margarine
3 cups brown sugar, packed
1 2/3 cups flour, sifted
3 eggs, unbeaten

1 tablespoon baking powder
1 teaspoon salt
1 1/2 teaspoons vanilla
1 cup coconut
1 cup chopped pecans

Set oven at 350° and grease 9x12-inch pan. Melt butter; stir in sugar. Add all other ingredients. Bake 45 minutes. Cut in squares.

MRS. FRANK G. TURPIN

DATE COOKIES

3 egg whites
3/4 cup sugar

2 cups chopped dates
Pinch of salt
1 teaspoon vanilla

Beat egg whites until very stiff, adding sugar 1/4 cup at a time. Mix in the remaining ingredients. Have flour convenient on paper; roll a teaspoon of the mixture in the flour. Place on a greased cookie sheet and bake at 350° for 18 minutes. Let cool; remove from cookie sheet and roll in confectioners sugar. Store in a closed can.

MRS. FANNIE ROBINS

CINNAMON COOKIES

2 sticks butter
1 cup sugar
2 egg yolks
1 cup flour

½ teaspoon baking powder
4 teaspoons cinnamon
2 egg whites
1 cup chopped nuts

Set oven at 300°. Cream butter and sugar. Add egg yolks, flour, baking powder and cinnamon. Spread thin on an ungreased cookie sheet. Over this spread two egg whites stiffly beaten. Sprinkle with chopped nuts. Bake for 40 minutes. Cut in squares to serve.

From the recipes of the late
MRS. CLARENCE SLAGLE
By: Mrs. Chauvin Wilkinson

DATE LOAF SQUARES

1 pound pitted dates
1 cup boiling water
1 teaspoon soda
1 cup sugar
1 cup pecans

½ cup butter
1 egg
2 cups flour
1 teaspoon vanilla

Cut up dates in boiling water mixed with the soda. Cream sugar and butter. Add egg, flour, vanilla, and pecans. Add dates to creamed mixture. Bake in pyrex baking dish that has been well greased at 325° for 1 to 1¼ hours. Cut into squares when cool.

MRS. WILLIAM F. CHISHOLM

DATE TORTE

3 whole eggs
1 cup sugar
1 tablespoon cream
2 tablespoons soft butter
3 heaping tablespoons flour

1 teaspoon baking powder
1 package pitted dates
½ cup chopped pecans
(optional)

Mix ingredients in order given. Spread thin in buttered baking pans. Bake in moderate oven 350° for 30 minutes. Cut in squares while warm and serve with whipped cream.

MRS. JAKE DAMPF

HOLIDAY FRUIT COOKIES

1 cup shortening
2 cups brown sugar (firmly packed)
2 eggs
½ cup sour milk
3½ cups all purpose flour

1 teaspoon soda
1 teaspoon salt
1½ cups chopped pecans
2 cups halved candied cherries
2 cups halved dates

Mix well the shortening, brown sugar, and eggs. Add sour milk. Sift flour, soda, salt and stir in. Mix in pecans, cherries and dates. Chill. Heat oven to 400°. Drop with teaspoon 2 inches apart onto greased baking sheet. Bake 8 to 10 minutes. Makes several dozen.

MRS. L. C. KUTTRUFF

FRUIT CAKE COOKIES I

1½ pounds pecans
½ pound candied cherries
¾ pound box raisins
1 cup flour
1 cup brown sugar
¼ pound butter
4 eggs, beaten well
3 scant teaspoons soda

3 tablespoons milk
2½ cups flour
1 teaspoon each cloves, nutmeg, cinnamon
1½ ounces whiskey
½-1 pound jar pineapple preserves

Mix together pecans, cherries, raisins, 1 cup flour, and set aside. Cream brown sugar and butter. Add well beaten eggs. Dissolve soda in milk, and add alternately with flour and spices. Add whiskey, pineapple preserves, nuts, and fruits. Drop onto greased cookie sheet and bake at 350° about 12 minutes. Makes quite a large batch of cookies that store well in air tight containers.

THE EDITORS

FRUIT CAKE COOKIES II

1 cup brown sugar
¼ cup butter
½ cup wine
2 eggs
1½ cups flour, heaping
½ pound mixed cherries, citron, and pineapple
½ teaspoon allspice

½ teaspoon nutmeg
½ teaspoon cloves
½ teaspoon cinnamon
1 pound pecans, cut fine
1 pound raisins
2 teaspoons soda
1½ tablespoons milk

Cream butter and sugar; add wine and eggs. Add gradually one half of the flour. Use rest of flour on fruit mixture. Add the spices. Mix all together; add soda dissolved in milk, and mix in. Drop from spoon onto cookie sheet. Put pan of water under cookies and bake 30 to 40 minutes at 300°.

MRS. RICHARD HUMMELL

GOLDEN APRICOT BARS

⅔ cup dried apricots
½ cup soft butter
¼ cup sugar or confectioners sugar
1⅓ cups sifted flour
½ teaspoon baking powder

¼ teaspoon salt
1 cup light brown sugar (packed)
2 eggs, well beaten
1½ teaspoons brandy flavoring or vanilla

½ cup chopped walnuts

Rinse apricots, cover with water and boil 10 minutes. Drain, cool and chop. Mix soft butter with sugar and 1 cup sifted flour. Pack into layer, covering bottom of greased 8-inch square pan. Bake at 350° for 25 minutes. Sift remaining ⅓ cup flour with baking powder and salt. Beat brown sugar slowly into eggs, beating well after each addition. Stir in sifted flour mixture, flavoring, walnuts, and chopped apricots. Spread over baked layer. Return to oven and bake 30 minutes more. Cool in pan and cut in squares.

MRS. EDWIN CHUBBUCK through
MRS. LOUIS McHARDY

CANADIAN TEA CAKES
(Variation of Golden Apricot Bars)

Make pastry base same as for Golden Apricot Bars. Substitute 1 cup of coconut for apricots. Use 2 tablespoons flour in place of ⅓ cup flour. Proceed same as above. Ice with plain butter frosting of 1 tablespoon butter, ⅓ cup powdered sugar, vanilla, and just enough evaporated milk for spreading consistency.

MRS. D. M. BENTON, SR.

HONEY SCOTCH COOKIES

¼ pound butter	1 egg
½ cup sugar	¼ teaspoon vanilla
¼ teaspoon salt	¼ cup sugar
1¼ cup flour	1 teaspoon cinnamon

Cream butter and sugar; add yolk of egg, flour, salt, and vanilla. Roll thin on a floured board (if chilled, it is easier to roll). Cut in small circles; brush top with stiffly beaten egg white. Mix ¼ cup sugar and 1 teaspoon cinnamon and sprinkle in center of cookies. Bake on ungreased cookie sheet in 370° oven for 10 minutes or until brown. Watch closely. Makes about three dozen cookies.

MRS. LEO SANCHEZ

Variation of Honey Scotch Cookies

Same as above except substitute 1 teaspoon almond flavoring for vanilla and add about 2 tablespoons more flour. In place of rolling on board, roll in 1 inch balls. Dip these in egg whites. Place on ungreased cookie sheet and place unblanched almond in center. Bake in 350° oven until golden brown (about 10 minutes).

MRS. ELLIS TWILLEY

May be rolled in 1 inch balls and then pressed with bottom of glass which is covered with a wet cloth. Spread a little slightly beaten egg white on each and sprinkle with white sugar.

MRS. J. M. CADWALLADER

LEMON DROP COOKIES

½ cup butter	1 teaspoon baking powder
¾ cup sugar	¼ teaspoon salt
1 egg	½ cup finely crushed lemon
1 tablespoon lemon juice	drops
1½ cups sifted flour	

Set oven at 350° and grease cookie sheet. Cream butter and sugar. Add egg and lemon juice. Mix together the sifted flour, baking powder, salt and lemon drops. Add to creamed mixture. Drop by ½ teaspoonfuls onto greased pan. Bake about 10 minutes, until sides begin to brown. Cool slightly and remove from pan. Makes about three dozen cookies.

MABEL A. WHITE

GUM DROP COOKIES

1 pound orange gum drop
slices (chopped fine)
4 eggs

1 pound brown sugar
2 cups flour
1 cup finely chopped nuts

1 teaspoon vanilla

Set oven at 350°. Chop gum drops very fine with scissors, dipping them in a glass ¾ filled with flour whenever needed to prevent gum drops from sticking together again. This takes a good while to do, but the cookies are excellent.

Beat eggs, and then add brown sugar beating until fluffy. Add flour and beat again. Fold in chopped nuts and gum drops. The gum drops should be slightly floured if they aren't already from the cutting. Add vanilla. Bake 40 to 50 minutes; cool and cut. They can be rolled in powdered sugar, will keep a long time in air-tight tins.

MRS. JULIUS O'QUIN

LEMON MARDI GRAS SQUARES

1½ cups sifted flour
½ teaspoon salt
¼ teaspoon double acting
baking powder
3 eggs, separated
1 cup confectioners' sugar

½ cup butter
1 cup sugar
⅓ cup lemon juice
2 tablespoons grated lemon
rind

Frosting:

1 cup confectioners' sugar
1 tablespoon cream

2 tablespoons butter
Chopped nuts

Sift together flour, salt and baking powder. Beat egg whites until soft mounds begin to form. Add confectioners' sugar gradually, beating after each addition. Continue beating until stiff, straight peaks are formed.

Cream butter; add sugar, creaming well. Add egg yolks, one at a time. Beat for one minute. Add lemon juice alternately with dry ingredients to creamed mixture, beginning and ending with dry ingredients. Blend thoroughly. Add grated lemon rind. Fold in beaten egg whites gently but thoroughly. Pour into well greased and lightly floured 13x9x2-inch pan. Bake in 350° oven 25 to 30 minutes. Mix the frosting ingredients and frost in pan while warm. Sprinkle with chopped nuts.

MRS. HAROLD DAVIS

BROWN SUGAR MACAROONS

1 egg white
⅞ cup sifted brown sugar

2 cups chopped nuts
½ teaspoon vanilla

Set oven at 250° and grease cookie sheet. Beat egg white very stiff. Beat in brown sugar gradually. Fold in nuts and vanilla. Drop on cookie sheet and bake about 45 minutes. Hint: May be dropped on waxed paper over cookie sheet. When done pull paper off onto wet tea towel for a few minutes; then remove.

MRS. GORDON W. PEEK

Variation: Smith's Pecan Royale

Do not chop nuts, but leave in halves. Stir in as many as mixture will cover. Separate pecan halves on waxed paper over cookie sheet. Bake at 350° for 7 minutes only.

MRS. WILLIAM R. SMITH

BEACON HILL COOKIES

1 cup semi-sweet chocolate chips	½ cup sugar
2 egg whites	½ teaspoon vanilla
Pinch of salt	½ teaspoon vinegar
	¾ cup nuts

Set oven at 350° and grease cookie sheet. Melt chocolate chips over hot water. Beat egg whites with a pinch of salt until foamy. Gradually add sugar, beating well. Beat in vanilla and vinegar. Fold in chocolate and chopped nuts. Drop by teaspoonfuls on greased cookie sheet. Bake for 10 minutes. These cookies are better if served the day they are made. This makes about 3 dozens.

MRS. JOHN BARTON

MINCEMEAT HERMITS

1 cup sifted flour	⅓ cup dark brown sugar, packed
¼ teaspoon soda	1 egg
¼ teaspoon salt	⅔ cup mincemeat
¼ teaspoon nutmeg	½ tablespoon sour cream or buttermilk
½ teaspoon cinnamon	
⅓ cup soft butter	

Sift flour, soda, salt, and spices. Cream butter and sugar. Add egg and beat until light. Add dry ingredients, mincemeat and cream. Mix well. Drop by teaspoonfuls onto greased cookie sheets. Bake in 400° oven, 10 to 12 minutes. Remove to racks to cool.

MRS. BERT S. TURNER

OATMEAL MACAROONS

1 cup shortening	1⅔ cups flour
1 cup brown sugar	1 teaspoon soda
1 cup granulated sugar	1 teaspoon cinnamon
½ teaspoon vanilla	½ teaspoon nutmeg
2 eggs, unbeaten	3 cups rolled oats
½ cup nuts	

Mix thoroughly the shortening, sugars, vanilla, and eggs. Sift together the flour, soda, cinnamon, and nutmeg, and add to mixture. Fold in rolled oats and nuts. Drop by teaspoonfuls onto greased cookie sheet. Bake 10 to 15 minutes at 350°. Makes about four dozen cookies.

MRS. SAMUEL E. GUYER
St. Louis, Missouri

PUFFED WHEAT MACAROONS

2 egg whites   1/4 teaspoon salt
1/2 cup sugar   2 1/2 cups crisp puffed wheat
1/2 cup shredded coconut

Set oven at 325° and grease cookie sheet. Beat egg whites and add gradually sugar and salt, then puffed wheat and coconut. Drop by dessert spoonfuls onto cookie sheet and bake for 20 minutes. You will have about 2 dozen delectable tidbits.

MRS. PRESTON BARNES

PECAN BARS

Pastry base:

1/2 cup butter   1 1/4 cups sifted all purpose
1/4 cup sugar   flour
1 egg   1/8 teaspoon salt
1/2 teaspoon vanilla

Cream·butter and sugar until well blended. Beat in egg. Combine flour and salt and add these dry ingredients in about three parts to the butter mixture, blending them well. Add vanilla. Use dampened hands to spread the dough evenly in a 9x12-inch pan. Bake in moderate oven 350° for 15 minutes.

Filling for pastry base:

2 beaten eggs   2 tablespoons flour
1 1/2 cups brown sugar   1/2 teaspoon baking powder
1/2 cup grated coconut   1/2 teaspoon salt
1 cup chopped pecans   1 teaspoon vanilla

Combine ingredients; spread this on the cooked pastry base; bake at 350° for 25 minutes. When cool spread it with: 1 1/2 cups confectioners sugar thinned to a good consistency to spread with lemon juice. (Or you may use milk.) Note: Coconut may be omitted if 1 1/2 cups nut meats are used.

MRS. LAURANCE BROOKS

SAND TARTS

1 cup butter or margarine   1 1/2 teaspoons baking powder
4 tablespoons powdered sugar   1/2 teaspoon salt
2 cups flour   1 tablespoon vanilla
1 cup finely chopped pecans

Cream butter and sugar. Sift flour and baking powder and salt. Gradually add flour mixture to creamed butter. Add vanilla and nuts. Drop in one inch balls on a greased cookie sheet, and then mash slightly flat. Bake in 375° oven until brown. If desired, roll in powdered sugar. Makes five dozen cookies.

MRS. HUGH A. NEAL

VARIATION OF SAND TARTS
OR
BROWN EYED SUSANS

Prepare sand tarts or sand cookies. Roll into balls. Place on greased sheet and flatten slightly. Bake in hot oven (400°) 10 to 12 minutes. Cool and frost in center of each cookie with following frosting. Top each cookie with blanched almond half.

Frosting

1½ cups confectioners' sugar   2 tablespoons hot water
2 tablespoons cocoa   ½ teaspoon vanilla

Combine sugar and cocoa; add hot water and vanilla.

MRS. HAROLD DAVIS

1 cup chocolate chips may be added to the dough and the pecans may be used to roll each cookie in.

MRS. WRAY E. ROBINSON, JR.

SHORTBREAD

¼ pound butter   ¼ cup brown sugar
7 tablespoons shortening   2 cups flour
¼ cup powdered sugar   Sugar
Nutmeg

Cream butter and shortening with sugar. Work in sifted flour. Roll about ¼ inch thick; cut in shapes or sticks. Sprinkle with granulated sugar and a little nutmeg. Bake on an ungreased cookie sheet in 350° oven until light brown. Makes 3 to 3½ dozens.

MRS. H. C. McCALL

SCOTCH SHORTBREAD

2 cups sifted all purpose flour   1 cup butter
½ cup confectioners' sugar

Sift flour; cream butter; gradually work in confectioners' sugar, again creaming thoroughly. Sift in flour a little at a time, mixing quickly and lightly. Chill dough for about thirty minutes in refrigerator. Roll out dough to thickness of ½ inch (no thinner) on lightly floured board. Cut shortbread with deep cookie cutter and place cookies on ungreased baking pan. Prick surface of cookies with prong of fork. Bake five minutes at 325°, and then turn oven down to 300° or slow oven and bake 20 to 30 minutes longer. Cookies should be light in color, not brown at all—slightly tan on bottom. If seasoned for a week or so in covered tin box and stored in cool spot they become much better. Will keep indefinitely.

MRS. THOMAS M. MIXON II

SNICKERDOODLES

1 cup soft shortening	2 teaspoons cream of tartar
1½ cups sugar	1 teaspoon soda
2 eggs	½ teaspoon salt
2¾ cups sifted flour	2 tablespoons sugar
2 teaspoons cinnamon	

Set oven at 400°. Mix shortening, sugar and eggs together thoroughly. Sift flour, cream of tartar, soda, and salt together and add to above mixture. Chill dough. Roll into balls the size of small walnuts. Roll in mixture of 2 tablespoons sugar and 2 teaspoons cinnamon. Place about two inches apart on ungreased cookie sheet. Bake 8 to 10 minutes, until lightly browned, but still soft. (These cookies puff up at first then flatten out with crinkled tops.) Makes about five dozen 2-inch cookies.

MRS. GERALD W. MIDDLETON

PIES

CARAMEL CANDY PIE

25-30 chewy caramels (light colored ones only)	2 teaspoons cornstarch
	Pinch of salt
2 cups milk	1 teaspoon vanilla
3 eggs	1 baked 9″ pie shell

Melt caramels in 1 cup of milk in top of double boiler. Beat egg yolks well and add to 1 cup milk and cornstarch. When caramels have melted, mix with egg mixture, adding salt. Return to top of double boiler to heat and cook until thick, stirring constantly. When thickened, add vanilla and pour into baked pie shell. Top with meringue or whipped cream.

MRS. HAROLD ·KNOX

DEEP DISH APPLE PIE

⅓ cup cinnamon candies (red hots)	½ cup sugar
	½ teaspoon nutmeg
½ cup sugar	⅓ teaspoon salt
½ cup water	1 tablespoon lemon juice
6 cups pared sliced apples	2 tablespoons butter
¼ cup flour	1 recipe for pie crust

Melt candies and sugar in water. Combine apples, flour, sugar, nutmeg, and salt. Add lemon juice to cinnamon syrup and pour over apples. Blend until apples are coated with syrup. Pour into 10″ deep dish pie pan or shallow baking pan. Dot with butter. Place a pastry crust over apples, trim edge. Seal by moistening edge of dish and pressing crust. Bake in hot oven 450° for 10 minutes, then in moderate oven 350° for 40 to 50 minutes or until apples are tender.

MRS. HUGH MIDDLETON

UPSIDE-DOWN APPLE-PECAN PIE

4 tablespoons butter	Juice of 1 lemon
⅔ cup brown sugar	⅓ cup brown sugar, firmly
⅔ cup pecans	packed
2 unbaked 9 or 10 inch	1 tablespoon flour
pastry circles	½ teaspoon cinnamon
6 cups sliced apples	½ teaspoon nutmeg

¼ teaspoon salt

In a 9″ or 10″ pie plate (1) spread evenly butter and brown sugar which have been combined; (2) arrange pecan halves in design, pressing into sugar; (3) cover with plain pastry, trim, leaving ½″ hanging over all around. Filling: Combine all dry ingredients with apples and lemon juice. Pile on pastry, leveling as much as possible. Cover with second crust. Fold bottom crust over top crust wetting edge of top as you go. Flute edges and prick top crust. Bake at 450° for 10 minutes. Reduce to 350° and bake 30-45 minutes longer. When syrup in pan stops bubbling, place serving plate over pie and invert. Remove pie plate. Serve with vanilla ice cream.

Mrs. Kenneth Kahao

CHESS PIE

1 tablespoon flour	6 egg yolks
1 rounded tablespoon	2 cups sugar
cornmeal	1 cup milk
½ cup softened butter	Juice of ½ lemon

2 uncooked 10″ pie shells

Mix flour and meal well. Add softened butter, beaten egg yolks and sugar. Mix well. Add milk and lemon juice slowly. Pour into 10″ pie shell which has been prepared by pricking bottom of uncooked pastry shell and rubbing mixture of 1 teaspoon flour and 1 teaspoon sugar into holes. (This prevents crust from becoming soggy.) Bake shell 10 minutes to 300°. Then add filling and bake 45 minutes at 350° or until filling is set. This will make two 9″ pies.

Mrs. Preston Barnes, Jr.

MAMMY'S LEMON CHESS PIE

¾ cup butter	Juice of three lemons
1 cup sugar	Grated rind of two lemons
5 whole eggs, separated	1 unbaked pie shell

Cream butter and sugar; add egg yolks and beat. Add lemon juice and grated rind. Fold in beaten egg whites. Pour into 9″ pie tin lined with unbaked crust. Bake about 30 minutes at 325° or until mixture sets and slightly browns.

Mrs. Floyd Williamson, Jr.

CHOCOLATE PIE

1 cup sugar	2 cups milk
⅓ cup cocoa	½ stick butter
⅓ cup flour	½ teaspoon vanilla
1 pinch salt	½ cup sugar
2 eggs, separated	1 baked pie crust

Mix dry ingredients in ¼ cup milk (make a paste); add egg yolks and whip together. Add balance of milk. Place on low heat and stir until mixture begins to boil. Add butter. Cool and pour into baked pie crust. Beat egg whites and add ½ cup sugar and vanilla. Place this mixture on top of pie and run under broiler until mixture is golden brown.

MRS. JAMES JOLLY

HERSHEY BAR PIE

6 small chocolate almond bars	½ cup milk
16 marshmallows	1 cup whipping cream

Melt above ingredients, except whipping cream, in double boiler and cool thoroughly. Beat whipping cream until stiff. Fold into above mixture. Pour into prepared cooked pastry crust or graham cracker (crushed) crust. Place in refrigerator until serving time. Can be made ahead of time and kept in deep freezer. Makes one 9″ pie.

MRS. R. E. (BERT) SMITH, JR.

BLACK BOTTOM PIE

1 tablespoon gelatine	3 eggs, separated
¼ cup cold water	1 tablespoon rum flavoring or vanilla
1½ ounces bitter chocolate	¼ teaspoon salt
1¾ cups milk	¼ teaspoon cream of tartar
½ cup sugar	¼ cup sugar
3 teaspoons cornstarch	

Soak gelatine in ¼ cup cold water. Melt chocolate over hot water. Scald milk. Combine ½ cup sugar and corn starch. Beat egg yolks until light. Add sugar and cornstarch to egg yolks; mix with scalded milk a little at a time and cook until thick. Remove from heat and take out one cup of custard. Blend in the melted chocolate. Pour into 9″ pie shell of crushed graham crackers or ginger snaps and chill. Dissolve soaked gelatine in the remaining custard. When cool, stir in rum flavoring or vanilla. Beat, until well blended, the three egg whites with salt and cream of tartar. Beat in gradually ¼ cup of sugar (just like a meringue). Fold egg whites into remaining custard and pour over chocolate in pie shell. Chill. Sprinkle top with a little grated chocolate.

MRS. W. D. FARR

FUDGE PIE

2 squares bitter chocolate
1 stick butter or margarine
2 eggs
1 cup sugar
¼ cup sifted flour

Melt chocolate and butter in double boiler. Mix flour and sugar. Beat eggs and combine with flour and sugar. Add chocolate and butter. Put in well greased 9″ pie tin and bake at 350° 30 to 45 minutes. Serve with topping of ice cream or whipped cream. Will cut into segments like a pie.

MRS. DUDLEY W. COATES

ROCKY ROAD CHIFFON PIE (CHOCOLATE)

1 package chocolate chiffon pie filling mix
1 cup scalded milk
¼ cup sugar
1 cup miniature or 10 large marshmallows, chopped
⅓ cup chopped pecans, optional
1 baked 8″ or 9″ pie shell, cooled

Place mix in a small deep bowl, about 1½ quart size. Add hot milk; mix well. Beat vigorously with rotary beater or at highest speed of electric mixer, or until filling stands in peaks (about 3 to 6 minutes). Add sugar slowly, while beating; beat a minute longer. Fold in marshmallows and pecans. Spoon into pie shell. Chill about two hours. Whipped cream may be added as a topping. A graham cracker pie shell may be used.

MRS. W. E. ROBINSON, JR.

CHRISTMAS PIE

1½ cups finely ground Brazil nuts (about ¾ pound unshelled)
3 tablespoons sugar
1 envelope unflavored gelatine
¼ cup cold water
1½ cups scalded milk
3 eggs, separated
¼ cup sugar
⅛ teaspoon salt
½ cup thinly sliced candied cherries
2 tablespoons white rum
¼ cup sugar
½ pint whipping cream
¼ cup Brazil nut meats

Combine 1½ cups ground Brazil nut meats (use food grinder) with 3 tablespoons sugar. Press to bottom and sides of 9″ pie pan up to rim with back of spoon. Bake at 400° 8 minutes or until lightly brown. Meanwhile soak gelatine in cold water 5 minutes. Scald milk in double boiler. Beat egg yolks; and add ¼ cup sugar, salt; slowly stir in milk. Cook in double boiler over very hot water until it coats spoon. Remove at once from heat and stir in gelatine thoroughly. Cool. Chill until it mounds when dropped from spoon; beat smooth with egg beater. Add cherries and rum. Beat egg whites until they peak; add slowly ¼ cup sugar. Then add to custard. Pour into cooled pie shell; chill. Whip cream and cover pie. Shave or grind ¼ cup Brazil nuts over pie. *"Spoon onto each plate any crust that crumbles off when pie is cut—it's too good to waste."*

MRS. W. FLOYD WILLIAMSON, JR.

COCONUT PIE

4 tablespoons butter (½ stick)
3 tablespoons flour
⅞ cup sugar

3 eggs, separated
½ cup milk
½ teaspoon vanilla
1 cup flaked coconut

Melt butter over low heat. Stir in mixed sugar and flour, egg yolks, and milk, blending well. Cook slowly until thickened. Immediately stir in ⅔ cup coconut and vanilla. Cool to lukewarm. Top with meringue made from the three egg whites and sprinkle remaining ⅓ cup coconut on top. Bake 325° about 20 minutes or until golden brown. The filling will be a bit thin in the crust but is too rich to be thicker. Serves 6 or 7.

MRS. LAURENCE SIEGEL

LEMON MERINGUE PIE

¾ cup sugar
2 tablespoons flour
2 tablespoons cornstarch
¼ teaspoon salt

1¼ cups hot water
2 lemons, juice and rind
3 eggs, separated
1 tablespoon butter

1 baked pie shell

Meringue:

3 egg whites
¼ teaspoon cream of tartar
6 tablespoons sugar

Mix first four ingredients in saucepan. Add hot water; cook over medium heat until mixture begins to thicken. Add lemon juice and rind. Mix well. Add slightly beaten egg yolks. Cook until mixture begins to bubble. Remove from heat; add butter. Cool and pour into cooled baked pie shell. Top with meringue. Bake in 350° oven for 15 minutes or until golden brown.

MRS. JOHN B. FRANCIONI, III

DEEP SOUTH LEMON PIE

5 egg whites
2 tablespoons sugar
1 can condensed milk
½ cup lemon juice

½ teaspoon yellow food coloring
1 baked graham cracker crust

Make graham cracker crust according to directions on box. Be sure to bake for eight minutes at 350°. Let cool. Reserve ½ cup crumbs for pie topping. Grate one tablespoon lemon rind and sprinkle on crust. Let stand while filling is being made. For filling, beat egg whites very stiff, adding sugar gradually. Mix in a separate bowl condensed milk, lemon juice and food coloring. When this is mixed well, fold into stiffly beaten egg whites. Pour mixture into graham crust, sprinkle with ½ cup graham crumbs. Keep refrigerated. This pie may also be frozen for future use.

MRS. G. W. COURTER

ORANGE PIE

1 package orange gelatin	Juice of 1 orange
1 cup boiling water	Juice of 1 lemon
½ cup sugar	1 can evaporated milk
⅛ teaspoon salt	1 package vanilla wafers

Dissolve orange gelatin in boiling water. Add sugar and salt. Chill in freezing tray until it begins to set; then add orange and lemon juice. Chill evaporated milk in freezing unit until it begins to freeze. Remove and whip until stiff; add to above mixture and place in pie plate lined with well pulverized vanilla wafers. Chill until set. Garnish with whipped cream and orange slices.

MRS. KIMBROUGH OWENS

FRESH PEACH PIE

6 medium sized peaches	1 cup sugar
1 9″ unbaked pastry shell	2 tablespoons melted butter
2 beaten eggs	

Peel peaches and cut into halves. Place in pastry shell, cut side up. Mix sugar, melted butter, and beaten eggs. Pour over the peaches. Bake in 425° oven for 30 minutes.

MRS. ALBERT L. McQUOWN

PECAN PIE

¼ cup butter	Pinch of salt
⅞ cup sugar, scant	4 whole eggs
1 tablespoon flour	1 cup broken pecan meats
1½ cups white corn syrup	1 teaspoon vanilla
1 unbaked pastry shell	

Cream butter. Add sugar and flour gradually and cream until fluffy. Add syrup. Beat well. Add salt and eggs, one at a time. Beat thoroughly. Add broken pecans and vanilla. Bake 350° about 50 minutes or until set. If crust gets too brown around edge, cut out a circle of foil and place over it.

MRS. THOMAS P. ROBERTS

PECAN PIE

3 tablespoons butter	1 cup dark corn syrup
1 cup sugar	1 cup pecans
3 eggs	1 teaspoon vanilla
1½ tablespoons flour	1 unbaked pie crust

Cream butter and sugar. Add remaining ingredients and pour in unbaked pie crust. Bake at 450° for 10 minutes and lower to 350° and cook for approximately one hour.

MRS. JOE M. MacCURDY

PECAN PIE

1 cup brown sugar	3 eggs, beaten
2 tablespoons flour	¼ teaspoon salt
1 tablespoon butter	1 teaspoon vanilla
1 cup light corn syrup	1 cup pecan halves

1 unbaked pie shell

Cream butter with mixed sugar and flour; add syrup and eggs. Beat until frothy. Add salt, vanilla and pecan halves. Pour into 9″ unbaked pie shell. Bake 40 minutes at 325°.

MRS. JOHN J. SEIP

PUMPKIN PIE

1 cup granulated sugar	2 eggs
½ teaspoon salt	2 or 3 teaspoons Pumpkin Pie
1½ cups canned pumpkin	Spice
1 large can evaporated milk	1 unbaked 9″ pie shell

Mix ingredients until smooth. Place in unbaked 9″ pie shell and bake in hot oven, 425° for 15 minutes. Lower temperature to moderate oven, 350°, and continue baking about 30 minutes longer or until custard is firm.

MRS. LOUIS I. TYLER, JR.

RUM PIE

2 cups milk	1 tablespoon butter
½ cup sugar	3 tablespoons rum
⅛ teaspoon salt	Whipped cream for topping
3 tablespoons flour	Grated chocolate for trim
1 egg yolk	

Scald 1 cup milk. Mix sugar, salt, flour and remaining milk together. Stir into hot milk. Cook over hot water five minutes. Add slowly to beaten egg yolk. Cook one minute longer. Add butter and rum. Cool. Pour into graham cracker crumb shell. Top with whipped cream and grated chocolate.

MRS. DAVID THOMAS

STRAWBERRY SHORT PIE

1 recipe of pie crust for a two crust pie	1 recipe hard sauce
	2 pints strawberries, sliced and sugared

Line a 9″ pie pan with uncooked pie crust and roll remaining crust on a cookie sheet. Bake both in a 450° oven until golden brown. Remove from oven, dot pie shell with hard sauce, add berries, dot again, then add another layer of berries. Cover with top crust and serve while hot.

MRS. BRYAN LUIKART

STRAWBERRY GLAZE PIE

1 quart strawberries
1⅓ cups water
1 cup sugar
3 tablespoons cornstarch
1 cup heavy cream, whipped

1 tablespoon confectioners'
  sugar
⅛ teaspoon nutmeg
9″ baked pie shell, cooled

Wash and hull berries. Mix 1 cup berries, 1 cup water and sugar together. Bring to boil quickly, then reduce heat and cook gently 15 minutes. Mix cornstarch and remaining water to form paste. Then add to the cooked strawberries. Cook over low heat stirring constantly until thick and clear. Strain and cool. Beat cream until stiff. Gently stir in confectioners' sugar. Spread half of whipped cream in bottom of pie shell. Sprinkle with nutmeg. Put 3 cups of the hulled berries on top of cream. Pour over glaze. Chill for 3 hours. Just before serving spoon on remaining whipped cream over glazed strawberries. Yield—8 servings.

MRS. D. V. CACIOPPO

TAFFY TARTS

2 cups light brown sugar
2 large eggs

1 tablespoon vanilla
1 tablespoon butter

Mix all ingredients until very creamy. Divide and pour into one dozen pastry shells which have been made in large muffin tins. Bake for 10 minutes at 350°; reduce heat to 275° and bake until crust is a golden brown.

MRS. G. W. COURTER

YAM PECAN PIE

1958 LOUISIANA YAMBILEE PRIZE WINNING RECIPE

Pastry:

1½ cups sifted all purpose
  flour
½ teaspoon salt
3 tablespoons water
½ cup shortening

Sift flour and salt into a bowl. Take out ¼ cup flour and blend with water to form a paste. Cut shortening into remaining flour until the pieces are the size of small peas. Add flour paste to blended shortening and flour mixture. Mix with a fork until the dough comes together and can be shaped into a ball. Roll out crust ⅛″ thick and line 9″ pie pan.

Custard:

1 cup mashed sweet potatoes,
  cooked or canned
⅓ cup brown sugar
¾ teaspoon cinnamon

¾ teaspoon ginger
Dash salt
¾ cup scalded milk
2 eggs, well beaten

Combine sweet potatoes, brown sugar, cinnamon, ginger, salt, milk

and eggs. (If fresh sweet potatoes are used, add ⅓ cup granulated sugar.)
Cool and fill pie shell. Bake at 375° for 20 minutes. Sprinkle with topping.

Topping:

¼ cup butter or margarine,   ½ cup brown sugar
   softened   ¾ cup pecans, finely chopped

    Combine ingredients. Continue baking for an additional 25 minutes.
Serve with whipped cream when cool.

ANN COIT
Winner of 1958 Yam Cooking Contest

CANDY

APRICOT BALLS

1 pound dried apricots,
    ground fine
¼ cup orange juice

Grated rind of one orange
1½ cups sugar
1 cup nuts, finely chopped

Cook all ingredients except nut meats in double boiler 30 minutes, stirring often. Add nut meats. Cook 5 minutes more. Cool. Form into small rolls or balls and roll in powdered sugar. If first sugar is absorbed too much, sift more over the balls later.

MRS. EMILY BLAKE

BUTTERMILK CANDY

2 cups sugar
1 cup buttermilk
¼ cup butter (½ stick)
½ teaspoon soda

2 tablespoons white corn
    syrup
A lot of pecans
1 teaspoon vanilla

Mix and heat over medium heat in a large pot until it comes to a boil and thickens. Set off heat and add vanilla. When lukewarm, beat until thick as for fudge. Pour out into buttered plate. *This candy turns a rich brown before your eyes!*

MRS. LEON KENYON

OLD FASHIONED DATE LOAF

3 cups sugar
1 cup milk

1 package dates, chopped
2 cups chopped pecans

Put sugar and milk into sauce pan and cook until mixture forms a soft ball when dropped in a cup of cool water (238°). Remove from heat and add chopped dates. Beat until dates are melted well into sugar. Add chopped pecans. Pour out in a long strip on a cold wet cloth and gradually fold cloth over and over shaping roll with your hands until candy is in a long loaf form. Let chill for about an hour or until thick enough to cut into slices.

MRS. JAMES H. HUGUET
MRS. PRESTON EGGERS

FRENCH COCOA BALLS

1 cup cocoa
3 cups powdered sugar
2 cups finely chopped nuts

1 cup condensed milk
2 teaspoons vanilla
2 tablespoons cocoa

2 tablespoons powdered sugar

Mix cocoa and sugar well. Blend into milk. Add nuts and vanilla. Mix well. Roll into small balls. Then roll balls in the cocoa and powdered sugar.

MRS. NAVEN O. COUVILLON

FUDGE

4 cups sugar	3 level tablespoons butter
¾ cup water	(unmelted)
¾ cup milk	⅛ teaspoon salt
½ or ⅓ cup cocoa	1 teaspoon vanilla

1½ cups nuts (broken)

Boil sugar, water, milk, cocoa, and butter without stirring to 238°F., or until mixture forms soft ball in cold water. Remove from heat and let stand undisturbed until lukewarm. Add salt, vanilla, and nuts. Beat well (until it begins to lose its gloss) and turn quickly into a buttered pan and cut into squares.

MRS. PERCY DOHERTY

CHOCOLATE DROPS

Fudge balls	½ pound bitter chocolate

⅓ scant teaspoon shaved cocoa butter

Using Mrs. Percy Doherty's Fudge recipe—instead of cutting into squares, pour onto a kneading board. Knead well; if it is too hard, wet hands and bring it together. Make it into balls the size of a walnut. Place on waxed paper. Melt cocoa butter and bitter chocolate in top of double boiler. When 85° F. on candy thermometer, or barely melted, take off stove. With a fork, dip each ball into chocolate; then drop into iced water. When all are dipped, take them out and wipe off with clean cloth. Wrap each candy in wax paper.

MRS. PERCY DOHERTY

KENTUCKY COLONELS

1 box confectioners' sugar	Bourbon
¼ pound butter	1 pound bittersweet chocolate
1 tablespoon undiluted	¼ block parawax
evaporated milk	Pecans (halves)

Combine in mixing bowl the sugar, butter, and milk. Shape by hand this fondant into balls about the size of a small English walnut. With the little finger, shape a cavity into this ball of fondant, making sure the sides and bottoms of the ball are not broken. With a medicine dropper, fill the cavity with bourbon—do not fill too full—pinch top together (extra fondant may be used to seal cavity) (bourbon must not spill out). Melt bittersweet chocolate with parawax over hot water. Chocolate mixture must be deep for dipping fondant balls. Place a bourbon-filled fondant ball on a fork and dip into melted chocolate. Remove from fork and place pecan half on top.

MRS. THOMAS R. DRISDALE

CHOCOLATE FUDGE TURTLES (5 Pounds)

4½ cups sugar
1 8-ounce can evaporated
　milk
3 packages chocolate chips

5 ounces marshmallow creme
½ pound butter
1 pound chopped nuts
2 teaspoons vanilla

Stir sugar and evaporated milk together. Bring to boil and boil gently for 9 minutes. Remove from heat and add chocolate chips, butter, marshmallow creme, and vanilla. Beat until blended and until chocolate bits are melted. Add nuts. Pour into buttered pan. Cut when cold.

MRS. J. L. HOCHENDEL

MAMA'S MINTS (FONDANT)

1 cup water
2¼ cups sugar
½ stick butter

6 drops of oil of peppermint
　(from drugstore)
Food coloring

Boil water and add sugar and butter. Boil until mixture spins a thread ("hard-crack stage"). Pour out on greased slab of marble. Add 6 drops of oil of peppermint and a few drops of green, yellow or red food coloring. Let cool only long enough so that you can pick it up with greased fingers (candy will still be hot). Work fast by pulling as for taffy. When candy toughens and starts turning silvery, twist and cut with scissors. Put cool mints in can containers and they will "cream" overnight. *This is my grandmother's old fashioned pulled mint recipe.*

MRS. J. H. BENTON

PEANUT BRITTLE

2 cups sugar
½ cup white corn syrup
¼ cup boiling water

2 cups raw peanuts (do not
　remove red hulls)
1 teaspoon baking soda

Put sugar, corn syrup, and water in large heavy iron pot and let come to a boil (use medium heat throughout). Add peanuts when mixture starts to boil. Cook until peanuts start popping and smell parched and syrup is medium brown in color, about 20 minutes. Remove pot from heat, immediately add baking soda. Stir and quickly pour on a well buttered large cookie sheet. Do not beat. Let cool and break in small size pieces.

MRS. FRED G. HOCHENEDEL, JR.

GLAZED PECANS

1 cup shelled pecans　　　　　¼ cup sugar
　　　　　Dash of salt

Put pecans, sugar, and salt in a large heavy skillet. Cover over medium heat, stirring the mixture constantly. Cook sugar-nut mixture until sugar melts and turns a rich, golden color. Transfer nut mixture to waxed paper and let cool slightly. Separate nuts.

MRS. LOUIS I. TYLER, JR.

NUT BUTTER CRUNCH

2 sticks butter (one-half may
  be margarine)
1 cup sugar

2 tablespoons water
1 tablespoon light corn syrup
½ cup chocolate chips

⅔ cup finely chopped nuts

Melt butter over low heat in pan. Add sugar and stir until melted. Add water and syrup. Continue cooking over low heat until syrup, dropped in cold water, becomes brittle (320° F.). Don't undercook. Remove from heat. Pour onto greased platter. This should be thin. Cool until hardened. Melt chocolate over hot water. Spread on crunch. Sprinkle nuts over top and pat in. Break into pieces. *This is quite similar to a Heath bar. You must hide it if you expect it to last at all!*

MRS. LAURENCE SIEGEL

ORANGE CANDIED PECANS

1¼ cups sugar
2 tablespoons white corn
  syrup
1 pinch cream of tartar

Juice and grated rind of 1
  orange
2 cups pecans

Mix all of the ingredients, except pecans, and cook to soft ball stage. Beat. Then add pecans; stir until pecans are well coated. Spread out on paper and separate.

MRS. P. CHAUVIN WILKINSON

ORANGE PECANS

2 cups light brown sugar
½ cup sweet milk

1 tablespoon vinegar
Grated rind of 2 oranges

1 pound pecan halves

Combine sugar and milk in saucepan. Add vinegar. Boil until it forms a soft ball in cold water. Pour mixture over pecan halves. Add grated rind and stir until nuts are coated.

MRS. J. W. C. WRIGHT

PRALINES

2 cups confectioners' sugar
1 cup maple syrup

½ cup cream
2 cups nut meats

Boil powdered sugar, maple syrup and cream together until a little dropped in cold water forms a soft ball. Remove from heat and beat until creamy. Add nut meats and drop from spoon into patties on waxed paper.

MRS. JAKE DAMPF

OLD FASHIONED PECAN PRALINES

2 cups brown sugar   1 cup water
1 cup white sugar   1 cup cream
                3 cups pecans

Combine sugar, cream and water in a sauce pan and cook to soft ball stage (238°). Remove from heat and beat until creamy. Add nuts and drop by spoonfuls onto buttered sheet.

THE EDITORS

LOUISIANA CARAMEL PRALINES

2 cups white granulated   1 or 2 teaspoons vanilla
  sugar   2½ cups chopped pecans
1 cup evaporated milk   (these may be toasted)
1 cup granulated sugar   2 tablespoons butter

Place 2 cups of sugar and milk in a large saucepan. Cook slowly, stirring often. At same time put other cup of sugar in another saucepan on low heat; stir until melted. Pour slowly into the milk and sugar that should be ready to boil; stir while adding. Cook slowly until a firm ball will form when dropped into cold water (238°). Set off the heat. Add vanilla, pecans, and butter. Beat or stir until this begins to thicken. Drop by spoonfuls as small as desired on wax paper. Should set up immediately.

MRS. C. E. PHILLIPS

RICH PRALINES

2½ cups granulated sugar   3 tablespoons butter or
1 teaspoon baking soda   margarine
1 cup buttermilk   2⅓ cups pecan halves
¼ teaspoon salt   ⅔ cup perfect pecan halves

Use large pan (8 quarts) and mix first four ingredients. Put candy thermometer in place. Cook over high heat 5 minutes or to 210° F., stirring frequently and scraping bottom. Add butter and 2⅓ cups nuts. Cook, stirring continuously and scraping bottom and sides of kettle, until a little mixture in cold water forms a very soft ball (about 5 minutes or to 230° F.). Remove from heat. Stand by while mixture cools slightly—just a minute or two. Then beat with spoon until thickened and creamy. Immediately drop by tablespoonfuls onto waxed paper, aluminum foil, or greased cookie sheet. Dot with ⅔ cup pecan halves.

MRS. WARREN MUNSON

TAFFY (OLD FASHIONED PULL)

3 cups sugar   2 tablespoons vinegar
¾ cup water   1 teaspoon butter

Cook until it forms a hard ball in a cold glass of water. Then take off stove and pour into a pan with 1 teaspoon butter spread in it. Soon as you can handle it grease hands slightly and pull until it becomes white and hard. Stretch into long ropes. When hard, chop into short pieces with a knife. It is best to pull with just your fingers if possible. This should be stored a day to soften.

THE EDITORS

PRESERVES AND RELISHES

APPLE CHUTNEY FOR INDIA CHICKEN CURRY

1 cup water
5 tablespoons sugar
3 tablespoons vinegar
½ teaspoon allspice
¼ teaspoon salt
1 teaspoon dry mustard

1 whole ginger root
6 tart apples, pared and
    cut in small pieces
1 green pepper, cut in small
    pieces
½ cup seedless raisins

Mix in sauce pan and boil for 5 minutes the water, sugar, vinegar, all-spice, salt, dry mustard, and ginger root. Add apples, pepper, and raisins and simmer for 45 minutes. Chill. Serve as condiment for curry.

MRS. J. H. BENTON

BEET MARMALADE

3 pounds peeled beets,
    julienned
1 pound honey

1 pound sugar
¼ pound sliced blanched
    almonds

White ginger, to taste

Cook noodle-like strips of beets in just enough water to cover, over slow fire. Strain when tender; add honey. Stir over slow heat until boiling. Add sugar, almonds and ginger. Cook until very thick and beets begin to turn brown. Seal in sterile jars or keep in refrigerator. Makes about 2 pints.

NOTE: If beets begin to darken before mixture is thick enough, remove beets and boil syrup a few minutes by itself. Canned julienne beets drained may be substituted. Juice can then be boiled briefly with lemon juice, brown sugar and salt to taste, and then cooled for beet soup to be served with sour cream and cut-up green onions, cucumber, radish and hard cooked eggs.

MRS. ALVIN RUBIN

BREAD AND BUTTER PICKLES

1 gallon cucumbers, sliced
    very thin
10 medium or 20 small onions,
    sliced very thin
2 green peppers (one red
    makes it pretty), sliced
    very thin

½ cup salt
2 trays ice
5 cups vinegar
5 cups sugar
½ teaspoon tumeric
½ teaspoon ground cloves
2 tablespoons mustard seed

1 teaspoon celery seed

Place the thinly sliced cucumbers, onions and peppers in a large container; sprinkle with salt; add ice and cover. Let stand 3 hours. Drain well. Add remaining ingredients. Place over low heat; keep turning pickles over until mixture reaches the scalding point. *Do not boil.* Bottle while hot in hot jars. Seal. Let stand 48 hours before eating. Yields 8 pints.

MRS. JEAN FREY FRITCHIE

CAULIFLOWER RELISH

2 tablespoons flour
1 teaspoon dry mustard
¼ teaspoon tumeric
1 cup cold water
¼ cup sugar
2 teaspoons salt
⅓ cup cider vinegar
⅛ teaspoon black pepper
½ teaspoon celery seed

⅛ teaspoon garlic powder
1 teaspoon whole mustard
  seed
2 cups small cauliflower
  clusters (raw)
½ cup onion rings
Pimento strips, enough to
  make relish colorful
Whole red peppers, to taste

Combine in 2-quart pot the flour, mustard, tumeric. Add water slowly and make a paste. Add sugar, salt, pepper, vinegar, celery seed, garlic powder, mustard seed and mix well. Stir in cauliflower and onions and bring to a boil. Cook 2 minutes. Add pimentos and red peppers and stir. Seal in sterile jars to keep indefinitely or let stand over night (at least) for immediate use. *Serve cold with sliced ham, turkey, or chicken. Good for Christmas giving!*

MRS. ROBERT SINGER

HORSERADISH SOUFFLE

1 package lemon gelatin
1 teaspoon salt
1 tablespoon vinegar

½ pint whipping cream
1 bottle horseradish
Parsley

Dissolve gelatin according to directions; add salt and vinegar. When partially set, whip the cream and add it with the horseradish. Pour into a mold and allow to set. Unmold and garnish with parsley. *This is very good served as a relish with almost any meat, or it can be served on lettuce as a salad. It tastes and looks much better than it sounds.*

MRS. EUGENE McCRORY

PEAR RELISH

4 quarts pears (after they
  are peeled and ground)
2 quarts onion (4 pounds)
8 green bell peppers
2 red bell peppers
12 dill pickles

1 cup salt
2 hot peppers
8 tablespoons sifted flour
4 cups sugar
2 tablespoons tumeric
6 tablespoons dry mustard

2 quarts dark vinegar

Grind pears, peppers, onions and dill pickles. Add salt and let stand ½ hour. Drain well. Mix dry ingredients and add some of vinegar to make smooth paste. Then add rest of vinegar to the paste. Stir and boil for five minutes. Turn off heat and add ground pears, peppers, onions and pickles. Let stand 3-5 minutes. Pour into jars while hot.

THE LATE MRS. J. M. CADWALLADER

CRANBERRY RELISH

1 pound cranberries	1 cup nuts
1 large orange	2 cups sugar

Wash cranberries. Peel orange, section and remove seeds. Put cranberries, orange sections, orange peel and nuts through food chopper. Add sugar. Mix thoroughly. Let stand 30 to 40 minutes. Pour into jars and cover, or store in covered dish in the refrigerator several days before serving. Keeps indefinitely. *This is an excellent substitute for cranberry sauce. Very good with pork.*

THE EDITORS

PEAR JAM

2½ pounds cooking pears	¾ cup drained crushed
1 orange	pineapple
1 lemon	5½ cups sugar

Peel and core pears. Grind pears, orange and lemon (including the rinds) using coarse blade of chopper. Add pineapple and sugar. Stir well. Heat to boiling point. Cook 20 minutes, stirring occasionally. Pour into hot sterilized jars. Makes 9 six-ounce jars or glasses.

MRS. T. P. ROBERTS

PEPPER-ONION RELISH

24 bell peppers	2 scant cups sugar
6 onions	3 tablespoons salt
3 cups vinegar	1 teaspoon celery seed

1 teaspoon mustard seed

Grind bell peppers and onions; cover with boiling water and let stand five minutes. Drain. Boil together vinegar, sugar, salt, celery seed, mustard seed. Add pepper-onion mixture. Simmer 15-20 minutes. Put in jars and seal.

MRS. TED DUNHAM, SR.

TOMATO RELISH

12 green tomatoes	4 quarts boiling water
6 tablespoons salt	1 quart white vinegar
24 green peppers	3 cups sugar
6 red peppers	1 teaspoon each of celery
12 large onions	seed, cinnamon, and allspice

Cut tomatoes up fine; add salt and let stand for 1 hour. Drain. Put peppers and onions through a coarse food chopper; pour over 2 quarts boiling water. Drain off at once. Pour over 2 quarts more of boiling water and let stand 10 minutes; then drain. Add tomatoes, vinegar, sugar and spices. Let come to boil and cook 30 minutes. Put into jars and seal.

MRS. THOMAS P. ROBERTS

NANNY'S RIPE TOMATO PICKLE

Chop:

1 gallon ripe tomatoes	1 quart onions
1 gallon cabbage	½ dozen red peppers (hot)
½ dozen bell peppers (red)	

Add:

1 cup salt—mix, let drain 2 hours

Boil:

2 quarts vinegar	2 teaspoons tumeric
6 cups sugar	1 tablespoon celery seed
2 teaspoons ground mustard	1 tablespoon ground cloves
2 teaspoons ginger	1 tablespoon cinnamon

Add chopped ingredients. Cook until thick. Put in sterile jars and seal.

MRS. P. M. SMITH, JR.

WATERMELON RIND PICKLES

Rind from 1 large melon	3¾ pounds sugar
(Usual yield—7 pounds)	1 quart vinegar
Lime water (about 1 cup lime	Cloves
juice and 2 gallons water)	Cinnamon sticks (1 package)

Select melon with deep rind. Remove all green rind and pink meat. Cut remaining rind into one-inch squares. Soak this over night or at least 8 hours in lime water. Drain fruit and place in preserving kettle. Cover with water and boil until easily pierced with a broom straw. This usually takes about 2 hours. Drain and cool fruit and stick each piece with a clove. Dissolve sugar and vinegar and add one package of stick cinnamon. Boil 5-10 minutes. Add fruit. Cook until rind is spotted. (About 2-2½ hours.) You may have to make more juice, using same proportion of 3¾ pounds sugar to 1 quart vinegar, as fruit takes up some of juice. If necessary, cook extra juice about 20 minutes, boiling. Place in jars while hot and seal. Makes about 10 pints.

MRS. IVY MORRIS

PARTY FOODS

In South Louisiana "that demitasse of café noir" may well be the center of many a mid-morning get-together, whether it be neighbors dropping in for a cup of coffee or planned outings for larger groups. Morning coffees are one of our most popular parties.

ANCHOVY COCKTAIL BISCUITS

1 3-ounce package soft cream   1 stick butter
  cheese   1 cup flour
Anchovy paste

Mix cream cheese, butter and flour together. Store in refrigerator until well chilled. Roll dough paper-thin. Cut round. Fill with anchovy paste and fold. Bake at 450° about 5 minutes. May be made ahead of time and stored, unbaked, in freezer.

MRS. ROBERT F. PARISH

CHEESE-ASPARAGUS CRISPS

1 pound New York State   1 loaf thin sliced fresh bread
  cheese   and round white hors
2 tablespoons mayonnaise   d'oeuvre picks
¼ teaspoon red pepper   1 large bell pepper, chopped
Horseradish to taste   fine
         1 can large green or white asparagus

Grate cheese and blend in mayonnaise, red pepper, and horseradish. Remove crusts from bread and spread cheese mixture thinly on bread slices; sprinkle with finely chopped bell pepper. Roll around asparagus stalks and fasten with picks. Toast under broiler until brown. (Do not toast too slowly, as cheese melts quickly.) Serve with cocktails, salad or in place of hot bread for luncheons. Makes 18 to 20. For cocktails, cut in half to make 36 to 40 small rolls.

MRS. ROY DABADIE

COCKTAIL PARTY CHEESE BALLS

1 pound sharp yellow cheese,   2 teaspoons Worcestershire
  grated   sauce
¼ pound Roquefort or Bleu   2 teaspoons onion, grated
  cheese, crumbled   Cayenne pepper
½ pound soft cream cheese   ½ cup pecans, chopped
         ½ cup parsley, chopped fine

Have cheeses at room temperature. Place in electric mixer and blend well. Add Worcestershire sauce, onion and pepper. Chill thoroughly in refrigerator. Form into balls. Mix pecans and parsley on waxed paper. Roll cheese balls in this mixture until completely covered. Place on attractive tray surrounded by assorted crackers. Serves 20 to 25 people.

MRS. H. PAYNE BREAZEALE

CHEESE OLIVE BALLS

1 pound sharp cheese, grated
1 cup flour
Red pepper to taste
Garlic to taste

Worcestershire sauce to taste
Large jar medium sized
   stuffed olives

Grate cheese on coarse end of grater. Let grated cheese soften at room temperature until consistency of butter. Add flour and seasoning, working into a dough. Press mixture around olives and bake on greased baking sheet for 10 minutes at 400°. Serve hot.

MRS. JACK HERGET

CHEESE AND WALNUT BALLS

1 cup Cheddar cheese, grated
2 tablespoons flour
½ teaspoon salt
½ teaspoon chili pepper

Pinch of oregano
Few drops of Tabasco
1 egg white, beaten
Walnuts, chopped fine

Mix together the cheese, flour, salt, chili powder, oregano, and Tabasco hot sauce. Fold in egg white. Form into small balls and roll in walnuts. Chill and fry in deep, hot fat until brown. Serve on hors d'oeuvre picks. Makes 2 to 3 dozen.

MRS. A. J. NOLAND

CHEESE ROUNDS

1 stick butter
2 cups grated sharp cheese
   (Cracker barrel or
   Wisconsin)

1 cup flour
1 teaspoon salt
Tabasco or red pepper to
   taste

Blend ingredients together. Divide mixture into 2 balls, then work each ball into long roll about one inch thick. Wrap in wax paper and chill. Slice very thin. Put whole pecan half on top of each. Place on ungreased baking sheet and bake at 350° for 10 to 15 minutes. Makes about 100 rounds.

MRS. MATT G. SMITH

GARLIC CHEESE ROLLS

½ pound sliced pimento
cheese, grated, or ½ pound
processed cheese and 2
pimentos, chopped and
drained

1 pound grated American
cheese
9 ounces soft cream cheese
3 buds garlic, grated
2 medium onion, grated

1 teaspoon salt

Mix ingredients well. Shape into 4 rolls about diameter of a cracker. Roll in paprika and wrap in waxed paper. Chill for a day. Slice thin and use on toast rounds or crackers.

MRS. HANSEN SCOBEE

CHEESE STRAWS

1 cup butter
2 cups grated sharp Cheddar
   cheese

2⅔ cups sifted flour
Dash red pepper
¼ teaspoon salt

Mix ingredients together well. Roll thin and cut in narrow strips. Bake in slow oven, 275°, until light brown. Makes about 4 dozen.

MRS. W. FLOYD WILLIAMSON, JR.

CHICKEN TURNOVER

3 sticks margarine
3 cups sifted flour
3 3-ounce packages soft
   cream cheese

1 flat can chicken
1 can mushroom soup
Paprika

Prepare pastry by mixing together margarine, flour and cream cheese; chill. Roll thin and cut into 2 inch rounds. Put dab of chicken mixed with mushroom soup on rounds and fold over. Press edges with a fork and prick pastry. Sprinkle with paprika before baking. Bake in 400° oven for 20 minutes. Yields about 200 small turnovers. These turnovers may be frozen before or after baking.

MRS. IRA WOODFIN

CHILI CON QUOTIS

2 large onions, chopped
1 bud garlic, chopped
¼ cup salad oil
1 tablespoon Worcestershire
   sauce

3 tablespoons chopped green
   chili peppers
1 pound processed cheese
1 No. 2 can red tomatoes,
   drained and chopped

1 tablespoon cornstarch

Sauté onions and garlic in oil. Add peppers and Worcestershire sauce. Melt cheese in top of double boiler; add to cheese the chopped tomatoes along with onion mixture. Add cornstarch, stirring until thick. Serve hot in chafing dish. Dip with corn chips.

MRS. J. M. CADWALLADER

CREAM CHEESE DIP

3 8-ounce packages soft
   cream cheese
½ cup mayonnaise
¼ cup milk
½ medium onion, grated

1½ tablespoons Worcester-
   shire sauce
1 teaspoon red pepper sauce
¾ teaspoon salt
¼ piece green bell pepper,
   grated

Mash cheese and make smooth by adding milk and mayonnaise. Add seasonings. Serve with waffle potato chips or corn chips. This will serve crowd of 45.

MRS. EGI FASCE

CHILI ROLL

¾ pound processed cheese
1 3-ounce package soft cream
  cheese
2 pods garlic, minced
¼ teaspoon salt

¼ teaspoon onion juice
¼ teaspoon Worcestershire
  sauce
⅛ teaspoon red pepper
¾ cup finely chopped pecans

About 1½ jar chili powder

Have cheeses at room temperature; mash processed cheese and add cream cheese, blending together. Add all other ingredients, excluding chili powder and pecans. Mix well and stir in pecans. Roll mixture into 4-inch rolls, approximately 1½″ in diameter to fit round crackers; roll each in chili powder. Place in refrigerator or freezer. When using from freezer, allow 1½ hours for thawing. Slice and serve on round crackers.

Mrs. A. E. McGrew

DEVILED HAM DIP

1 jar pimento cheese spread
½ cup mayonnaise

2 tablespoons deviled ham
1 teaspoon grated onion

Have all ingredients at room temperature. Blend together in electric mixer or with a fork. *Serve with potato chips or flowerettes of cauliflower.*

Mrs. P. J. LeBlanc, Jr.

FIESTA DIP

1 8-ounce package soft cream
  cheese
2 tablespoons of cream
3 tablespoons of French
  dressing

⅓ cup catsup
1½ tablespoons grated onion
½ teaspoon salt
Red pepper sauce to taste

Soften cream cheese and add remaining ingredients, blending until smooth. Very good with raw celery, cauliflower and corn chips. Will serve 10 to 12 persons.

Mrs. Dwight Martin

SHRIMP DIP

2 pounds boiled shrimp,
  coarsely ground
1 8-ounce package soft cream
  cheese
Juice of one lemon

10 green onions, minced
Mayonnaise
Hot sauce, Worcestershire
  sauce
Salt, pepper to taste

Soften cream cheese with lemon juice. Add shrimp and green onions to cream cheese mixture. Add enough mayonnaise to give a consistency for dipping potato chips or crackers. Season with hot sauce, Worcestershire sauce, salt and pepper. Much better if made 8 hours prior to serving time. Add more seasonings if necessary. Serves 15 generously.

Mrs. Don R. McAdams

DIP FOR SHRIMP

1 tablespoon salad mustard
1 tablespoon catsup
1 tablespoon mayonnaise
About 1 cup salad oil, chilled
Hot sauce, 2 or 3 drops

Salt, pepper
½ teaspoon Worcestershire
sauce
Juice of ½ lemon or little less

Combine mustard, catsup, and mayonnaise and beat with fork or wire whip. Add cold salad oil very, very slowly (the secret to thickening the dip), beating constantly. Add oil until thickened. Stir in all seasonings, mixing well. Enough for 3 pounds of shrimp.

THE EDITORS

HOT SWISS 'N CIDER DIP

½ pound Swiss processed
cheese, diced
1½ tablespoons of flour
1½ cups sweet apple cider or
apple juice
Dash of garlic salt

½ teaspoon salt
⅛ teaspoon pepper
¼ teaspoon nutmeg
1 tablespoon parsley or
chives, finely chopped

Sprinkle diced cheese with flour. Heat cider to boiling point, then reduce heat to simmer. Add floured cheese, gradually stirring until all cheese is melted. Add seasonings. A good zippy dip used with toasted French bread wedges or potato chips. Serves about 15.

MRS. PRESTON BARNES, JR.

DEVILED OYSTERS

9 dozen oysters (3 pints),
drained
1 large onion, chopped fine
1 small bell pepper, chopped
fine
3 cloves garlic, chopped fine
1 rib celery, chopped fine
1 stick butter
1 teaspoon salt
½ teaspoon mustard

½ teaspoon red pepper
½ teaspoon black pepper
1 tablespoon Worcestershire
sauce
Juice of 1 lemon
1 loaf French bread
2 eggs
½ cup milk
½ cup chopped parsley
½ cup chopped green onion
tops

Sauté the onion, bell pepper, garlic and celery in butter in a large skillet. Grind oysters on large blade in meat grinder and add to mixture in skillet. Add seasonings, bring to boil. Remove from heat and cool. Toast bread and roll into crumbs. Add to oyster mixture. Beat the eggs in the milk and add to oyster mixture. Mix in parsley and onion tops. If serving as individual entree, place in ramekins, top with bread crumbs. Bake in 400° oven for 20 minutes. If serving as casserole, top with bread crumbs and place in 375° oven for ½ hour. If serving as hors d'oeuvre, place in chafing dish and serve with crackers. Serves 8 to 10 as entree. Serves 30-40 as hors d'oeuvres. Other deviled oyster recipes are found in Seafood Section.

MRS. ALEXIS VOORHIES

DEVILED HAM PUFFS

1 8-ounce package soft cream
  cheese
1 egg yolk, beaten
1 teaspoon onion juice
½ teaspoon baking powder

Salt to taste
¼ teaspoon horseradish
¼ teaspoon hot sauce
24 small bread rounds
2 2¼-ounce cans deviled ham

Blend together the cheese, egg yolk, onion juice, baking powder, salt, horseradish and hot sauce. Toast the bread rounds on one side. Spread the untoasted sides with deviled ham, and cover each with a mound of the cheese mixture. Place on a cookie sheet and bake in a moderate oven (375°) for 10 to 12 minutes, or until puffed and brown. Serve hot.

Note: These can be made ahead of time and placed in a freezer. Remove and allow to thaw before baking as above. If in a hurry, Melba Toast (plain or rye) in rounds or oblongs may be substituted for the bread rounds.

MRS. RALPH DUFF

EGGPLANT CAVIAR

1 large eggplant
1 large onion, chopped
1 green pepper, chopped
1 bud garlic, crushed
  2 tablespoons dry white wine

½ cup olive oil
2 fresh tomatoes, peeled
  and chopped
Salt and pepper to taste

Put a whole eggplant in a 400° oven and bake until soft, (about one hour.) Sauté onion, garlic and pepper and olive oil until tender but not brown. Peel and chop eggplant; mix with tomato; add to sautéed seasoning. Add salt and pepper to taste. Add dry white wine. Mix everything thoroughly and continue to cook gently until the mixture is fairly thick. Cool, then place in refrigerator. *Serve well chilled with pumpernickel or thin pieces of ice box rye bread.*

MRS. WILLIAM R. SMITH

LOBSTER IN CHAFING DISH

2 or 3 small lobster tails,
  boiled and cut in small
  pieces
3 tablespoons butter
1 can sliced mushroom caps
1 tablespoon flour
½ pint heavy cream
  2 egg yolks, slightly beaten

1 can shrimp, drained and
  cut in small pieces
Salt, black pepper, nutmeg
  to taste
⅓ cup sherry wine
1 tablespoon Parmesan
  cheese

Melt 3 tablespoons butter in pan and sauté lobster and mushrooms for 5 minutes. Sprinkle in flour and stir. Add cream. Add shrimp. Season with salt, pepper, nutmeg, sherry and cheese. Add egg yolks slowly to prevent curdling. Place in chafing dish and allow to thicken. If necessary, can be thinned with cream. Serve on melba toast rounds.

MRS. FRANK JORDAN

PICKLED MUSHROOMS

3 medium onions	½ teaspoon celery seed
¾ cup water	½ teaspoon mustard seed
¾ cup vinegar	1 tablespoon salt
½ teaspoon leaf marjoram	Few drops hot sauce
¼ teaspoon whole cloves	½ pound fresh mushrooms

¼ cup olive oil

Cut onions in ½-inch slices and cook in water, vinegar, and spices for 5 minutes. Add mushrooms and cook 5 minutes longer. Remove mushrooms and add olive oil to remaining liquid and onions. Bring to boil and pour over mushrooms. Let stand for 3 hours or longer and serve as hors d'oeuvre or salad.

MRS. WILLIAM BAILEY SMITH

OLIVE ROLLS IN BACON

Large olives stuffed with pimento, pecans, or anchovy	Bacon slices Parsley

Roll each olive in piece of bacon and fasten with hors d'oeuvre pick. Place in wire basket and fry in deep hot fat at 375°. Arrange in circle on platter and garnish with parsley.

Bon Appétit

STUFFED ONION CANAPÉ

4 large white or yellow onions	⅓ pound highly seasoned fresh sausage

½ box frozen meatless dressing

Boil onions until soft; cook sausage very crumbly and add to thawed dressing. When onions are cool, separate layers. Fill each "leaf" lengthwise with dressing and fold over; will have the appearance of 2 cigarettes placed side by side. Store in refrigerator until ready to serve. Run directly under broiler to brown and heat through. This makes about 40 to 50 sticks.

MRS. WILLIAM T. BAYNARD

PARTY MIX

1 package Cheerios	1 tablespoon garlic salt
2 packages Rice Chex	1 tablespoon celery salt
1 box "Slim Jim" stick pretzels	½ teaspoon red pepper
¾ pound butter	2 tablespoons Worcestershire sauce

Salted nuts

Break pretzels in half. Pour cereals into large roaster and sprinkle with salt and garlic salt. Melt butter with red pepper and Worcestershire sauce and pour this over mixture. Cover and bake at 250° for 1 hour, stirring every 20 minutes. Remove cover and bake 30 minutes longer. Mix in any kind of salted nuts. Cool and store in airtight containers. This will keep indefinitely.

MRS. F. M. ROBERTS

SHRIMP BALLS

1 pound shrimp, boiled and cleaned	¼ cup celery, finely diced
3 tablespoons cream cheese	2 tablespoons green pepper, finely diced
1 tablespoon chili sauce	1 hard cooked egg, chopped
1 teaspoon Worcestershire sauce	1 tablespoon onion, grated
2 teaspoons horseradish	1 tablespoon parsley
	¾ teaspoon salt

Dash of black and cayenne pepper

Chill shrimp. Then mash very fine with fork or blender. Add all other ingredients and mix well. Roll into small balls, size of large marbles. Roll lightly in finely chopped parsley. Chill. Makes 2½ dozen.

MRS. J. H. BENTON

PICKLED SHRIMP

2 to 2½ pounds raw shrimp	2 large bay leaves
15 to 20 whole allspice	2 pinches dried or 1 sprig fresh thyme
6 to 8 peppercorns	Several sprigs parsley
⅛ teaspoon black pepper	Few bits dried red pepper
Juice of ½ lemon and rind	1 tablespoon Worcestershire sauce
15 to 20 cloves	4 medium onions, sliced thin
6 buds garlic, sliced	Box of bay leaves
3 small onions, sliced	
2 large stalks of celery, crushed or broken	

Season 2½ quarts of water with 3 tablespoons of salt; then add above ingredients except the shrimp, 4 onions and box of bay leaves. Bring to a boil and allow to simmer 20 minutes. Add shrimp and bring to boil again; simmer 12 to 15 minutes. Cool and devein shrimp. In a large pan arrange the shrimp in layers with 4 medium sized onions sliced thin and the bay leaves. Pour over each layer the following sauce (all ingredients being combined):

1¼ cups salad oil	2½ tablespoons capers and juice
¾ cup warmed white vinegar	Dash of hot sauce
1½ teaspoons salt	¼ cup Worcestershire sauce
2½ teaspoons celery seed	

1 tablespoon yellow mustard

After pouring sauce over shrimp, onions and bay leaves, cover pan and store in refrigerator not less than 24 hours. *Will keep a week or more. When serving, arrange the entire mixture on large platter. Have cocktail picks handy. Nice with crackers. This is worth the time it takes.*

MRS. JOHN SUTTON

SWEDISH MEAT BALLS

6 pounds ground meat (beef with approximately ¼ pork)
6 slices stale bread, soaked in milk
3 whole eggs, beaten
Garlic salt, black pepper, salt

½ cup parsley, finely chopped
½ cup green onion tops, finely chopped
2 medium white onions, finely chopped
4 stalks celery, finely chopped

Sauce:

2 large cans barbecue sauce

2 cans mushroom soup

Mix ingredients and roll into bite-size balls. Fry in small amount of fat. Pour off excess fat and mix barbecue sauce and mushroom soup in remaining drippings. Pour over meat balls which have been placed in large saucepan and simmer 40 to 45 minutes. Makes between 400 and 450 meat balls.

MRS. J. B. ESNARD

WALNUT BOURBON BALLS

2½ cups (5 dozen) finely crushed vanilla wafers
2 tablespoons cocoa
1 cup confectioners' sugar

1 cup finely chopped walnuts
3 tablespoons white corn syrup
¼ cup bourbon

Confectioners' sugar, sifted

Mix well the wafer crumbs, cocoa, sugar and nuts. Add corn syrup and bourbon. Blend well. Form into one-inch balls (in diameter). Roll each of these in the sifted sugar. Makes about 3 dozen.

MRS. LANCASTER COLLENS

HOW MEN COOK

And this is precisely how these men cook! We give to you their recipes—untouched—just as they gave them to us. To standardize would have wasted their wording; to edit would have lost their charm. To change them in any way would be unfair, and so the wording, the methods, as well as the recipes themselves are how men cook!

HOT APPETIZERS

Do they ring a gustatory bell? Maybe so, but groans from the hostess-cook because a hot appetizer means a separate course. Oh well, why be so practical! So let's be bold and start the meal off with something a little different. Well, here they are, and please try them out on the family before "Company night."

STUFFED MUSHROOMS

The problem here is to find the mushrooms. I recommend the large canned mushrooms, because the fresh article is too hard to find in the South and often dried up. Remove the stems and dig a nice niche for stuffing. Then sauté mushrooms in butter; if you like, add a *clove of garlic to butter* for flavor. Lump crab meat is admirable substitute for oyster, but let's use the bivalve. Cut up oysters and mushroom stems, and add to sautéed minced shallots, along with *2 tablespoons minced parsley*. If you wish, pitch in a little *breadcrumb-Parmesan cheese* mixture. Cook all for a spell; then further bind with an *egg*, or better still, a *white sauce* to which *sharp Cheddar cheese* has been added. Stuff mushrooms, crumb, and put under broiler for browning. Serve with or without extra cheese sauce at table, depending on how dry and rich the remainder of dinner will be. I'd suggest $\frac{1}{3}$ to $\frac{1}{2}$ *bunch of shallots* (tops and all), *2 tablespoons parsley*, to 2½ *dozen oysters*. This, with the other ingredients, will fill the *large can of about 17-18 mushrooms* which are at least one inch in diameter. Some are larger. Serve about 3 to a person.

ERNEST GUEYMARD

OYSTERS OLGA

This little number can be thrown together ahead of time and stored. I won't give proportions here, just a general idea. Naturally, you first make a *roux*, and for goodness sake, use *creamery butter*. Sauté *green onions*, add *oyster water*, and if needed a little additional *water or broth;* cook a little while, then add *oysters* and *boiled artichoke bottoms* that have been cut up, along with scrapings from leaves and seasoning to taste. Cook all about 10 minutes. Then drop this insipid looking goo in pastry shells, ramekin size, cover with *buttered bread crumb-Parmesan cheese mixture,* and place in hot oven for browning. If you plan to serve two dinner wines, serve this first course, naturally, with a dry white wine, and, voilà, your guests should scrape their plates.

ERNEST GUEYMARD

BOUILLI

Of course, in French this means "boiled" but foodwise it denotes "boiled beef." For this, use best brisket obtainable and boil, with all seasoning and vegetable ingredients, as if making soup. (Save soup and serve at later date.) Trim fat from meat before serving and drain. Serve hot with tomato-horseradish sauce.

ERNEST GUEYMARD

OMELET

1 tablespoon green onions, chopped fine	2 eggs
1 teaspoon parsley, chopped fine	Salt and pepper, to taste
Butter	½ cup drained small green peas

Sauté green onions and parsley in sauce pan with butter. Heat peas with this mixture. Put salt and pepper in eggs and beat well. Heat greased 8-inch black skillet (not too hot) and pour in eggs. When eggs have cooked through (not hard), sprinkle with onions and parsley mixture and green peas. Fold over and serve at once on hot plate.

JOE MICHAEL

VEAL BRUCCIALUNA AND TOMATO GRAVY

Gravy:

2 cans tomato paste	Parsley to taste
1 medium onion	2 teaspoons sugar
2 ribs celery	3 tablespoons fat or bacon drippings
3 cloves garlic	

3 cans water

Chop all vegetables fine, brown lightly in fat. Add water, sugar and salt and pepper to tomato paste. Cook over slow heat for 20-30 minutes. Add vegetables. I often add hard grated Italian cheese to gravy; add slowly, so it won't lump up.

Now start on meat dish.

Meat: However many pieces of $\frac{1}{4}''$ thick (or thin as butcher can slice) round steak you may need. Use pieces cut about 4" x 8"; have scraps ground coarse and save.

Ground meat	Parsley
Bread crumbs	Coarse grated Romano cheese
Eggs	Salt
Garlic	Pepper
Green onions	Fresh mint

Spread thin layer ground meat over round steaks, season with salt and pepper. Sprinkle grated cheese over ground meat. In a bowl, mix vegetables and eggs, not too soft, makes a rather firm sticky mess! Spread this mixture (pat in hands and lay on steaks, really can't spread the stuff) over steaks. Roll the steaks and tie securely (I make 4 ties on each piece,

don't want them to come unrolled or loosen enough to lose the dressing).
Brown, turning frequently. Put into gravy, cook long and slowly. Serve
with spaghetti, green salad, homemade bread, red Italian wine. The bruc-
cialuna is best made a day ahead of the time you intend to use it, and don't
skimp on seasoning. Everything absorbs some of the seasoning and it
usually turns out OK—if not, you have a day to "doctor" it up a bit.

JIM MARTIN

SUKIYAKI

Sukiyaki is the usual Japanese party or formal dinner. Translated
sukiyaki means, "I like it fried." The dish is, according to legend, said
to have originated in rural Japan where farmers prepared it on the blade
of a turned plow using meats and garden vegetables. Some of the present
ingredients of sukiyaki, such as tofu, are only available on the west coast
of the USA; however, a most enjoyable meal may be prepared using the
readily available components.

The *veal or beef* is boned and trimmed of fat. Using a 10 setting on
an electric meat slicer, butcher slices meat; and then the stacks of these
thin slices are cut to size of a strip of bacon, perhaps a little shorter and
wider. (When cooked this size is a mouth full.) About ½ *pound per person* is suggested. *Two small heads of cabbage per 4 people* are sliced
1 inch wide. *White onions, 8 per 4 persons*, are cut in 4-6 slices, and 2
bunches green onions per person are cut in 3-4 inch lengths including
green tops. *Soya sauce and sugar* are used for seasoning. *Whole canned
mushrooms*, 1 large can per 4 people, are optional. A hot plate, using
electric skillet at 250°-300° or a large frying pan and the atmosphere for
sukiyaki is established by sitting on the floor around a coffee table. Chopsticks are used instead of conventional silverware.

When skillet is warm, the bottom is greased with a piece of beef suet.
Then strips of meat are laid on bottom of skillet, and as frying begins,
mushroom water is poured into skillet to cover bottom and then *equal
handfuls of onions and cabbage* are added to make a heaping skillet full.
About *2-3 tablespoons sugar* are added, sprinkled over vegetables followed
by ½ bottle soya sauce. Allow to simmer or "stew" until done. More meat
may be added as well as other ingredients to suit demand. Mushrooms
are added after vegetables are almost cooked. More mushroom water or
plain water may be added, but usually water fom vegetables will suffice.
When finished cooking all reach into skillet with chopsticks and pick up
a mouthful of sukiyaki and hold it over a cup to cool, then bring to
mouth with cup under food particles to catch drip or dropped food. More
advanced sukiyaki eaters whip a raw egg in their individual cups and dip
each mouthful in egg before consuming. Second, third, etc. skilletfuls are
similarly prepared except after first batch there is a gravy remaining in
which the meat is started. Plain boiled rice is served with final dish and
the rice should be somewhat "gummy" to facilitate eating with chop sticks.
Sake (rice wine) is warmed and sipped from small jigger size cups during
meal.

JAMES W. LORIO, M.D.

CHINESE SWEET AND SOUR PORK

1 pound raw lean pork, 1"
chunks
1 cup sugar
1 cup vinegar, cider or wine
1 teaspoon salt
½ cup water

2 green peppers, ¼" slivers
2 tablespoons cornstarch in
½ cup water
1 small can pineapple chunks,
drained

Score all sides of pork with very sharp knife. Coat with mixture of egg and 2 tablespoons cornstarch. Deep fat fry light brown. Bring to boil in a saucepan the sugar, vinegar, salt, and water. Add green peppers and boil 1 minute. Stir in cornstarch and water and simmer 2 minutes (until thickened and translucent). Add drained pineapple chunks with pork. Stir until heated. Serve with steamed rice on the side. Individual servings are "salted" to taste with soy sauce.

FONVILLE WINANS

HOT TAMALES

2 pounds lean boneless pork,
or 1 3½-pound shoulder
butt or loin
4 tablespoons chili powder
4 tablespoons paprika
2 teaspoons ground comino
seed

1 teaspoon oregano
1 teaspoon cayenne pepper,
ground
2 teaspoons black pepper
1 teaspoon salt
4 cloves garlic, pressed,
mashed, or minced
1 cup stock

Cut pork in large 3" to 4" chunks and boil in two quarts of plain water for 45 minutes. Then remove bones and excess fat. Put through meat grinder. Reserve the stock. Add all the seasoning and 1 cup stock to the ground pork and mix well.

Paste Mixture:

1 pound tamalina
½ pound softened lard

4 teaspoons salt
2⅔ cups warm stock

Work lard well into tamalina by hand or mixer. Add salt, then add the stock, using electric mixer. This will make a thick paste, which is called "masa."

Soak 50 to 60 nice corn shucks for several hours in hot water, each trimmed to about 4"x6". The paste is applied with a table knife to the lower left hand corner of the shuck in an area about 2"x4" and about ⅛" thickness. Then about a tablespoon full of the pork mixture is applied along the center of this, like making a cigarette. Then the tamale is rolled up (like a cigarette) and the "empty" end of the shuck folded up alongside of the tamale. This wrapping is done rather loosely to allow for the eventual swelling of the masa when the tamales are steamed. The tamales are put in a steamer, on the steaming tier in bundles of 6, or placed side by side, so as to hold their shape. A canning type pressure cooker is good for the steaming operation, used as a steamer and not as a pressure cooker (just put the lid on and don't "seal" it). Steam over boiling water for 1 hour.

NOTES:

Tamalina (Mexican corn meal) and packaged corn shucks are available at Messina's Food Mart, 915 Decatur, New Orleans, in the French Market area. Keep refrigerated.

Shuck scraps boiled with the meat increase shuck flavor of tamales. Also shuck scraps in the steaming water are helpful flavorwise and also enhance the aroma of the kitchen. You will notice you have about 3 cups of stock left. Make a sauce for the tamales with this: Thicken the remaining stock with tamalina to a nice sauce consistency. This will take about 1 tablespoon tamalina for each 5 ounces of the stock or 5 tablespoons for 3 cups stock. Then stir in chili powder to taste (3 cups of stock will take about 2½ tablespoons of chili powder.) Add 1 teaspoon of salt, taste, then add more if desired.

Excellent "tamales" can be made with white corn meal, in which case the stock added must be scalding. The resulting "paste" should be thick but workable. Lacking cornshucks (which may be green as well as dried), many people use pieces of brown paper grocery bags, or parchment paper made for cooking. Some misguided souls even use banana leaves, which I don't think much of. I think grape leaves would work, however. The meat may be beef, or a mixture of beef and pork. Chicken is also used, in which case it would be desirable to cut down on the seasoning so as not to overpower the "chickeny" flavor. I have even made Shrimp Tamales with success. "Fancy" tamales are made by tying both ends, either with string or strips of corn shucks, in which case the shucks are buttered so as to leave end free of the paste. Another and quicker way to make tamales is to mix filling and paste together.

FONVILLE WINANS

Q'S CHARCOAL BROILED HAMBURGERS

3 pounds ground meat
Salt and pepper to taste
¼ cup cooking oil
3 tablespoons Worcestershire
  sauce
¼ cup catsup
¼ teaspoon curry powder,
  optional
2 or 3 pounds charcoal, regular or briquets
2 or 3 large hickory chips

Mix meat with salt, pepper, cooking oil, Worcestershire sauce, catsup and curry. Allow 3 to 4 patties per pound of meat. Pat out meat ½" thick and 5 or 6 inches in diameter. These patties may be made ahead of time and stored in the refrigerator. Use a plate to press meat into patties on waxed paper. Put charcoal in pile on grill and ignite. Allow fire to burn down slightly, usually 15 or 20 minutes. The fire will still be very hot. Add soaked hickory chips. Place patties on grill three to six inches above fire; cook 5 minutes. Do not turn too soon because meat might break apart. Turn patties and cook 3 minutes. If grill is uncovered, use water to keep fire from flaming. Makes 12 hamburgers.

CALVIN L. SIMPSON, II

BREAST OF CHICKEN KIEV

3 large chicken breasts
6 mushrooms, finely chopped
Butter
½ pound sweet butter,
   unsalted
1 clove garlic

2 tablespoons chopped
   parsley
Salt and pepper to taste
2 eggs
1 tablespoon vodka
Fine breadcrumbs

Debone 3 large chicken breasts and separate each in 2 halves. Place each half between waxed paper and flatten till they look somewhat like pancakes. Sauté the chopped mushrooms in about 1 tablespoon of butter for about 5 minutes. Cream together ½ pound sweet butter, minced garlic, chopped parsley, and the sautéed mushrooms. Chill in refrigerator, then shape into 6 rolls about 3 inches long and about 1 inch wide. Refrigerate again. Season flattened chicken breasts with salt and pepper. Place one of the refrigerated butterrolls on each of the chicken breasts and roll meat around butter roll, folding the ends in carefully so that the butter roll is encased. This is important, otherwise, butter will leak out as it melts. Secure rolled breasts with wooden toothpicks. Beat eggs with vodka and roll prepared chicken breasts in breadcrumbs, then in beaten eggs and in breadcrumbs again. Fry in plenty of not too hot butter until rolls are golden brown. Drain on paper towel and place in hot oven for about 5 minutes or until chicken meat is tender. Serve at once. Makes 3 servings.

KURT MICKLEY
City Club of Baton Rouge

TURKEY JAMBALAYA

2 tablespoons salad oil
1 cup green pepper, chopped
1 cup onion, chopped
1 clove garlic, minced
2 teaspoons salt
Pepper to taste
2 teaspoons (or more)
   Worcestershire

¼ teaspoon thyme or marjoram, or both
3 cups water
1½ cups uncooked rice
1 to 2 cups cubed cooked turkey or chicken
1 to 2 cups cubed cooked ham
1 small can mushrooms

Heat oil and cook green pepper, onion, and garlic until tender. Stir in seasonings and water and simmer for 10 minutes. Mix in rice, turkey, and ham. Cook covered over low heat for 25 minutes or until rice is done. Add mushrooms with a little of their liquid. Cook about 5 minutes longer. Serves 6.

HARRY BARTON

CHARCOAL BROILED BARBECUED CHICKEN

2 fryers, 2 or 2½ pounds
   each
Salt and pepper to taste

1 recipe of barbecue sauce
3 pounds charcoal briquets
3 or 4 hickory chips, optional

Halve fryers, either with knife or poultry shears. Salt and pepper chickens to taste. Make barbecue sauce and cool until slightly congealed. I use Mrs. George Simon's Chicken Barbecue Sauce. (See p. 158.) Build fire on covered grill and let it burn down until only a bed of good coals is evident. Place halves of chicken on grill 8 or 10″ above fire and "sop" with sauce. Turn chickens each fifteen or twenty minutes for 1½ to 2 hours. Soaked hickory chips may be added to the fire for the last 30 minutes to an hour for added flavor.

HUGH A. NEAL

STEWED CHICKEN

1 large fryer
Salt and pepper to taste
2 tablespoons shortening
2 tablespoons flour
2 medium onions, finely chopped

1 cup water
1 large bunch green onions, chopped
1 small bunch parsley, chopped
1 bay leaf

2 ribs celery, chopped

Cut chicken into serving pieces; salt and pepper to taste and place in a large sauce pan. Put shortening in a skillet; add flour, and brown well. Add onions and cook for a minute or two. Add water, stir well, and then add the green onions, parsley, bay leaf, and celery. Pour this mixture over the chicken. Cook chicken for 30 minutes or until tender over medium heat. Stir from bottom frequently to prevent sticking. Serve with steamed rice.

A. S. PAINE

SMOKED WILD DUCK OR TURKEY

Marinade:

2½ cups vinegar
2½ cups water
½ cup onion, chopped
1 lemon, sliced
½ teaspoon celery salt
½ teaspoon oregano

8 ducks or 1 turkey

3 bay leaves
3 cloves of garlic
6 whole black peppers
1½ teaspoon salt
Dash of hot sauce
Dash Worcestershire sauce

1 quart of your favorite barbecue sauce

Combine all of the marinated ingredients in a very large pyrex dish or crock. After thoroughly washing ducks put them in the marinade and store in refrigerator 24 hours or at least over night. The ducks should be turned several times. Cover with foil, if you prefer. When ready to start smoking the ducks, wipe very dry. Soak hickory chips in water over night if possible. This creates lots of smoke and gives a "woodsy" flavor. After starting your fire be sure the charcoal has burned down to a low even heat before putting the ducks on the spit. Add chips and charcoal as needed to keep the temperature at 300°. Place the ducks evenly on the spit so they will be balanced. The ducks should be placed on the opposite end from the fire. (The damper over the ducks should be opened to create a draft.) Baste occasionally with the barbecue sauce. The cooking time varies with the size of the duck but approximately 4 hours at 300°

is sufficient. The meat will be quite pink when done. Serve on a platter with "dirty rice." Serves 14 to 16 people.

When smoking a turkey follow the same procedure except do not marinate. Eight hours cooking time is usually required. A meat thermometer is a more accurate guide.

W. E. ROBINSON, JR.

WILD DUCK

Marinate over night or for several hours in a vinegar, salt and water solution.

When ready to cook, slit skin of breast and insert 2 strips of bacon between meat and skin. This keeps the meat moist and adds flavor. Salt and pepper bird. Stuff onion, celery, bell pepper into cavity. Brown well in iron pot; cover, let cook slowly until tender. Wine can be added to the soaking solution or to the gravy.

LOUIS MORGAN
New Roads, La.

WILD DUCK

4 whole ducks	½ bunch parsley, chopped
Bacon drippings	1 small can water chestnuts
2 cans consommé or bouillon	½ pound fresh mushrooms,
1 cup sherry or dry red wine	or 1 can
6 green onions, chopped	Salt and pepper to taste

Wash and dry ducks thoroughly. Rub inside and out with bacon drippings; salt and pepper to taste (coarse ground pepper). A small onion, a quarter section of apple and a rib of celery may be inserted in the carcass during cooking and removed before serving. Place in Dutch oven or roaster. Cover ducks with water to which has been added 1 can of the consommé or bouillon and ½ cup of the sherry or red wine. Cook at 300° until half the water has evaporated. Add second can of consommé and remaining sherry. Cook until ducks are completely tender.

Remove ducks from pan. Add green onions, half of the parsley, mushrooms, water chestnuts, and simmer until onions are cooked. Halve the ducks, and sprinkle with chopped parsley to serve. Serves 8.

In this recipe the ducks brown themselves in the long, slow cooking. A "Cajun" guide in the duck blinds gave this recipe to me.

CHARLES DUCHEIN, JR.

DUCKS

(Cookout in Woods)

Clean ducks. Get good fire going. Use heavy black iron Dutch oven with feet to keep it above flame.

Salt and pepper ducks. Place a piece of onion inside each one. Brown lightly in a little hot lard or salad oil. Pour off any excess fat. Add a little water. Cover pot. Turn and baste while cooking. When almost tender, add an ounce of sherry per duck. Add canned mushrooms and juice if available. Cook until tender. This will require at least two hours.

JOHN BARTON

VENISON ROAST
(Hind Quarter, 8-10 Pounds)

2 medium onions, sliced	1 cup red wine
1 heart and 3 ribs celery, chopped	1 dozen black pepper pods crushed
1 bunch (stem only) parsley	½ dozen cloves
1 cup water	½ dozen cracked allspice
1 cup vinegar	2 carrots, coarsely grated

Remove from the venison ham the covering membrane layer; bone if desired. Place in earthen container. Then mix together the carrots, celery, and parsley and marinate. Cover the roast with this; then top this with the sliced onions; add cracked pepper, cloves and allspice. Cover top of the onion with ½ teaspoon of cloves and 1 teaspoon allspice. Pour over the marinade the mixed wine, water and vinegar. Cover container with top or aluminum foil and place roast in refrigerator. Turn the roast every morning and evening for 5 days, basting well each time. The morning of the 6th day remove roast from the marinade and liquor and wipe with a dry cloth. Strain through a collander the marinade from the liquor and save both.

After drying the venison, lard about every 2 inches with a piece of salt meat. This should give you about 8 to 10 lardings to the ham. Larding is the cutting of a hole straight down into a roast with a knife and inserting into the hole first ¼ teaspoon salt, ⅛ teaspoon red pepper and ¼ inch thick salt meat.

Then sear roast in hot Dutch oven. Bake in oven with the top off at 325° until meat thermometer registers "done lamb." Remove venison from Dutch oven and add sufficient fat to sauté marinade. At this stage you can convert your roast gravy to sauerbraten or regular gravy.

If you prefer the regular roast gravy, you add to the sautéed marinade 3 bouillon cubes and 1 can of consommé, 1 can water. Bring to boil for 10 minutes. Strain this through a collander to remove marinade and serve gravy on sliced roast. If you prefer thicker gravy, you thicken it with a roux or cornstarch or cup of cream.

If you prefer sauerbraten gravy, then omit consommé and bouillon cubes and add to contents of Dutch oven enough of the liquor drained from the marinade to make as sour as you prefer. This also may be thickened in the above mentioned manner.   FRED A. BLANCHE, SR.

REMOULADE SAUCE

3 tablespoons horseradish	2 tablespoons paprika
½ cup hot mustard	4 stems parsley, chopped
3 cloves garlic, crushed	1 cup salad oil
1 large onion, chopped	Salt and pepper to taste
4 leaves celery, chopped	1 ounce Worcestershire sauce

Combine all ingredients and serve over boiled shrimp on shredded lettuce. This sauce may be refrigerated and kept for a period of time.

CHARLES BRANDT
Baton Rouge Country Club

SAUCE PIQUANTE

8 chickens, turtle, squirrel or rabbit
40 quail
8 kitchen spoons flour
1 quart oil
10 pounds onions, chopped
16 garlic cloves
6 bell peppers, chopped

6 small cans tomato sauce
15 to 20 pounds raw meat
2 cups water
1 fifth Burgundy or any dry wine
1 handful parsley
1 handful onion tops
3 or 4 bay leaves

Make a roux using flour and oil. Add onions, garlic and bell pepper. Cook until tender. Add tomato sauce. Cook about 35 minutes. Add approximately 15 to 20 pounds raw meat and water. When meat is tender, add a fifth of Burgundy or any dry wine. Let cook on slow heat for about 1 hour. Before serving, add a handful of parsley and onion tops and bay leaves. Let remain on fire until parsley curls.   EDGAR BECNEL
New Roads, La.

CRAWFISH BISQUE

Bisque:

¾ cup peanut or salad oil
¾ cup flour
3 cups fat
3 quarts hot water

¼ cup finely chopped green onion
¼ cup celery
Salt and pepper to taste

Into a skillet put the oil and flour. Make a brown roux. Strain 3 cups fat, saved in cleaning the crawfish. Add this to the roux. Then add the roux to 3 quarts hot water with green onion and celery. Bring to a boil and simmer. Add salt and pepper to taste.

Dressing:

3 cups crawfish tails
2½ cups bread crumbs
¾ cup parsley

1¼ cups chopped green onion
¼ stick butter
Salt and pepper to taste

Chop the crawfish tails, but do not grind. Add bread crumbs and parsley, green onion, butter, salt and pepper. Wet the dressing with some of the stock from the roux. Put the dressing in a heavy iron skillet with a little cooking oil and cook until the tails have turned pink. Then stuff the heads with this dressing. Roll heads in flour and fry or bake at 350° until brown.

Add another quart of water to the roux, together with a handful of crawfish tails and the stuffed heads, and simmer for ½ hour.

FRED A. BLANCHE, SR.

MARINADE SAUCE FOR SEAFOOD

¾ small jar Louisiana hot mustard
½ cup vinegar

¾ cup salad oil
2-3 teaspoons paprika
3 chopped green onions

Salt and pepper to taste

Mix all ingredients together and refrigerate before serving over boiled shrimp, crawfish, etc.

FRED A. BLANCHE, SR.

COURTBOUILLON

1 3- to 4-pound red snapper
  or redfish
6 to 8 tablespoons bacon
  drippings
6 to 8 tablespoons flour
2 large onions, chopped
1 bell pepper, chopped
½ bunch celery, chopped
2 cloves garlic, chopped
2 #2 cans peeled tomatoes or
  fresh tomatoes

2 small cans tomato paste
3 bay leaves
Stock saved from boiled fish
1 teaspoon allspice
Red pepper to taste
Worcestershire sauce to taste
Parsley
Salt and pepper
1 large can mushrooms,
  stems and pieces
1 cup olive oil

1 cup red wine

Tenderloin the fish. Boil bones and head. Save stock. Make roux from bacon drippings and flour. When dark brown add onions, bell pepper, celery, garlic, and sauté. When tender add tomatoes, tomato paste, bay leaves, stock and other seasonings. Simmer about one hour. Salt and pepper filets of fish. Put in Dutch oven and add sauce. Simmer on top of stove about ½ hour. Just before serving add mushrooms, olive oil and wine. Serve in soup bowls over rice. Serves 8. Note: Remove any fish left on bones and add to sauce. Do not break up filets any more than necessary while simmering.

ROY DABADIE

SHRIMP OR CRAWFISH FRICASSÉE

1 tablespoon crab boil mix
2 cups water
3 or 4 lemon slices, thin, cut
  up
1 10-ounce package frozen
  shrimp or as much as 1
  pound headless shrimp
½ cup flour
⅓ cup salad oil
⅔ cup shrimp stock

1 cup onion, diced
3 cloves garlic, minced, or
  garlic powder
⅛ teaspoon thyme
⅛ teaspoon cayenne
½ teaspoon black pepper
1 teaspoon salt
¼ teaspoon sugar
1 tablespoon parsley or onion
  tops, minced

Simmer the crab boil mix, water, and lemon slices for 15 minutes. Add shrimp; bring to boil, simmer 5 minutes. Drain, and save liquid. Peel. Save lemon slices. Make a roux in an iron skillet of the flour and oil. Stir over medium fire until dark brown. Add shrimp stock, onion, garlic, thyme, cayenne, black pepper, salt and sugar to the roux and cook slowly, stirring frequently until onions are very soft. If too thick add a little of remaining shrimp stock. Stir in peeled shrimp and heat. Mix in parsley or onion tops and heat. Serve with steamed rice or very fresh soft white bread. This makes 2 nice servings.

FONVILLE WINANS

SHRIMP CURRY

1 package crab boil
1½ quarts water
1 tablespoon salt
3 oranges, juice and some peeling
3 lemons, juice and some peeling
2 pounds shrimp, raw and headless
1 egg, beaten
4 tablespoons flour, rounded

4 tablespoons curry powder, rounded
1 teaspoon salt
½ teaspoon cayenne pepper
¼ teaspoon cinnamon, powdered
1 stick of butter or margarine, melted
2 cans fruit cocktail, juice and all
1 cup milk

⅛ cup shrimp stock

To prepare the shrimp bring crab boil, water and salt to boil; boil for 10 minutes, add orange and lemon juice and peeling. Add shrimp and bring to boil again; remove from heat and let cool; then peel and cut up. Don't throw away the stock. Stir the beaten egg into flour, curry powder, salt, cayenne pepper, and cinnamon; then add the melted butter. Stir in the fruit cocktail. This does well in the upper pan of a double boiler. Place the pan over the boiling water of the lower pan, stirring and blend in the milk. Add the shrimp stock, stirring all the while as the sauce reaches its nice consistency. Add more shrimp stock if sauce is too thick. Stir in the cooked shrimp, bring to heat and serve with rice.

FONVILLE WINANS
JOHN E. UHLER, JR.

An excellent amateur cook, John soaked up a little about curry cookery during a military stint in India. He undertook this culinary caper with such a show of confidence and know-how that my curiosity prompted me to take notes. This was fortunate. Now, whenever he brags about his curry and gets invited out to cook he has to wrangle me an invitation, too. He can't remember how he did it and he is above asking me for "his recipe."

FONVILLE WINANS

TURTLE STEW

3 pounds turtle meat
3 tablespoons cooking oil or lard
3 tablespoons flour
1 pound dry onions, chopped
2 cloves garlic, minced
2 No. 2 cans tomatoes
1 can tomato paste
Boiling water
1 rib celery, chopped fine
1 bunch green onions, chopped fine

2 bell peppers, chopped fine
1 cup sherry wine
½ dozen eggs, hardcooked
Red pepper to taste
Salt to taste
4 bay leaves
8 whole cloves
½ teaspoon allspice
1 tablespoon sugar
¼ pound butter
1 lemon, sliced

Parboil turtle meat. Make a brown roux of fat and flour. Add onions, garlic, tomato paste, and tomatoes. Cook slowly 20 to 30 minutes. Add to turtle meat. Add enough boiling salted water to cover meat. Boil down.

Add celery, green onions, peppers, wine, and seasoning. Cook covered over high heat for 30 minutes. Mash egg yolks; chop whites. Add to thicken stew. If stew gets too thick, add a little water. Cook slowly for about three hours. One half hour before serving add sliced lemon and butter. To increase amount add ½ pound turtle meat per person. Serves 6.

Hoo Shoo Too Club
Baton Rouge, Louisiana

CHARCOAL BROILED STEAKS

Steaks, any kind, sirloins,
tenderloins or filets
½ pound butter
1 lemon
Hot sauce

3 cans mushrooms, chopped
or sliced
White onions
Bell peppers
Tomatoes

Salt and pepper to taste

Prepare ahead of time lemon sauce by melting butter, juice of one lemon and the peel of ½ lemon and a dash of hot sauce. Just before ready to put on the meat, add mushrooms. Prepare to cook over fire at the same time that the steaks are cooking sliced large white onions, sliced bell peppers, and sliced tomatoes arranged in a wire grill that closes to hold them securely. When vegetables and steaks are ready, arrange them on a stainless steel platter or tray. Spoon mushrooms from the sauce over the steaks. Pour the remaining sauce over the vegetables. Return platter to the charcoal fire and bring to a boil. Remove from the fire and serve.

Tom Singletary

SUGAR STEAKS

1 4″ thick sirloin steak   Sugar
Salt and pepper to taste

(To prepare this steak, it is necessary to have an adjustable grill or a way to remove some of the coals at the appropriate time.)

Buy a 4-inch thick sirloin steak. It may weigh anywhere from 6-11 pounds but usually is about 10 pounds. Coat the steak heavily with sugar. Let stand for an hour, continuing coating during that time. Meanwhile, build a charcoal fire. Cook on a medium fire. Put the steak close to the coals. Cook 6 or 7 minutes on one side; turn, and cook 5 or 6 minutes on other side. (Both sides will flame.) Raise the grill or remove part of the coals. Continue cooking (no violent flames on steak now) for 25 minutes on each side. It will be medium rare. Salt and pepper to taste. Slice (a tray or platter with grooves and a well for the juice is especially nice) and serve. Serves 10 to 12.

Jimmie Boyce

CHATEAUBRIAND

CHARCOAL BROILED WHOLE TENDERLOIN OF BEEF

1 8-pound tenderloin	½ pound butter
Salt and pepper	½ lemon (juice and peel)
Monosodium glutamate	Dash of hot sauce
	3 cans mushrooms

Buy an 8-pound whole tenderloin. Salt, pepper and apply mono-sodium glutamate to taste. Cook over a medium charcoal fire for 1¼ hours. Decrease the heat by adding more coals and continue cooking another ½ hour. Total cooking time 1¾ hours. The tenderloin should be turned 3 times during cooking, at 40 minutes, at 1 hour and 5 minutes, and at 1½ hours. Have ready ½ hour before the meat's done the following lemon but-ter sauce: Melt butter, add lemon juice and peel of ½ of a lemon, and a dash of hot sauce. Just before ready to put on meat, add mushrooms to sauce, may be whole, sliced, mixed, or chopped.

Vegetables:

3 cans whole new potatoes	2 cans asparagus
2 cans whole tiny onions	3 cans small whole carrots

One half hour ahead prepare the vegetables: Place opened cans in pots of boiling water and heat vegetables through. Place the meat when done on a stainless steel platter and slice in ½″, or better, thick slices. Drain all the vegetables and arrange around the meat. Spoon the mushrooms over the meat. Pour the remaining sauce over the vegetables. Return the platter to charcoal fire and bring to a boil. Remove from fire and serve. Serves 9 to 10.

TOM SINGLETARY

BAR-BE-CUE

This is for a dug out pit, preferably, brick lined to retain heat. Grill should be 2 feet from coals. Start fire about 9 P.M. the night before bar-be-cue. Use green oak for fire. Add more wood at about 5 A.M. Coat meat with salt. (Note—no salt in sauce.)

MEAT	SIZE	TIME
Mutton	**quartered**	**5-6 hours**
Beef roast	**8-10 pounds**	**7-8 hours**

Goat, venison, or pork can be used, also. Allow 1½ pounds per person. Keep coals real hot and put meat on grill about 10 A.M. Turn. After meat is almost done, begin dipping in real hot sauce. Let simmer in sauce 10 to 15 minutes at a time. (Dip instead of mop, because mopping makes too much smoke to see and also wastes sauce.) Put meat back on fire for a while and dip again before serving. Meat should be ready about 6 P.M.

Sauce

(Serves 50 people)

10 pounds butter
12 cans tomato paste
2 bottles tomato catsup
3 bottles Worcestershire
    sauce
2 whole onions
2 whole lemons
3 cloves garlic
¼ cup vinegar
Pinch of sugar
Louisiana hot sauce

3 tablespoons prepared
    mustard
Pod of red pepper
2 bouillon cubes
3 or 4 small cans black pepper
Bay leaf
Celery seed
Thyme
Parsley
Celery tops
Clove

D. C. JOHNSTON
Lindsay, Louisiana

STEAK

Use T-bone or sirloin strip (do not use sirloin steak—too much meat area) about 1½ to 2 inches thick. Have a good bit of hot coals—brush off ashes. Place steaks right on coals—*no grill.* Leave for 5 minutes. Turn on a new surface of brushed coals and leave 5 minutes. Now place on the grill and pour sauce over steaks.

Sauce

Butter
Salt and pepper

Worcestershire sauce
Lemon juice

EDWARD WALL

BAR-B-CUED FISH

2 red snappers or trout
    (about 4 pounds)
1 stick butter
3 tablespoons grated onion
2 lemons

2 tablespoons parsley
2 tablespoons Worcestershire
    sauce
2 dashes hot sauce

Salt and pepper fish. Place on sheet of heavy foil. Pour sauce over fish. Seal foil, making sure that there is no leakage. Place on grill (one with hood, if possible). Turn every 20 minutes, being careful not to tear foil. Cook for 1½ hours. Remove from foil and place fish on grill. Leave on grill for 10 minutes; turn and leave another 10 minutes, basting with sauce saved from package or make up a little more.

EDWARD WALL

BUTTER SAUCE

(To serve with barbecued chicken or fish—serves 25)

6 pounds oleo or butter
Small bottle Worcestershire
  sauce
Juice of 6 lemons
½ can dry mustard

1 tablespoon garlic powder or
  puree
2 lemon rinds, whole—
  remove before serving

Let simmer for 15 minutes. Just before serving, add a handful of chopped parsley. Leave on fire just long enough for parsley to curl.

EDGAR BECNEL
New Roads, La.

PAPA J. B.'s FRENCH DRESSING

1 tablespoon salt
½ cup vinegar
1 tablespoon Worcestershire
  sauce
¼ teaspoon hot sauce
1 teaspoon black pepper
2 teaspoons paprika

2 teaspoons mustard
  (French's)
2 teaspoons creamed
  horseradish
2 crushed garlic buds
½ medium onion, grated
1 cup salad oil

This is a very interesting tart dressing, and it is perfect for fruit salads such as avocado, grapefruit and orange salad. It is also excellent for a tossed green salad of avocado, tomatoes, lettuce, parsley, celery, etc.

PROF. J. B. FRANCIONI, JR.

BOILED CORN

1½ gallons water
1½ dozen ears of corn

3 pounds salt meat

Cut salt meat into chunks. Boil until tender, about 1 hour. Drop corn in with meat; boil until tender. Serve chunks of meat with corn. Rub meat on corn and eat both corn and meat. It is not necessary to use butter and salt.

JOE BEAUD
New Roads, La.

PUNA'S POTATOES

1 tablespoons butter
2 tablespoons flour
1 cup milk
1 can whole new potatoes

3 shallots
¼ pound Cheddar cheese
Salt to taste
Pepper to taste

Dice the potatoes; chop the shallots, white and green parts. Grate the cheese. Make a white sauce by blending together the butter and flour over medium heat and adding milk gradually, stirring constantly. Add potatoes, shallots, seasoning and most of the cheese to the sauce. Put into a baking dish and top with remaining cheese. This may all be done ahead of time. About 20 minutes before serving, heat in 350° oven until bubbling. This is good with steaks.

LEWIS W. EATON, JR.

PINTO BEANS

8 pounds beans
4 pounds salt pork
12 onions
20 cloves garlic

4 bell peppers
½ can dry mustard
Small can chili powder
Salt and pepper, to taste

Boil beans on slow fire, until the beans are tender. Fry meat and remove from pot. Fry onions, garlic, and bell peppers until medium brown. Add meat and seasoning to beans. Stir well. Add rest of ingredients and cook 4-5 hours or until beans begin to break up.

EDGAR BECNEL
New Roads, La.

SWEET 'N HOT BEANS

¼ pound bacon, cut up
4 onions, chopped (enough to fill bean can)
1 pound can "pork and beans"

½ cup dark brown sugar (packed)
¼ teaspoon cayenne pepper (ground), for children, or ½ teaspoon for adults

Fry, or render, bacon in suitable pot. Add onions and cayenne, and cook until half done. Stir in sugar and beans; simmer a few moments before serving. Nice with barbecued chicken, hot dogs, etc. You may also use black strap molasses in this recipe instead of as much sugar as asked above. This serves two generously and can serve 4.

This one is "sure-fire," especially for that "patio" affair. And is it easy to make!

FONVILLE WINANS

WHITE BREAD

1¼ cups luke warm water
1 cake compressed yeast, or 1 package granular yeast
1 cup milk, scalded
2 tablespoons sugar

2 teaspoons salt
2 tablespoons shortening
7-7¼ cups sifted all-purpose flour

Dissolve yeast and 1 teaspoon sugar in ¼ cup luke warm water, taken from above amount. Let stand 10 minutes. Scald milk. Add sugar, salt, water and shortening. Cool to lukewarm. Add yeast mixture and flour gradually, beating thoroughly after each addition. Turn dough out on slightly floured board and knead until smooth and satiny, about 10 minutes. Shape into a ball and place in a greased bowl. Brush top lightly with melted shortening. Cover. Let rise until double in bulk, about 1½ hours. Divide into two portions. Shape into loaves and place in two greased bread pans. Brush top lightly with shortening. Cover. Let rise until double in bulk. Bake at 375° for 45-50 minutes. This straight dough method yields 2 loaves.

ASHTON STEWART

YEAST RAISED DONUTS

Dissolve and let stand for 20 minutes:

2 packages yeast	**About ½ cup luke warm water**

Cream:

1½ cups sugar	**1 teaspoon nutmeg**
½ cup shortening	**1 teaspoon salt**

Add:

8 eggs, one at a time	**2 teaspoons vanilla**

Sift and add:

4 cups cake flour	**2 tablespoons baking powder**
5 cups bread flour	

Add slowly:

1½ cups milk

Do not make dough too soft. Let set for 30 minutes. Roll out and cut with a donut cutter. Fry in deep fat at 350° Dip cooked donuts in sugar glaze below:

2 pounds powdered sugar	**Pinch of salt**
¾ cup water	**¼ teaspoon vanilla**

Let donuts drain on rack.

IVY GARON

COFFEE-SPICE CAKE

½ cup butter	**¼ teaspoon mace or nutmeg**
1½ cups brown sugar	**¼ teaspoon cloves**
2 egg yolks, well beaten	**⅓ cup evaporated milk**
2 cups flour	**⅓ cup cool, strong, dripped**
2 teaspoons baking powder	**coffee**
1 teaspoon cinnamon	**1 teaspoon vanilla**

2 egg whites, stiffly beaten

Cream butter; add sugar and egg yolks. Mix and sift flour, baking powder and spices. Add alternately with milk. Beat until smooth. Add vanilla. Fold in egg whites. Bake at 375° for 25 - 30 minutes.

Caramel Frosting

1¼ cups sugar	**2 tablespoons butter**
¾ cup brown sugar	**1 cup evaporated milk**

1½ teaspoon vanilla

Blend milk and sugar. Add butter. Cook to soft ball stage. Cool. Add vanilla. Beat until thick enough to stay on cake.

NORMAN SAURAGE, JR.

COFFEE EGGNOG

1½ cups sugar
3 cups boiling water
2 cups ground coffee

10 egg yolks
2½ quarts milk
10 egg whites

Add sugar to boiling water and stir until dissolved. Let come to a boil. Remove from heat; add coffee; stir well; let stand 15 minutes. Let drip through 2 thicknesses of wet cheese cloth in a strainer. Let cool. Beat egg yolks, stir in coffee syrup slowly. Add milk, blend well; fold in well beaten egg whites. Pour into punch bowl. Serve in punch cups. Sprinkle with nutmeg. Serves 40.

NORMAN SAURAGE, JR.

COFFEE DATE NUT LOAF

2 cups sifted flour
1 teaspoon salt
⅓ cup broken nuts
1 cup strong coffee
1 egg, beaten well
4 teaspoons baking powder

⅔ cup sugar
¾ cup dates, finely cut
⅛ teaspoon baking soda
2 tablespoons melted shortening

Mix and sift flour, baking powder, salt and sugar. Stir in nuts and dates. Combine coffee, baking soda, egg and shortening; add all at once to dry ingredients. Stir only enough to dampen dry ingredients. Turn into greased loaf pan. Let stand 20 minutes. Bake at 375° for 1 hour.

NORMAN SAURAGE, JR.

EGGNOG

1 dozen eggs
1½ cups granulated sugar
⅓ cup confectioners' sugar
1 quart homogenized milk
1 quart vanilla ice cream

1 pint whipping cream
1 pint bourbon
1 pint dark rum
1 pint vodka
1 cup sweet sherry

Nutmeg

Separate yolks from whites of eggs. Beat egg yolks until fluffy and very light in color. Add 1 cup sugar. Add slowly, while beating mixture constantly, the bourbon, rum, and vodka. While still beating mixture, add the milk. Reserve 2 tablespoons sherry. Blend remainder of sherry with vanilla ice cream and beat into egg mixture. Whip cream until it forms soft peaks. Whip in ⅓ cup powdered sugar, folding into this the 2 tablespoons sherry. Set aside. Beat whites of six eggs until stiff and dry and add ½ cup granulated sugar. Sprinkle with nutmeg. Fold whipped cream into egg mixture and top with whites of eggs. If it is desired to increase or decrease alcoholic content of this eggnog, the same ratio of alcoholic beverages should be maintained. The virtue of this recipe lies in the fact that authoritative strength may be achieved without an excessively strong bourbon taste. Serves about 25.

DR. JOHN A. THOMPSON

COFFEE-EGGNOG PIE

2 envelopes unflavored
  gelatin
½ cup cold coffee
2 cups hot coffee
½ cup sugar
2 eggs, separated

1 teaspoon brandy flavoring
1 cup heavy cream
⅛ teaspoon salt
1 square unsweetened
  chocolate
1 9" baked pie shell

Soften gelatin in cold coffee. Dissolve in hot coffee. Add sugar, stir to dissolve. Pour slowly in well-beaten egg yolks. Chill until consistency of unbeaten egg whites. Add flavoring. Whip cream; fold in. Beat egg whites with salt; fold in. Spoon into pie shell. Chill until set. Garnish with shaved chocolate.

NORMAN SAURAGE, JR.

FIG CONSERVE

2 pounds ripe figs
1 cup crushed pineapple
2 medium lemons, cut in
  small pieces

½ teaspoon salt
1 cup chopped pecans
Sugar

Wash figs and cut in pieces. Mix with pineapple and lemons and put into a boiler with an equal amount of sugar and the ½ teaspoon salt. Bring slowly to boiling point and simmer gently until thickened, but still a little runny. Stir in nuts; put in hot jars.

GEORGE REYNAUD

STRAWBERRY PRESERVES

6 pounds ripe strawberries
  and juice

5 pounds sugar
Juice of 1 large lemon

Strawberries to be preserved should first be washed thoroughly in cool water. Do not stem berries until after washing. After washing and stemming berries, place in shallow container and sprinkle with sugar. (This is extra sugar and is not measured from the five pounds to be used later.) Let berries stand in sugar for three hours; or if desired, place in refrigerator overnight. Using a large perforated spoon, gently mash berries and juice, leaving some berries whole. Weigh berries and juice. For every 6 pounds of berries and juice, use 5 pounds of sugar. Place berries, juice of berries, and juice of the lemon into a preserving kettle. Bring to boil over a high fire and, stirring constantly, add sugar. After mixture comes to a boil again, then lower heat to a slow boil and continue cooking for 1 hour. Stir occasionally and skim the top. Place hot preserves into prepared jars and seal. This recipe will make a dozen ½-pint jars.

ADRIAN DE MONTLUZIN

EQUIVALENTS

LIQUID MEASURE VOLUME EQUIVALENTS

60 drops = 1 teaspoon
3 teaspoons = 1 tablespoon
2 tablespoons = 1 fluid ounce
4 tablespoons = ¼ cup
5 ⅓ tablespoons = ⅓ cup
8 tablespoons = ½ cup or 4 ounces or 1
  gill or 1 tea cup

16 tablespoons = 1 cup or 8 ounces
⅜ cup = ¼ cup plus 2 tablespoons
⅝ cup = ½ cup plus 2 tablespoons
⅞ cup = ¾ cup plus 2 tablespoons
1 cup = ½ pint or 8 ounces
2 cups = 1 pint or 16 ounces
1 quart = 2 pints or 64 tablespoons
1 gallon = 4 quarts

DRY MEASURE VOLUME EQUIVALENTS

2 cups = 1 pint
2 pints = 1 quart

4 quarts = 1 gallon
2 gallons or 8 quarts = 1 peck
4 pecks = 1 bushel

MISCELLANEOUS MEASURE EQUIVALENTS

A few grains = Less than ⅛ teaspoon
Pinch = As much as can be taken between
  tip of finger and thumb
Speck = Less than ⅛ teaspoon

1 jigger = 2 ounces
1 minim = 1 drop
10 drops = dash
6 dashes = 1 teaspoon
8 teaspoons = 1 ounce

WEIGHT OR AVOIRDUPOIS EQUIVALENTS

1 ounce = 16 drams

1 pound = 16 ounces
1 kilo = 2.20 pounds

METRIC ABBREVIATIONS

cc = cubic centimeter
l = liter
ml = milliliter
cm = centimeter
m = meter
mm = millimeter

mμ = millimicron
°C = degrees Centigrade
g = gram
kg = kilogram
mcg = microgram
μg = microgram
mg = milligram

METRIC LIQUID MEASURE VOLUME EQUIVALENTS

1 teaspoon = 5 milliliters
1 tablespoon = 14.8 milliliters
66⅔ tablespoons = 1 liter
1 cup = ¼ liter, approximately, or 236.6
  milliliters

1 gill = .118 liters
1 pint = .4732 liters
1 quart =.9464 liters
1 gallon = 3.785 liters
1 liter = 1000 milliliters or 1.06 quarts

METRIC DRY MEASURE VOLUME EQUIVALENTS

1 pint = .551 liters
1 quart = 1.101 liters

1 peck = 8.81 liters
1 bushel = 35.24 liters

WEIGHT EQUIVALENTS IN GRAMS

1 ounce = 28.35 grams
1 pound = 453.59 grams
1 gram = 0.035 ounces

1 kilogram = 2.21 pounds
1 microgram = 0.001 milligram
1 milligram = 1000 micrograms
1 gram = 1000 milligrams

METRIC LINEAR EQUIVALENTS

1 centimeter = 0.394 inches

1 inch = 2.54 centimeters
1 meter = 39.37 inches

TEMPERATURE CONVERSIONS

To convert Fahrenheit to Centigrade:
   Subtract 32, miltiply by 5, divide by 9
To convert Centigrade to Fahrenheit:
   Multiply by 9, divide by 5, add 32

CAN SIZES

Can size	Weight	Approximate Cups
8 ounces	8 ounces	1
Picnic	10½ to 12 ounces	1¼
12 ounces	12 ounces	1½
No. 300	14 to 16 ounces	1¾
No. 303	16 to 17 ounces	2
No. 2	1 lb. 4 ounces or 1 pint 2 fluid ounces	2½
No. 2½	1 lb. 13 ounces	3½
No. 3 Cyl.	3 lb. 3 ounces or 1 quart 14 fluid ounces	5¾
Baby Foods	3½ to 8 ounces	
No. 10	6½ lbs. to 7 lbs. 5 ounces	12 to 13
Condensed Milk	15 ounces	1½
Evaporated Milk	6 ounces	⅔
Evaporated Milk	14½ ounces	1⅔

BUTTER OR MARGARINE MEASUREMENTS

1 pound = 4 sticks or 2 cups
1 cup = 2 sticks

½ cup = 1 stick
¼ cup = ½ stick

CHEESE MEASUREMENTS

1 pound American cheese = 4 cups grated
1 pound Cheddar cheese = 4 cups grated
4 ounces Cheddar cheese = 1 cup grated, sieved or chopped
1 pound Cottage cheese = 2 cups
½ pound Cottage cheese = 1 cup or 8 ounces
½ pound Cream cheese = 1 cup or 8 ounces
6 ounces Cream cheese = 12 tablespoons or ¾ cup
5 ounces Cheese spread = 8 tablespoons or ½ cup

APPROXIMATE INGREDIENT SUBSTITUTIONS AND EQUIVALENTS

1 teaspoon baking powder = ¼ teaspoon baking soda plus ½ cup buttermilk
= ¼ teaspoon baking soda plus ½ teaspoon cream of tartar
Leavening
(per cup flour) = Use 1¼ teaspoon baking powder, or ¼ teaspoon soda with 2 tablespoons vinegar
1 pound sifted flour = 4 cups
1 cup sifted all purpose flour = 1 cup plus 2 tablespoons sifted cake flour
1 cup sifted cake flour = ⅞ cup sifted all purpose flour
1 pound granulated sugar = 2 to 2¼ cups
1 teaspoon sugar = ¼ grain saccharin
= ⅛ teaspoon non-caloric sweetner
1 pound confectioners sugar = 4 to 4½ cups
1¾ cups packed confectioners sugar = 1 cup granulated
1 pound brown sugar = 2¼ to 2½ cups
1 cup packed brown sugar = 1 cup granulated
1 cup honey = 1 to 1¼ cups sugar plus ¼ cup liquid
1 cup corn syrup = 1 cup sugar plus ¼ cup liquid
1 cup butter = 1 cup margarine
= 14 tablespoons hydrogenated fat and ½ teaspoon salt
= 14 tablespoons lard and ½ teaspoon salt
1 cup fresh milk = ½ cup evaporated milk plus ½ cup water
= ½ cup condensed milk plus ½ cup water (reduce sugar in recipe)
= 4 teaspoons powdered whole milk plus 1 cup water
= 4 tablespoons powdered skim milk plus 2 teaspoons butter plus 1 cup water
1 cup buttermilk or sour milk = 1 tablespoon vinegar or lemon juice plus enough sweet milk to make one cup (let stand 5 minutes) or 1¾ teaspoon cream of tartar plus 1 cup sweet milk
1 cup yogurt = 1 cup buttermilk
1 cup coffee or light cream = 3 tablespoons butter and about ¾ cup milk
1 cup heavy cream = ½ cup butter and about ¾ cup milk

1 cup whipping cream = 2 cups or more after whipping

2 large eggs = 3 small eggs

1 ounce chocolate = 1 square or 3 tablespoons cocoa plus 1 teaspoon to 1 tablespoon fat (less for Dutch-type cocoa)

1 tablespoon flour = ½ tablespoon cornstarch or arrowroot, or 2 teaspoons quick-cooking tapioca (as thickener)

1 tablespoon cornstarch = 2 tablespoons flour (as thickener)

1 tablespoon potato flour = 2 tablespoons flour (as thickener)

1 teaspoon lemon juice = ½ teaspoon vinegar

Herbs, ½ to 1½ teaspoon dried = 1 tablespoon fresh

⅛ teaspoon garlic powder = 1 small clove

1 tablespoon candied ginger, washed of sugar or 1 tablespoon raw ginger = ⅛ teaspoon powdered ginger

1 tablespoon fresh horseradish = 2 tablespoons bottled

1 cup raw rice = approximately 3 cups cooked

1 cup uncooked macaroni = 2 to 2¼ cups cooked

1 cup uncooked noodles = 1¾ cups cooked

1 pound fresh mushrooms = 3 ounces dried or 6 ounces canned

15 pounds whole crawfish = 1 pound peeled tails

METRIC CONVERSION TABLE

COMPARISON OF AVOIRDUPOIS AND METRIC UNITS OF WEIGHT

Ounces to Pounds to Grams			Pounds to Kilograms		Grams to Ounces		Kilograms to Ounces	
1	0.06	28.35	1	0.454	1	0.035	1	2.205
2	0.12	56.70	2	0.91	2	0.07	2	4.41
3	0.19	85.05	3	1.36	3	0.11	3	6.61
4	0.25	113.40	4	1.81	4	0.14	4	8.82
5	0.31	141.75	5	2.27	5	0.18	5	11.02
6	0.38	170.10	6	2.72	6	0.21	6	13.23
7	0.44	198.45	7	3.18	7	0.25	7	15.43
8	0.50	226.80	8	3.63	8	0.28	8	17.64
9	0.56	255.15	9	4.08	9	0.32	9	19.84
10	0.62	283.50	10	4.54	10	0.35	10	22.05
11	0.69	311.85	11	4.99	11	0.39	11	24.26
12	0.75	340.20	12	5.44	12	0.42	12	26.46
13	0.81	368.55	13	5.90	13	0.46	13	28.67
14	0.88	396.90	14	6.35	14	0.49	14	30.87
15	0.94	425.25	15	6.81	15	0.53	15	33.08
16	1.00	453.59	16	7.26	16	0.56	16	35.28

COMPARISON OF U. S. AND METRIC UNITS OF LIQUID MEASURE

Ounces (fluid) to Milliliters		Quarts to Liters		Gallons to Liters	
1	29.573	1	0.946	1	3.785
2	59.15	2	1.89	2	7.57
3	88.72	3	2.84	3	11.36
4	118.30	4	3.79	4	15.14
5	147.87	5	4.73	5	18.93
6	177.44	6	5.68	6	22.71
7	207.02	7	6.62	7	26.50
8	236.59	8	7.57	8	30.28
9	266.16	9	8.52	9	34.07
10	295.73	10	9.46	10	37.85

Milliliters to Ounces (fluid)		Liters to Quarts		Liters to Gallons	
1	0.034	1	1.057	1	0.264
2	0.07	2	2.11	2	0.53
3	0.10	3	3.17	3	0.79
4	0.14	4	4.23	4	1.06
5	0.17	5	5.28	5	1.32
6	0.20	6	6.34	6	1.59
7	0.24	7	7.40	7	1.85
8	0.27	8	8.45	8	2.11
9	0.30	9	9.51	9	2.38
10	0.34	10	10.57	10	2.64

FOOD TO SERVE FIFTY

AMOUNTS OF FOOD TO SERVE 50 PEOPLE
Approximate amounts of foods as purchased to serve 50

FOOD	SERVING UNIT	PURCHASE
Beverages		
Coffee	5 ounces	1 pound coffee plus
	100 Demitasse	2¼ gallons water
	5 ounces	½ pound coffee plus
	50 Demitasse	1 gallon water
Fruit Juice, frozen	½ cup	4 to 12 ounce cans
Canned Fruit and	½ cup	Four 46 ounce cans
Vegetable Juice	⅓ cup	5 quarts
Cereals and Cereal Products		
Noodles	5 ounces	4 pounds
Rice	5 ounces	3 to 4 pounds
Spaghetti	5 ounces	4 to 5 pounds
Dairy Product and Eggs		
Butter for table	1 to 1½ pats	1 to 1½ pounds
Cream, coffee	1 teaspoon	3 quarts
Cheese, cottage	⅓ cup	10 pounds
Cheese for sandwiches	1¼ ounces	4 pounds
Eggs	1 to 2	4 to 8 dozen
Ice Cream	⅓ cup	2 gallons
Milk	6 ounce glass	2½ gallons
Fruits		
Canned Fruits	½ cup	6 to 7 pounds
MEATS		
Beef		
Creamed Beef, ground meat	3 ounces	10 pounds
Ground Meat Patties	3½ ounces	14 pounds
Pot Roast, chuck	3 ounces	20 to 22 pounds
Stew with vegetables	5½ ounces	15 pounds
Swiss steak, round ¾ inch	3½ ounces	16 pounds
Veal		
Breaded veal round	3 ounces	12½ pounds
Chops, 3 to 1 pound	1 each	17 pounds
Cutlets, 4 to 1 pound	3 ounces	12½ pounds
Fish		
Fish, fillets	4 ounces	12½ to 15 pounds
Oysters, large		1½ to 2 gallons

FOOD	SERVING UNIT	PURCHASE
Shrimp	2½ ounces, ¼ cup	10 to 12 pounds
Lamb		
Roast Leg, 6 pounds each	2½ ounces	4 legs
Pork		
Cold cuts	2 ounces	6 to 8 pounds
Frankfurters	2 each	8 to 10 pounds
Ham		
Baked, sliced	2 ounces	16 to 20 pounds
Pork chops	1 each	12½ to 16 pounds
Sausage	1 cake each	12½ pounds
Sausage link	2 each	6¼ pounds
Poultry		
Chicken, ready to cook		
Baked	4 ounces	30 pounds, 8 hens 5 to 6 pounds each
Creamed	5 ounces	18 to 20 pounds, 4 hens 4½ to 5 pounds each
Fried	¼ or ½ chicken	13 to 25 fryers 2½ to 3½ pounds each
Stewed	5 ounces	35 to 40 pounds, 8 hens 4½ to 5 pounds each
Turkey, roast	2½ ounces	35 to 40 pounds
Turkey, roll	3 ounces	12 to 15 pounds
Vegetables		
Canned Vegetables	½ cup	Ten no. 2 cans
Dried Peas and Beans	½ cup	5 pounds
Asparagus, fresh	3 ounces, ¼ cup	18 to 20 pounds
Beans, green, fresh	3 ounces	10 to 12 pounds
Beans, lima, fresh	3 ounces	22 to 25 pounds
Broccoli, fresh	3 ounces	16 to 20 pounds
Cabbage, raw	1 to 2 ounces ⅛ to ¼ cup	8 pounds
Carrots, topped	3 ounces	12½ pounds
Cauliflower, fresh	3 ounces	28 to 32 pounds
Celery	1 to 2 pieces	2 pounds
Cucumber, 9 inch	2 slices	4
Eggplant, 1¼ pounds each	2 to 2½ ounces ¼ cup	8
Lettuce, head	1½ to 2 ounces	8 to 10 heads
Potatoes, to mash	½ cup	12 pounds

FOOD	SERVING UNIT	PURCHASE
Potatoes, to scallop	½ cup	15 pounds
Potatoes, sweet	½ cup	18 to 20 pounds
Spinach, to cook	¼ cup	12 to 15 pounds
Spinach, for salad	⅛ cup	5 to 6 pounds
Squash, to bake or mash	3 ounces	12 to 15 pounds
Miscellaneous		
Jelly	2 tablespoons	3 pounds
Syrup	¼ cup	3¼ quarts
Sugar, granulated	1½ teaspoon	¾ pound

APPROXIMATE AMOUNTS OF PREPARED
FOOD TO SERVE 50

FOOD	SERVING UNIT	PURCHASE
Beverages		
Tea, Iced	8 ounces, 1 glass	3 gallons
Punch	3 ounces, 1 punch cup	1¼ gallons
	6 ounces	2½ gallons
Breads		
Bread, thin for sandwiches	2 slices	7 pounds / 4½ to 5 loaves
Bread, quick loaf brown, nut, orange	2 to 3 loaves	5 loaves, 4x9-inch
Desserts		
Ice Cream, plain, bulk	⅓ cup	8 quarts

Emily Wray Lamont

INDEX

INDEX

River Road Recipes

The Junior League of Baton Rouge, Inc.
5280 Corporate Blvd.
Baton Rouge, LA 70808
(504) 924-0298

Please send me information on ordering additional copies of *River Road Recipes* or our second cookbook, *River Road Recipes II.*

Name _____

Address _____

City _____ State _____ Zip _____

Phone ( ) _____

- -

River Road Recipes

The Junior League of Baton Rouge, Inc.
5280 Corporate Blvd.
Baton Rouge, LA 70808
(504) 924-0298

Please send me information on ordering additional copies of *River Road Recipes* or our second cookbook, *River Road Recipes II.*

Name _____

Address _____

City _____ State _____ Zip _____

Phone ( ) _____

- -

River Road Recipes

The Junior League of Baton Rouge, Inc.
5280 Corporate Blvd.
Baton Rouge, LA 70808
(504) 924-0298

Please send me information on ordering additional copies of *River Road Recipes* or our second cookbook, *River Road Recipes II.*

Name _____

Address _____

City _____ State _____ Zip _____

Phone ( ) _____